D0899300

Between Politics and

China's transition from a centrally planned to a market-oriented economy has brought new roles for state agencies and new rules of the game for firms seeking to succeed. It also challenges social scientists to explain why the old economic system has fallen apart and what has shaped the process and outcome of economic institutional change since the late 1970s. Yi-min Lin addresses these questions through an in-depth analysis of the forces driving state action and offers a striking portrait of the changing nature of state–firm relations in China's transitional economy.

Lin traces the decline of central planning to the interplay between two emerging markets: an economic market for the exchange of products and resources and a political market for the diversion to private interests of state authority and assets. He argues that the two markets have been mutually accommodating, that the political market has grown also due to the decline of the state's self-monitoring capacity, and that the competition among economic actors for special favors from state agents has played a key role in redefining the rules of the economic game and fashioning its outcomes.

Through richly detailed accounts of complex and differentiated dealings between firm leaders and government officials, Lin explains why certain firms benefit more than others from the growing exchange relations in the political process. The case studies presented here, featuring a dozen different firms and two local governments, illustrate both the many ways that state action has continued to influence the selection of winners and losers despite the marketization of the economy and the strategies that Chinese firms have pursued to adapt to the political realities and costs of doing business. They also suggest, in contrast to some existing views, that the expansion of concrete markets for products and resources does not necessarily signify the ascendance of "the market," nor does it bear a linear correlation with the rise of a legal–rational state.

Yi-min Lin is Associate Professor in the Social Science Division of Hong Kong University of Science and Technology.

Structural Analysis in the Social Sciences

Mark Granovetter, editor

Other books in the series:

Mark S. Mizruchi and Michael Schwartz, eds., *Intercorporate Relations: The Structural Analysis of Business*

Barry Wellman and S. D. Berkowitz, eds., *Social Structures: A Network Approach*

Ronald L. Breiger, ed., *Social Mobility and Social Structure*

David Knoke, *Political Networks: The Structural Perspective*

John L. Campbell, J. Rogers Hollingsworth, and Leon N. Lindberg, eds., *Governance of the American Economy*

Kyriakos Kontopoulos, *The Logics of Social Structure*

Philippa Pattison, *Algebraic Models for Social Networks*

Stanley Wasserman and Katherine Faust, *Social Network Analysis: Methods and Applications*

Gary Herrigel, *Industrial Constructions: The Sources of German Industrial Power*

Phillipe Bourgois, *In Search of Respect: Selling Crack in El Barrio*

Per Hage and Frank Harary, *Island Networks: Communication, Kinship, and Classification Structures in Oceania*

Thomas Schweizer and Douglas R. White, eds., *Kinship, Networks, and Exchange*

Noah E. Friedkin, *A Structural Theory of Social Influence*

David Wank, *Commodifying Communism: Business, Trust, and Politics in a South China City*

Rebecca Adams and Graham Allan, *Placing Friendship in Context*

Robert L. Nelson and William P. Bridges, *Legalizing Gender Inequality: Courts, Markets, and Unequal Pay for Women in America*

Robert Freeland, *The Struggle for Control of the Modern Corporation: Organizational Change at General Motors, 1924–1970*

Structural Analysis in the Social Sciences 18

Between Politics and Markets

Firms, Competition, and Institutional Change in Post-Mao China

YI-MIN LIN

Hong Kong University of Science and Technology

CAMBRIDGE
UNIVERSITY PRESS

PUBLISHED BY THE PRESS SYNDICATE OF THE UNIVERSITY OF CAMBRIDGE
The Pitt Building, Trumpington Street, Cambridge, United Kingdom

CAMBRIDGE UNIVERSITY PRESS
The Edinburgh Building, Cambridge CB2 2RU, UK
40 West 20th Street, New York, NY 10011-4211, USA
10 Stamford Road, Oakleigh, Melbourne 3207, Australia
Ruiz de Alarcón 13, 28014 Madrid, Spain
Dock House, The Waterfront, Cape Town 8001, South Africa

http://www.cambridge.org

First published 2001
First paperback edition 2004

Printed in the United States of America

Typeface Sabon 10/12 pt.   *System* QuarkXPress™ [BTS]

A catalog record for this book is available from the British Library

Library of Congress Cataloging in Publication Data

Lin, Yi-min
Between politics and markets: firms, competition, and institutional change in
post-Mao China / Yi-min Lin.
p. cm. – (Structural analysis in the social sciences)
Includes bibliographical references.
ISBN 0-521-77130-7 (hb)
1. China – Economic conditions – 1976– 2. China – Politics and government
– 1976– 3. Mixed economy – China. I. Title. II. Series.
HC427.92 .L55 2000
338.0951 – dc21 00-027206

0 521 77130 7 hardback
0 521 60404 4 paperback

Part of Chapter 4 (pp. 99–103) contains material modified from the following:

Yi-min Lin and Zhanxin Zhang, "Backyard Profit Centers: The Private Assets of Public
Agencies." In *Property Rights and Economic Reform in China*, eds. Jean C. Oi and
Andrew G. Walder (Standford: Stanford University Press, © 1999 by the Board of
Trustees of Leland Stanford Jr. University): 203–25. Reprinted by permission of Stanford
University Press, www.sup.org.

For Irene and Our Parents

Contents

Tables and Figures

Tables

xi

Figures

Acknowledgments

This book has taken a long time to come to fruition. Along the way I received help from many people, whom I want to thank here. The theme of the book was conceived in my doctoral dissertation at Yale University. David Apter, Deborah Davis, and Charles Perrow guided me through course work and supervised my dissertation. A number of other teachers, especially Paul DiMaggio, Charles Lindblom, and John Michael Montias, also had important influence on my initial thinking about the subject.

During 1991–2 the Center for Chinese Studies at the University of California at Berkeley offered a postdoctoral fellowship for me to revise the dissertation for publication. Thomas Gold chaired the Center at that time. His advice and friendship made my stay a fruitful experience. While at Berkeley, I benefited from discussions with Lowell Dittmer, Joyce Kallgren, Hong Yung Lee, Elizabeth Perry, Frederic Wakeman, and Wen-hsin Yeh.

Much of the book was rewritten after 1992. Andrew Walder and Mark Granovetter substantially shaped the undertaking in many ways. Each read three earlier versions of the manuscript and provided searching comments that led to several major rewrites. Mark Selden, Alvin So, and Jonathan Unger were kind enough to read the entire manuscript and offered insightful suggestions. Discussions with Jean Oi helped improve parts of Chapter 5 and Chapter 7. Deborah Davis and Charles Perrow provided further guidance during their respective visits to Hong Kong in 1997–8. Revisions of the manuscript also benefited from comments and questions from anonymous reviewers for Cambridge University Press, University of California Press, Oxford University Press, and Routledge. Mary Child, Louise Calabro, and Cathy Felgar guided me through the publication process; Sue Avery copyedited the manuscript.

In mainland China, many people facilitated my fieldwork and data collection. In particular I want to thank Chen Wangtao, Li Qiuhong,

Lin Bin, Ma Changhai, Shi Xianmin, Sun Bingyao, and Wang Hansheng. I am also most grateful to my interviewees for the time, information, and thoughts that they shared with me. In Hong Kong, May Chong, Tony Chung, Fang Huirong, Lai Ganfeng, Daniel Lee, Wang Jian-ping, Eilo Yu, and Zhang Zhanxin provided research assistance.

Initial fieldwork for the book was supported by a Mun Yew Chung Fellowship from the Yale Center for International and Area Studies and a Dissertation Fellowship from the Yale Graduate School. Research after 1992 was funded by grants from the Hong Kong University of Science and Technology and the Hong Kong Research Grants Council. Hsi-sheng Ch'i and Min-min Chang made available special funds for data acquisition at a critical stage of the revision process.

Over the years my work on the book was greatly aided by the encouragement and moral support from many friends and colleagues, especially An Chen, John Huang, Vivian Lu, Janet Rogers, Terry Schmidt, Xinyang Wang, and Chan-liang Wu in New Haven; Stephen Cass, Thomas Gold, Wendy Locks, and Jane Turbiner in Berkeley; Yanjie Bian, Gaochao He, James Kung, William Liu, Jerry Patchell, Barry Sautman, Alvin So, Edward Tu, Kung-chia Yeh, and David Zweig in Hong Kong. This undertaking would not have been completed without the care, understanding, and support of my family. I dedicate the book to them.

Introduction: Economic Market and Political Market

> The market and bureaucracy are not a gin and tonic that can be mixed in any proportion wanted. There may be a certain level of bureaucratic market restrictions which still allows breath for the market. But beyond a critical limit, bureaucratic restriction cools down the live forces of the market, kills them – and only the appearance of a market remains. And there exists a combination of market and bureaucracy which unites, as it were, only the disadvantages of the two, while the separately existing advantages of both are lost.

Janos Kornai, the dean of socialist economics, wrote these remarks before the collapse of communism in Eastern Europe (1990: 14). His focal concern was the intermittent, largely unsuccessful attempts to incorporate market mechanisms into centrally planned economies in the Soviet Bloc during the preceding two decades. Indeed, the setbacks to such attempts were so severe and widespread that there was a growing consensus that in a partially reformed command economy market forces were unlikely to outgrow and redefine the institutional parameters set by the communist state,[1] much less become the primary driver of sustained economic growth.

China's reform experience since 1978, however, tells a different story. The central planning system, along with strict state ownership, has steadily declined. Markets have grown to become the center of economic activities. The net output of the economy has on average increased by 9.7% per year (GJTJJa 1999: 58), and the standard of living has greatly improved, as reflected in the World Bank's recent re-classification of the country from the "low income" to the "lower middle income" category (World Bank 1998: 187–91). These changes have taken place without an overhaul of the political system. This poses a challenging

---

[1] See, for example, the articles on Eastern Europe in Nee and Stark (1989).

1

question: What has driven and sustained marketization in the shadow of bureaucratic interests, habits, and restrictions while keeping the economy from being trapped in the worst of the two worlds described by Kornai?

A further intriguing twist in China's recent economic transformation is that it has been accompanied by a significant growth of political corruption and, relatedly, rent-seeking activities.[2] In 1995, for example, Chen Xitong, Mayor of Beijing and a member of the Politburo of the Chinese Communist Party (CCP hereafter), was arrested (along with a number of his deputies) on corruption charges (*RMRB*, July 3, 1995). In 1998, Luo Ji, Director of the Anti-Corruption Bureau,[3] was removed from office for making illicit use of illegal funds uncovered in the Bureau's investigations (*RMRB*, March 11, 1999). In 1999, Cheng Kejie, a vice chairman of the Standing Committee of the National People's Congress, was arrested (and later executed) for taking bribes in return for granting, among other things, government contracts, quotas, and loans (*China Daily*, August 23, 2000, September 15, 2000). The diversion of public authority and assets as represented by these high-profile cases has become so widespread and deep-seated throughout the state apparatus that CCP leaders have openly recognized the seriousness of the problem, calling the fight against it a matter of "life and death" for the communist state (*RMRB*, February 27, 1998).

Political economists have long argued that pervasive corruption and rent seeking are detrimental to economic growth (e.g., Krueger 1974; Myrdal 1968; Olson 1982; Tullock 1967). They have substantial evidence to point to, ranging from economic retardation in many developing countries to stagnation and decline in some industrialized economies. How, then, should the contrast between their argument and what has happened in China during the past two decades be explained?

This book seeks to address these puzzles by analyzing the mechanisms – causal processes (Elster 1989) – of economic institutional change. I focus on the industrial sector – the largest contributor to China's eco-

---

[2] Political corruption refers to illicit use by government officials of public authority and assets for private purposes (Nye 1967; Rose-Ackerman 1978: 7). Rent seeking has to do with the socially costly pursuit of redistributive gains (e.g., monopoly profit) (Tollison 1982). Rent seeking may or may not involve political corruption, as it may take place within the confines of existing regulations or in the "gray area" between legal and illegal behavior. In this study, however, I will use the more encompassing term "favor seeking" to describe the exchange relations between state agents and economic actors. See the discussion below.

[3] The Anti-Corruption Bureau operates under the People's Supreme Procuratorate. Along with the Ministry of Supervision and the Central Discipline Inspection Commission of the CCP, it is one of the major internal watchdog agencies of the Chinese state.

nomic output,[4] and examine the forces that have shaped the paces, strategies, and outcomes of the transition of industrial firms from the central planning system to the economic space outside it.[5] The lead question of my investigation is how the competitive advantage of firms has been formed in two emergent markets, the economic and the political. The economic market involves the exchange of goods, services, and factors (capital, labor, and land) among economic actors. In the political market,[6] state-controlled resources, opportunities, and exemptions from societally shared liabilities are exchanged by state agents with each other and with outsiders for self-defined purposes – especially for private gain – that often deviate from publicly announced agenda of the state.[7] Neither market was highly developed in the Mao era (1949–76). Both are pervasive today. An account of their growing role in shaping the behavior and performance of firms thus sets the stage for a close examination of why and how these markets have evolved from a system of central planning and ideological control, how the rules of the economic game have been redefined along the way, and why the economy has steadily grown despite the state's increasing inability to maintain its own organizational health.

Competing to Win

A central feature of post-Mao China is that the economic landscape has become increasingly crowded and competitive. From 1978 to 1998, the number of industrial enterprises rose from 1.2 million to nearly 8 million (GJTJJa 1987: 233, 1999: 421; ZGXZQYNJBJWYH 1988: 573). Most of the newly formed enterprises are domestically funded, but foreign investors have also entered the scene and steadily increased their presence since the adoption of the "open door policy" in 1979. By the end of 1997, the total number of foreign capital enterprises was in the order

---

[4] In 1998 the industrial sector contributed 42.2% of China's gross domestic product (GDP) (GJTJJa 1999: 13).

[5] In this study, the term "firms" is used interchangeably with "enterprises" and "economic organizations" to refer to for-profit organizations that transform inputs into output.

[6] The notion of a political market is sometimes used in studies of vote manipulation and swapping in the West (e.g., Pelzman 1990; Ramseyer and Rosenbluth 1993; see also Mueller 1989 and North 1990). As I will show below, the political market that has emerged in post-Mao China is not driven and constrained by competitive party politics. Rather, it involves a wide range of state action beyond voting and thrives on favor exchange through diffused social networks.

[7] By state agents I mean functionaries of the government and the CCP who have varying levels of authority in the three areas mentioned here. They are also referred to as "officials" in this book. Managers of public enterprises, along with private entrepreneurs, are regarded as "economic actors" in that they do not have allocative and regulatory authority beyond their own organizational boundaries.

of 300,000, including those set up by over three hundred *Fortune 500* corporations (BJWYH 1998: 9). Starting from the manufacture and retail of low-end consumer goods, the newcomers have gradually made their way into almost all the other economic sectors, competing directly with existing enterprises and with each other in input supplies and output sales. After more than two decades of disappearance, marketing made a comeback in the spring of 1979, when the Shanghai TV station aired a commercial for the Swiss watchmaker Rado (*BJWB*, March 14, 1999). Since then advertisements have multiplied and flooded the mass media and other channels of communication. New domestic brands such as Changhong (electronic products), Haier (household electrical appliances), and Wa Ha Ha (food and beverages), along with Coca Cola, Kodak, 555, and their likes, have become widely recognized names.

This sea change has captured the attention of analysts. A group of economists has developed a theory, referred to below as the "economic competition thesis," to explain the central role of competition in driving China's recent economic growth and institutional change.[8] They argue that growing competition in product and factor markets developed from the periphery of central planning has drawn increasing numbers of enterprises from the plan to market-oriented economic activities by rewarding those that can make efficient use of resources and penalizing those that fail to do so.

Together with interfirm competition in product and factor markets, however, there has grown another type of competition – that between local governments. Many of the enterprises formed in the reform are "owned" by local governments and operate outside the central plan. Their growth and competitiveness have drawn greatly on the resource support, regulatory flexibility, and managerial incentives provided by their owners. Before the plan's demise in the mid-1990s,[9] many local governments even used their administrative power to back local enterprises against nonlocal ones in what has been described in Chinese media as "raw material wars" – fierce competition for locally produced industrial inputs that were in short supply, such as cotton, silkworm cocoon, tobacco leaves, and wool (e.g., *RMRB*, July 21, 1986, December 17, 1986, April 22, 1988, August 12, 1989). Following the example of cen-

---

[8] For elaborate accounts of this view, see Jefferson and Rawski (1994a, 1994b), Naughton (1992b, 1994a, 1994b, 1995a), McMillan and Naughton (1992), and Rawski (1994a, 1994b, 1995, 1999).

[9] In October 1992 the 14th CCP Congress formally abandoned the traditional emphasis on central planning and redefined China's transforming economy as moving in the direction of a "socialist market economy." In 1993 and 1994, the CCP spelled out detailed plans to bring this vision to reality, which were accompanied and followed by a constitutional amendment and a host of new laws and regulations aimed at clearing up the remains of central planning. See *RMRB* (December 12–14, 1998) for a chronology of the sequence of relevant events.

trally designated special economic zones in southern coastal areas, lower level governments have also established within their own jurisdictions various special policy enclaves, totaling 4,210 in 1997 (*RMRB*, January 23, 1998), to compete for investment, technology, and other resources from domestic and international sources.

In view of these developments, some scholars have proposed another explanation, which I call the "local developmental state thesis," to account for the driving forces behind the transition of enterprises from the plan to markets.[10] It is mainly concerned with the responses of local governments to the incentives created by fiscal decentralization during the reform, which has significantly strengthened the tie between local officials' financial and career rewards and the growth of local government revenue. According to this theory, efforts to expand the revenue base have led local officials to mobilize resources and bend existing rules for local enterprises' market-oriented activities that compete with those promoted by governments in other localities. The result is a weakening of commitment to the plan and a broadening of avenues to markets.

These contrasting views highlight two different drivers of economic change: market and hierarchy, which Charles Lindblom (1977) defines as being based on exchange relations and authority relations respectively. The economic competition thesis emphasizes the push-and-pull effects of cumulative competitive forces generated by the self-arranged exchanges of firms in product and factor markets. The local developmental state thesis recognizes the increasing market orientation of firms' activities and extends the notion of competition to interlocality interactions. Nevertheless, it focuses on the relationship between firms and local governments and treats it as a principal-agent issue involving control, monitoring, and incentives under restructured authority relations, rather than as a market phenomenon.

I see both views as capturing important aspects of reality and, despite the tension between them, complementing each other. Drawing on the insights from these views, this study seeks to cast light on what lies between them – i.e., the relationship between market and hierarchy, which I think holds a key to understanding the economic change in post-Mao China. I argue that market may be embedded in hierarchy and erode its foundation from within, instead of being spatially separated from it. In the reform era exchange relations have grown not only among economic actors, but also under hierarchical settings of interaction – between economic actors and state agents and among state agents themselves. It is the concurrent growth and mutual reinforcement of exchange

---

[10] There are differences, though, in the focus of analysis among various studies sharing this view. For details, see Byrd and Lin (1990), Lin (1995), Oi (1992, 1995, 1999), Montinola, Qian, and Weingast (1995), Qian and Xu (1993), and Walder (1995a, 1998).

relations in the economic and political processes that have driven much of the observed changes in China since 1978.

The working hypothesis that I use to develop a further explanation is the following: In the reform era, effective manipulation of state action – i.e., making gains from ad hoc favorable treatment by the state – constitutes a necessary condition for the success of firms. By scrutinizing evidence that confirms, qualifies, or contradicts this hypothesis, I search for clues to understanding a central feature of the post-Mao Chinese political economy. That is, the communist state has been transformed from the central leadership's tool of social engineering, guided by ideology and organized through close-knit authority relations (Schurmann 1968), to a marketlike place where the center loses coherent control and public authority and assets are extensively traded by state agents at various levels for self-defined purposes.

To see how this change has been related to the behavior and performance of industrial firms and what such a relationship reveals about the mechanisms of economic institutional change, it is important to take a look at the influence of state action on the distribution of advantages and disadvantages among firms before and since the reform.

Particularism under the Plan

The constraints and opportunities that firms face in their environments have a direct bearing on the selection and outcome of their strategies. In modern society the road to a firm's success may be seen as originating from two major sources: interaction among economic actors, and actions of the state. Identifying promising opportunities for value creation, making productive use of resources through coordinated efforts of employees, and realizing intended gains through smooth transactions with suppliers and buyers are among the important factors that contribute to the ability of a firm to excel. On the other hand, because the state usually allocates considerable amounts of financial, physical, and human resources, regulates economic opportunities, and distributes societally shared obligations (such as the costs for providing public goods and fixing negative externalities), differential treatment by the state in these aspects may significantly tilt the balance of gains among firms. Therefore, unless the state is impartial to all firms, variations in the direction and impact of state action are of great relevance to how firms behave and fare.

For over two decades after the "socialist transformation" in the mid-1950s, the influence of state action on the choices and rewards among Chinese enterprises was so overwhelming that the role of independent decisions and actions by economic actors was reduced to a minimum.

Under the central planning system, the state monopolized the allocation of all the economic resources and opportunities and tightly controlled the decision making regarding their use. Enterprises with high priority in the pecking order of centralized resource allocation were systematically better accommodated in the supply of factors and material inputs, given generally more favorable terms of trade, and granted more generous packages of financial and material rewards for their employees, than enterprises with low status.[11] The former included large, centrally controlled capital goods producers in the state sector; the latter were represented by small, locally controlled consumer goods producers in the so-called "collective" sector (Eckstein 1977; Solinger 1991a; Walder 1986).

Although vertical bargaining existed between enterprises and their supervising authorities, it was mainly pursued as a way for enterprises to finesse for breathing space by maintaining a certain level of organizational slack rather than to maximize financial returns (Rawski 1975). Whether an enterprise could be upgraded to a higher status in the hierarchy of resource allocation was mainly a matter of the interaction between different administrative levels of the state rather than between the enterprise and its supervising authorities (Granick 1990; Lieberthal and Oksenberg 1988). Moreover, although the central planning system was not without loopholes, the discretion of individual officials to change the terms of treatment for different enterprises was severely restrained by long and complex decision chains, difficulties of finding grounds of justification, and divisive organizational politics (Harding 1981; Shirk 1982; Walder 1986). Consequently, a clear and stable pattern of winners and losers was centrally defined and sustained. What this pattern signified was a highly institutionalized particularism in resource allocation and regulation, and an underdevelopment of exchange relations in both the economic and the political process.

The reform era has seen drastic changes. The once overwhelming shadow of central planning has faded away, and economic decision making has been significantly decentralized, especially at the level of the firm (Naughton 1994a, 1995a; World Bank 1992). Many previously disadvantaged enterprises, such as those formerly known as commune and brigade enterprises in rural areas and now called township and village enterprises (TVEs hereafter), have become prominent winners (Byrd and Lin 1990; Ma Rong, Huang Chaohan, Wang Hansheng, and

---

[11] Under the prereform system, much of the surplus (accounting profit) of enterprises was extracted and redistributed by the state. As a result, the ratio between input and output did not bear a clear correlation with the actual gains accruing to different enterprises. The advantages of the most favored enterprises consisted mainly in the quantity, quality, and stability of the resources allocated to them and in the allowance for the provision of extra benefits to their employees. See Chapter 2 for more discussion of this.

Yang Mu 1994; Oi 1999; Walder 1998).[12] They are joined by increasing numbers of other new forms of economic organization, such as foreign capital enterprises, private enterprises, and joint ownership enterprises, which have risen from nonexistence to a solid segment of the economy, accounting for 40% of the gross industrial output and 63% of the total retail sales of consumer goods in 1998 (GJTJJa 1999: 421, 546–7). In contrast, many previously privileged enterprises, especially those in the state sector, have lagged behind in performance; some have even fallen to the ranks of losers (Steinfeld 1998; Woo 1999; Zheng Haihang 1998). As a result, one can no longer construct a clear profile of winners and losers by using a few structural indicators, such as ownership classification, administrative rank of an enterprise's immediate supervising authority, sector, and size.

Many changes have accompanied and contributed to such reshuffling of winners and losers.[13] The most obvious development is the rise of markets for products and (to a lesser degree) factors, as well as a concurrent intensification of competition in these markets. This raises two questions. Does the expansion of concrete markets represent a corresponding growth of a particular modus operandi of economic activities, known as "the market," where winners and losers are determined by the anonymous interplay between demand and supply? How has the role of the state in the selection of winners and losers changed?

Competitive Advantage in Economic Transition

To address these questions, let me begin with the notion "market." The simplest way to define market is to see it as a nexus of trade. In *Webster's Ninth New Collegiate Dictionary*, for example, the first definition of market is "a meeting together of people for the purpose of trade by private purchase and sale and usually not by auction." But such a definition often fails to capture the whole meaning of the term in use – not only in academic literature but in journalism. When market is referred to as a mode of resource allocation and economic coordination – often

---

[12] I define winners and losers in the reform era as enterprises with above or below average financial performances (see Chapter 1 for a discussion of performance indicators). I focus on the relative standing of individual cases rather than the absolute level of their performance. Seen in this light, losers need not be in the red or face immediate threat to survival, which may be sustained by a variety of economic and noneconomic factors (Meyer and Zucker 1989). Nor do those with above average performance necessarily achieve it through efficient use of resources in economic activities.

[13] For overviews and comprehensive discussions of the Chinese reform, see Bell, Khor, and Kochhar (1993), Davis and Vogel (1990), Harding (1987), Naughton (1995a), Perkins (1988, 1994), Perry and Wong (1985), and Walder (1995b).

known as "the market" – its rudimentary function of providing a nexus of trade is seen as being integrated with two other functions: a locus of information and incentives, and a screen through which the relative payoffs to the participants in exchange are determined. The levels and ups and downs of prices may carry important information (and misinformation) to economic actors, thereby forming a frame of reference and posing positive and negative incentives to their decision making. Also, given equal protection of property rights and freedom of enterprise and trade, the payoffs to each economic organization may be subjected to the independent decisions of other participants in economic activities (especially output buyers, input and factor suppliers, and competitors) on price, quantity, and transaction. Consequently, the economic prize goes to the most efficient players while the inefficient players are penalized and weeded out. When all these three functions are brought into full play, what emerges is the ideal-typical picture of a market economy (Samuelson and Nordhaus 1985; Stiglitz 1993).

How far and in what ways the reality in advanced capitalist economies differs from this ideal type has been a matter of debate.[14] The relevant issue here is how this conception contrasts with economic change in a transitional economy like China's where concrete markets have been expanding and affecting the decision making and performance of economic organizations.

Economic Competition

The economic competition thesis argues that the growth of markets for products and factors in the reforming Chinese economy represents a mutual inducement and consequently more or less concurrent expansion of the above three roles that markets may play.[15] Such a process has taken place through piecemeal economic reform that opens up limited spaces for self-arranged trade among economic actors, especially those operating on the periphery of central planning. The competitive forces spawned

---

[14] The conventional view, based on neoclassical economic theory, of Western capitalist economies as resembling this ideal type has been challenged by many studies. See, e.g., Galbraith (1967), Granovetter (1985), Lazonick (1991), and Lindblom (1977).

[15] A contending view is the so-called big bang theory, championed by Jeffrey Sachs, of economic change in former communist economies. Despite explicit statements made by some of those sharing the economic competition thesis to criticize the works of Jeffrey Sachs and his associates (e.g., Rawski 1994a, 1995), the main difference between them is not concerned with what a well functioning market system is like – both seem to see it in the light of the ideal-typical image described above. Rather, it lies in the institutional and organizational prerequisites for such a system to emerge and take shape. See Sachs and Woo (1994a, 1994b) and Woo (1994, 1999) for summaries of the focal issues under debate and critiques of the economic competition thesis, and Rawski (1995) for a spirited rebuttal (see also Rawski 1999).

in such openings have in turn amplified the role of markets in signaling information and incentives and screening winners and losers, thereby intensifying the drives and pressures for further reform. Although the economy has yet to be fully marketized, it is increasingly "marketlike." In the words of Rawski (1994a):

> In essence, institutional changes arising from partial reform created a virtuous circle in which the growing intensity of competition not only rewarded winners and punished losers, but by crippling the growth of fiscal revenues, diminished the ability of the state to protect losers from the consequences of high costs, poor quality, and other long-standing habits carried over from the planned economy . . . Partial reform has produced 15 years of strong growth and stimulated massive shifts from plan to market, from rent-seeking to profit-seeking, and from innovation-by-direction to decentralized technical change.

Findings from studies in line with this argument indicate indeed that the decision making of enterprises in both the rapidly expanding non-state sector and the traditional state sector has been increasingly responsive to the information conveyed by price movements in markets, and that much of the gains accruing to enterprises has been realized through the sales of their output (e.g., Jefferson and Rawski 1994a, 1994b; Jefferson and Singh 1999; Naughton 1995a; Rawski 1994b). What is left open to question, however, is whether the terms of trade among enterprises are determined mainly by the decisions and actions of interacting economic actors.[16] If such terms are significantly shaped by other forces (e.g., the decisions and actions of state agents) despite an expansion of self-arranged transactions between economic actors, then the potential role of markets as a screen through which to determine the relative payoffs among enterprises is severely restrained. Under such a condition, it is questionable to equate an expansion of concrete markets for products and factors to an expansion of the conceptual abstraction of market as a particular mode of economic activity.[17] Equally questionable

---

[16] An oft-cited example to support the economic competition argument is the growing inability of many state enterprises to enlist particularistic support from the state to protect their previously privileged status and contain their losses (see, e.g., the above quotation from Rawski). But in no way does this indicate that the better performing enterprises (especially those in the nonstate sector) do not get ad hoc favorable treatment from the state.

[17] Failure to recognize this important difference between concrete markets and the ideal-typical image of market as a mode of economic coordination and regulation appears to have led some studies (e.g., Nee 1989, 1991) to see markets and state power as mutually exclusive phenomena and conclude that in post-Mao China the rise of the former has led to the decline of the latter. For a critique of the tautological logic in the analysis developed from this dichotomized view, see Walder (1996).

is the related argument that it is primarily the "anonymous forces" generated by competing economic actors in such markets that have rewarded efficient enterprises (mostly operating outside the plan) and penalized inefficient ones (mostly situated under the plan), making the plan unsustainable and thereby leading to a gradual decrease of the scale and scope of central planning.[18]

Empirically, there is ample evidence of strong influence of state action on both the expansion of the economic space outside the plan and the outcomes of economic activities motivated and mediated by markets. Take the example of TVEs, which are a major driving force of economic change in the reform era. Their phenomenal growth has been closely related to the actions of local governments. Lowering or removing entry barriers, providing or facilitating factor supplies, relaxing or bending existing rules and regulations, offering tax reductions and exemptions, and improving local infrastructure are among the measures taken by local officials to help *selected* local firms to develop and expand their competitive edge. Such a powerful helping hand has been at work not only in the initial stage of rural industrialization but all along the way of its expansion, as has been detailed by existing studies (e.g., Byrd and Lin 1990; Ma Rong et al. 1994; Oi 1995, 1998, 1999; Walder 1995a, 1998).

Another example is the pursuit by state agents of private gains through active involvement in market-oriented economic activities. It is widely reported that in the reform era favor exchange has extensively taken place between state agents and economic actors operating outside the plan (e.g., Bruun 1993; Liu 1992; Odgaard 1992; Solinger 1993; Wank 1996, 1999; Young 1995). Such exchange channels physical, financial, and human resources away from the plan, perpetuates ad hoc modifications of existing regulations initiated by economic actors, and creates a highly uneven economic opportunity structure that shapes the distribution of competitive advantages and disadvantages both within and outside the plan. In return, state agents secure various private benefits, ranging from outright bribes to various hidden forms of personal enrichment. Moreover, large numbers of state agencies, including communist party organizations and the military, have formed their own front organizations for profit making (*Far Eastern Economic Review*, August 6, 1998: 68–9; Lin and Zhang 1999; *RMRB*, July 14, 16, 23, 1998; see also Chapter 4). Operating outside the regular budgets and administrative functions of their sponsoring agencies, these entities divert plan-allocated resources for arbitrage, broker ad hoc regulatory favors, and compete directly with ordinary enterprises. The double role of state agents as referee and player

---

[18] The rationale of this argument is that economic competition drives down the profits of inefficient state enterprises, thereby eroding the revenue base of their supervising authorities and intensifying the financial pressures and enterprise lobbying faced by such authorities. See Rawski (1994a, 1995) and Naughton (1995a).

in market-oriented economic activities weakens their commitment to the enforcement of the plan, drains its resource pool, and adds more twists to the distribution of rewards and penalties in the economic space outside the plan.

Proponents of the economic competition thesis do take partial notice of such evidence (e.g., Naughton 1995a; Rawski 1995). But their accounts fall short of showing its relevance to the decline of the plan and the formation of the economic space outside it. Their focus of analysis instead centers on the interactions among enterprises, which they see as the main driving force behind the changes in government economic policy. Given the importance that they attach to the competitive pressures generated from outside the plan, this omission obscures a major linkage in the economic institutional change that they seek to explain.[19] Bringing to light this linkage will further reveal the causal mechanisms in the chain of events that their accounts have masterfully illustrated.

The Local Developmental State

In contrast, the role of state action in China's recent marketization is brought to the center of the picture by studies sharing the local developmental state thesis. Their common view is that market expansion in the reform era has been greatly advanced by promarket policies of local governments, ranging from tolerating economic actors' self-arranged activities outside state plan to actively providing regulatory and resource support for such activities (Montinola et al. 1995; Oi 1992, 1999; Walder 1994, 1995a, 1998). In this view, the main driver of such policy orientation is the fiscal decentralization started in the early 1980s to address shortfalls in public finance, leading to an increase of the decision-making power of local governments in regulating local economic activities and allocating public resources. The resultant restructuring of authority relations within the state apparatus has greatly strengthened the tie between local officials' financial and career rewards and the growth of local government revenue. To advance their interests in the face of such institutional incentives and in view of the growing interregional competition for resources and markets, local officials have sought to promote revenue growth by facilitating market-oriented economic activities carried out by selected local (and predominantly public) enter-

---

[19] In fact, similar omission is also evident in their discussion of changes in the state sector economy, where promarket policy outcomes are portrayed as expedient responses to unexpected consequences of earlier actions by policy makers who, according to Naughton (1995a: 23), are only "weakly rational." In this light, state action is largely seen as reactive and yielding to cumulative market pressures rather than as opportunistic and proactive.

prises under their purview. As a result, enterprises with strong backing from the local state have been able to grow and compete in the economic space outside the plan.

These findings bring into sharp focus some of the obscurities in the economic competition thesis. They convincingly show that state agents have played a vital role in shaping China's marketization process. They also suggest that to account for the changes in the economy it is crucial to investigate the changes that have taken place within the state apparatus. In order for the potential of this line of inquiry to be fully brought out, however, three important issues need to be further examined.

First, the local development state thesis is developed mainly on the basis of investigations into rural political and economic change in the wake of decollectivization. Although rural jurisdictions constitute the majority of China's local – subprovincial – governments, there are also a significant number of local administrative centers in urban areas, where the magnitude of economic activities assumes even greater significance.[20] How and why actions of the local state in rural and urban areas are similar or different in their effects on the transition from the plan to markets need to be explored.

Second, although there seems to be little doubt that local officials have become more concerned about revenue growth in the reform, how they generate and use revenues needs to be scrutinized. This issue is important because it holds clues to revealing the driving forces of the economic decision making of local officials, which is regarded by the local development state thesis as being largely consistent with the public agenda tied to the formal institutional incentives faced by local officials.

An argument that extends from the thesis is that local enterprises that can contribute the most to local government revenue growth tend to receive from local officials the most favorable treatment in regulation and resource allocation. The causality implied in this relationship, however, is qualified by empirical evidence, including that reported in the studies of some proponents of the thesis. Successful local enterprises indeed have close relationships with local officials, but they are oftentimes the ones that continuously receive substantial exemptions from formal revenue obligations to the local government.[21] On the other hand,

---

[20] In 1997, there were 1,693 counties (excluding county-rank cities), 44,689 townships and 739,400 villages in the countryside, whereas there were 664 cities and 737 districts in large cities (GJTJJa 1998: 3, 385). In the same year, the output produced in 226 medium and large cities (above the level of prefecture) accounted for 44% of China's GDP (GJTJJa 1998: 55; ZGCSFZYJH 1998: 105).

[21] In a study of rural industry in a county in Shandong province, for example, Oi (1998) reported that in 1990 nearly 30% of the tax breaks in the county went to a single enterprise favored by the local government. For similar findings, see Byrd and Lin (1990), Ma Rong et al. (1994), and Oi (1999).

the burden of revenue generation weighs heavily on parties that are less favored by local officials, and such a pattern has become increasingly prevalent with the deepening of marketization.[22] This disparity points to a need to ascertain whether the preferential allocative and regulatory treatment that local officials extend to their favored enterprises is motivated primarily by concerns about the growth of local *public* resources, and whether other considerations, such as promoting the private interests of the key decision makers on both sides, have also played an important part in this regard.

A phenomenon widely noted in studies of enterprise reforms and their fiscal implications is that the enterprises favored by local officials are often where large sums of taxes are not collected as budgetary revenue of the government, but deposited as resources that can be accessed and disposed of by local officials for self-defined purposes (e.g., Ma Rong et al. 1994; Wang Shaoguang and Hu Angang 1994). Indeed, there is evidence that what local officials are most keen to expand are not the revenues that end up in the pool of budgetary resources, which are subject to relatively tight regulation and monitoring by the fiscal authority (Wong, Heady, and Woo 1995; Wong 1997). Rather, it is the various "off-budget" revenue categories – "extra-budgetary funds" and hidden slush funds, which have drastically increased in the reform[23] that constitutes the focus of local officials' attention and efforts.[24] The main reason for this is that such resources can be used in a more discretionary fashion by local officials than budgetary revenue (Deng Yingtao, Yao Gang, Xu Xiaobo, and Xue Yuwei 1990), where the boundary between "public" and "private" uses is much more clearly defined.

This brings up the third issue that needs to be further examined, i.e., mutual monitoring among officials, which has been the primary mechanism by which the communist state maintains its organizational health. It is important to note that, although economic policies are often made and enforced collectively by local officials, they are not a homogeneous group. In terms of behavioral orientation, they can be categorized as committed communists, self-seeking opportunists, and "middle-of-the-roaders" with mixed motives (Nee and Lian 1994). In organizational politics, they experience latent or open interpersonal rivalries and face factional divisions. Yet, bending existing rules for local market expan-

---

[22] A large part of this burden consists of various nontax levies contrived and imposed by various government agencies. See the discussion in Chapter 7.

[23] See Chapter 5.

[24] Oi (1999: Chapter 6) has an extensive discussion of extra-budgetary funds under local governments. The focal point is that there has been a weakening of central monitoring over this growing pool of locally disposed resources, which she sees as being mainly used to finance the development of local public enterprises.

sion and giving differential treatment to economic actors often involve unorthodox, deviant, or even illicit use of the authority under the collective control of local officials. In order for these actions to be effective, peer consent is indispensable.

The local developmental state thesis suggests that the basis for such consent has been broadened in the reform because decentralization has aligned the interests of local officials closely with the shared goal of revenue growth. Under restructured authority relations within the state apparatus, local officials tend to act like real owners of local public assets and take concerted collective action to exert close monitoring over the use of such assets in government administration and in local public enterprises. The underlying assumption is that the formal financial and career rewards for local officials are strong enough to contain the extent of their self-seeking behavior that is inconsistent with the public agenda of the local government.

The pattern of revenue generation and disposal discussed above suggests a need for caution in the use of such an assumption. Moreover, findings on local officials' behavioral change in the reform, especially those from accounts of widespread corruption, strongly indicate that mutual monitoring within the state apparatus has been seriously weakened by collusion among the guardians of public authority and assets for various self-defined purposes.[25] The "public" facade of local state action, therefore, should not be taken at face value. To shed sharper light on the process of economic institutional change and its consequences, it is important to explore how and why collusion has grown among state agents in a system where "divide-and-rule" has been the modus operandi (Harding 1981; Lee 1978; Shirk 1982; Walder 1986), and how such collusion between officials has been justified to cover up the extent to which it contradicts or undermines publicly announced agenda of the state.

Addressing these issues requires further investigation into what has taken place in the process of decentralization. Delegation of decision-making authority and reassignment of property rights to administrative loci at lower levels may indeed be conducive to consensus building among local officials. But this change does not in itself attain the end result of expanding common interests among them, especially those based on shared private agenda. Local officials, for example, may have divergent goals and different priorities with regard to the use of delegated authority. Reassignment of property rights to local jurisdictions

---

[25] For discussions on various aspects of corruption in the post-Mao era, see Dickson (1990), Gong (1994), Kwong (1997), Lee (1990), Lu (2000), Ma (1989), Manion (1996b, 1997), Oi (1989b), Rocca (1992), Sands (1989), Sun (1991), and Wedeman (1996).

indeed increases the financial power of local officials, thus making them look more like "principals" than "agents" of public assets as compared to their previous status (Oi 1999). But this does not change the fact that the officials there are not de jure owners of such rights and thus cannot legitimately use public assets for private purposes. Nor does it change the qualitative difference between true owners and local officials acting as pseudo owners in terms of risk bearing and immunity to opportunism in asset use.[26]

On the other hand, there is nontrivial evidence, cited above and to be presented below, that collusion has become a significant feature of local state action, and the motives of local officials to intensify efforts to extract revenue may be more diverse than a coherent response to the formal institutional incentives under decentralization. It is therefore important to examine more closely the mechanisms that facilitate the development of mutually beneficial agenda among local officials, raise the opportunity cost of alternative routes (e.g., whistle-blowing) of self-interest accommodation, and neutralize potential saboteurs of collusive collective action. In particular, the strategies for peer co-optation and fabrication of justification for self-seeking behavior – both representing attempts to weaken traditional constraints based on mutual monitoring within the state apparatus – merit close attention.

Dual Marketization

What the above discussion suggests is that to account for the mechanisms of China's recent economic change attention needs to be extended from exchange relations between economic actors to two other types of exchange relations: those between economic actors and state agents and those among state agents themselves. The first type constitutes a key element in the strategies of economic actors to move away from the plan and to compete in the growing economic space outside it. The second type provides a major avenue through which interdependence is enhanced among state agents and developed into mutually beneficial collusive actions that redefine the process and outcome of the state's decision making. Investigating how these two types of exchange relations interact with each other, with the growing exchange relations between economic actors (which the economic competition thesis focuses on), and with the restructuring of authority relations within the state (which is emphasized

---

[26] For a discussion of the moral hazard associated with this, see Chapter 7 and Whiting (1996, 1999).

by the local developmental state thesis), may lead to more revealing findings on the forces that have driven the changes in the rules governing economic activities and fashioned their outcomes in the post-Mao era.

To this end, it is useful to look beyond the narrow view of market as an arena of interaction among economic actors and to see, by extending Lindblom's analysis of social control mechanisms (1977),[27] all exchange relations in the economic and the political process as market phenomena. Based on such a conception, a distinction can be made between two types of market: an economic market where the exchange of goods, services, and resources takes place between economic actors, and a political market where exchange takes place between economic actors and state agents and among state agents themselves with regard to the use of state authority and assets.[28] The expansion of the former need not be accompanied by a concurrent expansion of "the market" – a simultaneous manifestation of *all* three potential roles (i.e., nexus of trade, locus of information and incentives, and screen for selecting winners and losers) that exchange relations among economic actors may play.[29] The latter may also be called the political marketplace in that the major items traded there – resources, opportunities, and exemptions from state-engendered liabilities – are often locality specific and lodged in concrete organizational and institutional settings of the state apparatus.

Both markets faced severe constraints under the prereform system, where command-driven central planning, the inhibiting shadow of Maoist ideology over open pursuit of self-interest, and deep interpersonal divisions in highly politicized organizational processes seriously limited the room for exchange relations to develop and multiply. Their concurrent rise in the reform, on the other hand, represents an essential feature

---

[27] Lindblom (1977) discerns three basic methods of social control: exchange, authority, and persuasion.

[28] Parish and Michelson (1996) categorize three types of political markets: bargaining between workers and managers and between managers and the state bureaucracy in the state sector; exchange ties between nonstate entrepreneurs and state bureaucracy and state enterprises; and patronage networks in electoral politics. Although I share their emphasis on the need to look beyond a narrow view of economic marketization, I regard the difference between state and nonstate (especially collective) firms with regard to the organizational and institutional legacies of state control as a matter of degree rather than kind. For the sake of simplicity, my discussion of the political market only includes exchange relations that directly involve state action, without assuming that exchange relations between economic actors are unaffected by their concurrent interactions with state agents.

[29] In the remainder of the book, I use "markets" to refer to concrete markets for products and resources. In contrast, the term "the market" denotes the three-pronged platform underlying a market economy.

of China's transforming economic and political institutions. My account of this process is built around three arguments.

First, the exchange relations between economic actors and those involving state agents are mutually inducing and accommodating. Exchanging favors with state agents helps reduce regulatory and resource constraints on favor seekers and thereby enhances their ability to enter and compete in the growing economic space outside the plan. It also brings direct benefits to state agents, thus stimulating their attempts to overcome existing constraints on their discretionary power.

Second, fabrication of justification for self-seeking behavior in public office and peer co-optation among state agents weaken mutual monitoring. Extensive use of these strategies by state agents in the reform era has facilitated the growth of exchange relations in the political process.

Third, competition among economic actors for favors from the state plays a key role in shaping the process and outcome of economic institutional change. Competitive favor seeking spreads the effects of ad hoc changes in the rules of the game, reducing entrenched barriers to economic freedom and growth. It also limits the gains from preferential treatment of firms, forcing them to look beyond special favors for ways to compete on economic grounds while exploring additional areas for rule bending. A result of these developments is the broadening of avenues for output growth. On the other hand, competitive favor seeking sows the seeds for problems that may fully manifest themselves down the road and affect future economic growth. It contributes to an overbuilding of production capacities and creates growing pockets of slack in underperforming enterprises. It also stimulates state agents' attempts to increase the diversion of public resources, which consequently drains the state's capacity to provide public goods and services. The resultant intensification of predation by state agents on less favored parties increases the tension between the state and the society.

It should be noted that the term "favor seeking" that I use in this context concerns a wide range of exchange relations between state agents and economic actors seeking allocative and regulatory favors. It covers what "political corruption" and "rent seeking" are often used to describe (see note 2). But I define it more broadly to include elements that these alternative notions often do not commonly or separately cover. The first one is the use by state agents of public office in exchange for private gains in "gray areas" of state action, which is often excluded from "political corruption" strictly defined in terms of the legality of state agents' behavior (Rose-Ackerman 1978: 7). The second one concerns collusion between state agents and outsiders for sheer embezzlement of state assets, which is largely outside the focus of rent-seeking theory – "the study of how people compete for artificially contrived transfers" (Tollison

1982).[30] The third one has to do with enlisting the help of state agents in overcoming pre-existing regulatory restrictions on economic freedom, which need not be illegal and hence may not amount to "political corruption." Efforts in this regard may give rise to monopoly profit for first movers who are able to capture new opportunities of value creation.[31] In contrast, the competitive rent seeking that conventional rent-seeking theory focuses on involves competition to create and sustain monopolies that thrive on pricing power rather than value creation (Tollison 1982; Tullock 1967).

It should also be noted that what is meant by a "favor" involves preferential treatment by state agents in the distribution of resources, opportunities, and state-engendered liabilities. It need not amount to an increase of net gain for the favor seeker, as it may refer to loss cutting – e.g., prevention or containment of officials' arbitrary levies and extortionary demands beyond the formal obligations of economic actors to the state, which is sometimes treated as a special case in the literature on political corruption and rent seeking (Bardhan 1997).[32]

Moreover, competition in favor seeking need not be open or face-to-face – favor seekers may remain anonymous to one another and go after the same or similar kinds of favors in different sectors and localities. Nor is competitive favor seeking necessarily a zero-sum game where a "winner-takes-all" rule applies among all participants – entry barriers, for example, may be lowered or removed by the same official(s) for multiple favor seekers. The multiplication of favor-seeking efforts, however, has an important bearing on the relative payoffs to different economic actors, as it directly affects their ability to undertake and sustain profit-oriented economic activities, the cost structure of their operations, or both.

---

[30] The rent-seeking literature, however, does cover competition for exclusive rights for government contracts, which the rent seeker(s) may overprice, resulting in a transfer of public funds to private contractors (Mueller 1989: 242–3). This may be seen as a special form of embezzlement of state assets.

[31] Buchanan (1980) defines such a phenomenon as "profit seeking" and distinguishes it from rent seeking, which is based on contrived restrictions on certain economic actors in selected areas of economic activities. An implicit assumption of his discussion is that in an economy where basic market institutions are in place to ensure free entry and exit, profit seeking by first movers can be independent of rent seeking. In a transitional economy such as China's, however, such an assumption may not hold. A first mover's advantage often stems from or is predicated on efforts to enlist ad hoc help of officials to relax or overcome the institutional constraints of the existing system. This type of uneven regulatory treatment thus may blur the line between profit seeking and rent seeking.

[32] See the last section of Chapter 7 for a discussion of this issue.

Outline of the Book

To bring to light the mechanisms of dual marketization, I explore the trajectories whereby industrial firms have moved from the plan to the economic space outside it. My investigation focuses on the variations in the pace, strategy, and outcome of different industrial firms during this process of institutional change. In particular, I seek to identify contributing factors for the unevenness between state enterprises and nonstate enterprises in these regards. The former have been the mainstay of the centrally planned economy, whereas the latter have become the leading force of market-oriented economic activities.[33] By examining how industrial firms compete and how the balances of advantage and disadvantage have been shifted among firms in the reform, I search for clues to understanding how the development of the political market has been coupled with that of the economic market, how the rules of the economic game have been changed by interacting economic actors and state agents,[34] and how such a course of institutional change has been related to the recent economic growth of China as well as to the economic and political challenges that the country faces.

My analysis combines macro-level accounts of structural changes in the reform with micro-level examination of the links and ramifications of such changes to the behavior and performance of firms. For the latter, I rely mainly on in-depth case studies. It is important to note that the findings, especially those from case studies, are intended to reveal the mechanisms at work. They are by no means exhaustive. What I hope to achieve through context-specific accounts of concrete causal links is to identify materials that can be used to develop testable hypotheses, thereby paving the way for further investigation. In view of the sensitivity of a large part of the information derived from the case studies, I use pseudonyms to refer to the persons, enterprises, and places that appear in the book, so as to avoid any adverse consequences to the informants.

As the point of departure, Chapter 1 offers an overview of the Chinese industrial economy. It provides a sketch of old and new forms of industrial firms and highlights major aspects of the process by which market-driven economic activities have expanded beyond the plan. It shows that state enterprises have lagged behind nonstate enterprises in terms of both the degree of participation in market-oriented economic activities and

---

[33] It should be noted that this does not imply a distinction between public and private ownership, as many of the enterprises in the latter category are owned by local governments.

[34] Although my discussion concerns both how old rules have been changed and how new rules have emerged, the focus of analysis centers on the former, as the process of institutional change is still unfolding and has by no means reached a point of stabilization.

the level of performance in the new economic game. On the other hand, there is evidence that the widely perceived superiority of the nonstate sector has been exaggerated, and that both groups have experienced deterioration in performance over time. This suggests a need to look beyond dichotomized ownership labels and investigate the forces that have shaped the formation of competitive advantage in concrete organizational and institutional settings.

Chapters 2 and 3 embark on this exploration with a close examination of case study materials focusing on the changing sources of advantages and disadvantages among different types of firms during the transformation from the plan to markets. The evidence indicates that the narrow view of firms' competitiveness as being based on what is commonly defined as economic efficiency tends to miss many of the critical elements that affect the variations in the behavior and performance of firms, resulting in oversimplified conclusions. Although the locus of decision making in the state apparatus has been decentralized in the reform, particularism has remained the defining feature of state action, which has direct implications for industrial firms. Localized state authority is found to be potent, resourceful, ad hoc responsive, and indeterminate with regard to whether to be helpful, neutral, restrictive, or exploitative. Whether a firm can excel depends greatly on whether it is perceived as an asset rather than a burden or threat to the collective and individual interests of state agents, whether it can maximize allocative and regulatory gains from the state apparatus, and whether it can avoid or minimize exploitation by state agents. Although the expanding markets for products and factors have become a key motivating and mediating force of economic activities, they are often overshadowed by particularistic state action in shaping the economic outcomes of firms. Also, the expansion of the extra-plan economic space itself depends greatly on ad hoc removal by state agents of pre-existing barriers to economic freedom.

To discern what re-orients particularistic state action and to shed further light on how such action affects the behavior and performance of industrial firms in the reform era, Chapter 4 explores the pursuit by state agents of entrepreneurial activities. The discussion focuses on various profit-seeking entities under the sponsorship of state agencies. The proliferation of these entities since the mid-1980s has driven state agents to re-prioritize their allocative and regulatory decisions in accordance with their re-configured collective and individual interests. The menaces and opportunities presented by these entities to industrial firms are examined in three aspects of the interaction between them: competition, transaction, and collusion. Enterprises that are able to steer such interaction to their advantage tend to have an edge over those extensively exposed to the downside. The evidence also indicates that the decline of the plan is due not only to the push-and-pull effects generated by interactions among economic actors, but to the corrosive effects of the self-seeking behavior of state agents.

Based on case studies of two local governments, Chapter 5 examines how exchange relations have grown in the political process and how differences in this regard affect the interactions among local government authorities in rural and urban areas and the enterprises under their purview. What the findings show is that the policy re-orientation from political mobilization and ideological indoctrination to economic development has broadened the common interests between local officials, especially political and nonpolitical functionaries. Also, the reform has been accompanied by a widening gap in administrative financing and an increase of uncertainties and inconsistencies in the policy process. In view of these developments, opportunistic officials have pursued various strategies to justify their self-seeking behavior, such as making the state's regular administrative functions dependent on off-budget funds and disguising self-defined agenda under the cover of reform. In the meantime, they have also made deliberate efforts to muffle whistle-blowing by sharing part of their spoils with those who are not actively involved in profit-seeking activities.

Due to differences in the path-dependent organizational structures of local governments, however, local officials have pursued different strategies to accommodate their individual and collective interests in the increasingly marketized local political and economic processes. Such strategies diverge between two types: externalization of the avenues for self-seeking pursuits from the formal organizational structure of the local government in urban areas, and internalization of such avenues in rural jurisdictions. Because of the dispersion of state agents' interests under the former regime, enterprises situated under it tend to face more adverse conditions of state action than those under the latter.

Chapter 6 explores the implications of such structural difference for the interaction between favor seekers and local officials. It focuses on the means of favor seeking – personal networks. The findings suggest that the use of this means faces greater constraint in urban jurisdictions, which are the homes of state enterprises, than in rural jurisdictions, where the majority of nonstate enterprises are located. The main reason is that urban enterprises are more extensively exposed than rural enterprises to the downside of what I call "third party effects" – the effects on a dyadic exchange exerted by one or both of the participants' interaction(s) with other parties. Such a difference, I argue, is an important contributing factor to the disparity in the process and outcome of marketization between state and nonstate enterprises.

In Chapter 7 I discuss the consequences of dual marketization. The focal issue is why economic growth has not been seriously hampered by the expansion of exchange relations in the political process. I take a two-step approach in this discussion: to examine the forces at work in the short run and to identify latent problems that have yet to manifest themselves fully. Competition in the economic and the political market is shown to have played a critical role in both regards. It has brought down entrenched barriers to economic freedom and eroded monopoly profits, thus unleashing enormous opportunities for output growth. But the growth of competitive forces in both markets has also led to growing organizational slack, intensification of predation by state agents on less favored parties, and consequently increase of tension between the state and the society. A full manifestation of these problems will likely pose serious challenges to further economic growth and institutional change.

1

Chinese Industrial Enterprises: A Bird's-Eye View

Industry as defined by the Chinese government includes manufacturing, mining, and production and supply of electricity, gas, water, and steam. It is China's largest economic sector. Its leading position was established by the government's concentrated effort to industrialize the economy during the three decades after the communist revolution. In 1949 the industrial sector contributed less than 13% of China's national income (GJTJJa 1983: 24).[1] In 1978 it accounted for 44.3% of the country's gross domestic product (GDP); in 1998 its share remained at 42.2% despite a significant increase in the contribution from the tertiary sector during the preceding two decades (GJTJJa 1999: 13).

The main avenue of state-engineered industrialization in the postrevolution era was central planning, and the main vehicles that carried it through were state enterprises. Since 1978, however, the central planning system has declined. The development of the state sector economy has also changed course toward markets. But state enterprises have been overtaken by nonstate enterprises, especially those formed in the reform, as the leading force of marketization. Indeed, many state enterprises have demonstrated a slow pace in participating in market-oriented economic activities, faced great difficulties in competition, and experienced steady deterioration in performance. To see how and why these changes have taken place, it is necessary to take a bird's-eye view of the transforming landscape of the industrial sector.

---

[1] Before 1992, "national income," which includes "net material product" (a form of value-added) in agriculture, industry, construction, commerce, transportation, and communications, was used in government statistics as the national account indicator for net output. Since then it has been replaced by "gross domestic product," which includes all the elements contained in "national income" as well as value-added in other sectors, such as banking, other financial services, education, and cultural activities (GJTJJa 1994: 49).

The Organizational Setting

Until the mid-1990s, industrial enterprises in China were classified by the government solely according to the identity of their owners.[2] In general, they fell into five major categories: state enterprises, urban and rural collective enterprises, (domestic) private enterprises, foreign capital enterprises, and joint ownership enterprises.[3]

State enterprises have been the mainstay of Chinese industry, though their dominance has been seriously undercut by the growth of industrial enterprises of other ownership forms in the post-Mao era (see Table 1.1). Their foundation was formed with (i) the industrial facilities taken over from the KMT regime and foreign industrialists in the late 1940s, (ii) the plants nationalized from private Chinese industrialists in the mid-1950s, and (iii) the massive economic aid provided by the Soviet Union in the 1950s (Wang Haibo 1994). But the majority of the enterprises in this group were built up over the ensuing three decades with substantial investment by the state, primarily via the resource allocation mechanism of the central planning system.

Administratively, state enterprises have been placed under the direct control of central government ministries, provincial governments, city or county governments, or a combination of these three levels. The higher the level of direct government control, the greater the importance attached to an enterprise and therefore the higher its priority ranking in resource allocation under the central plan. Before the 14th Congress of the Chinese Communist Party in 1992, members of this group were referred to as *guoying qiye* or state-run enterprises. Since then, their classification label has been modified to *guoyou qiye* or state-owned

---

[2] On July 1, 1994, the *Company Law* came into effect, with the explicit goal of instituting a new governance structure for newly established or reorganized economic organizations, including industrial enterprises. It discards the existing ownership labels and regroups economic organizations into two categories: those registered as limited liability companies and those as limited liability stock companies. Although the old classification has remained in effect, the government has planned to phase it out gradually and to make the *Company Law* the cornerstone of China's "modern enterprise system" (*RMRB*, August 8, 1997).

[3] In addition to ownership, industrial enterprises are also classified into two categories in government statistics: independent accounting units and nonindependent accounting units. According to the State Statistical Bureau (GJTJJa 1995: 401), independent accounting industrial organizations need to meet three criteria: They must (i) register as a legal person, have independent organizational form and location, and bear legal responsibility; (ii) have independent possession of assets, debt-bearing status, and authority to enter into contracts with other parties; and (iii) conduct independent profit-loss accounting and maintain independent balance sheets. In contrast, nonindependent accounting units are those affiliated with other organizations and do not meet the above three criteria.

Table 1.1. *Shares of state and nonstate enterprises in the industrial sector (unit: %)*[a]

Year	Gross Industrial Output			Number of Employees			Total Assets		
	State	Collective	Other	State	Collective	Other	State	Collective	Other
1978	77.6	22.4		72.1	27.9		87.3	12.7	
1980	76.0	24.0		64.6	35.4		80.9	18.1	1.0
1985	64.9	32.1	3.1	58.4	40.7	0.9	75.8	20.6	3.6
1990	54.6	35.6	25.0	57.3	40.4	2.4	58.9	19.1	22.0
1995	34.0	34.0	32.0	52.1	36.0	11.9	55.9	17.3	26.8
1997	25.5	38.1	36.4	49.5	34.0	16.5			

[a] The figures for the number of employees and the amount of total assets are those of independent accounting enterprises at and above the level of township. The definition of these indicators experienced modifications in the 1990s, which may cause some comparability problems for time series data. For details, see Holz and Lin (2000).

Source: GJTJJa (1998: 433); GJTJJb (1993: 90, 103, 116; 1994: 81–6; 1995: 79–87, 93–5; 1998: 78–9, 103–11); GYPCBGS (1996: 18–19; 54–5).

enterprises,[4] suggesting a formal recognition by the central leadership of the important distinction between management and ownership.

Collective enterprises include two major groups: urban collectives and rural collectives undertaking industrial activities. Urban collectives were created in the mid-1950s as an organizational form for bringing under state control (in the name of "cooperativization") small private industrial concerns and handicraft shops in the urban sector. Subsequently, they were retained as a way to provide job opportunities for unemployed urban residents in the wake of the failure of the Great Leap Forward campaign (1958–9). During the following two decades, urban collectives persisted through the economic contraction of the early 1960s and the 1967–8 disorder at the height of the Cultural Revolution (1966–76), and continued to grow, especially during the administrative decentralization in the early 1970s (Ji Long 1991). They played a supplementary role in industrial production (mainly of consumer goods) and in the provision of employment to urban residents.

It should be pointed out that the word "collective" used in this context is a misnomer. Neither the members of these enterprises nor the residents in their surrounding communities had any authority to make independent decisions on the use and transfer of the "collectively owned" assets or to dispose of the gains accruing to them. Under the central planning system, the main difference between urban collectives and state enterprises consisted in two aspects. First, the former were given much lower priority than the latter in the allocation of resources, and their employees had lower wages, poorer nonwage benefits (such as housing, health care, community services, etc.), and thus lower prestige. Second, with few exceptions, the former were exclusively controlled by governments below the provincial level and their activities were not so tightly integrated with the central plan as those of state enterprises. In fact, from time to time, some of the larger collective enterprises were even turned into state enterprises so that their activities could be more closely monitored by higher levels of state authority (Ji Long 1991).

Rural collectives are industrial undertakings controlled by grassroots governments in the countryside. Before the reform, they were called *shedui qiye* or commune and brigade enterprises.[5] Their origin can be traced to the Great Leap Forward campaign when large numbers of rural industrial enterprises were formed to boost output growth and accelerate China's industrialization. In the subsequent economic contraction

---

[4] State enterprises have also been referred to as *quanmin suoyouzhi qiye* or enterprises owned by all the people.

[5] Under the prereform people's commune system, rural socio-economic activities were organized under a hierarchical structure consisting of three tiers – the people's commune, production brigade, and production team (Zhu Rongji 1985).

between 1960 and 1962, the majority of them were closed down. In the early 1970s, they experienced a second spurt of growth, in large part as a result of the efforts by local governments to respond to the central leadership's call for agricultural mechanization and to address the problem of serious shortages in the supply of consumer goods (Byrd and Lin 1990). Although various constraints on their further growth were imposed by radical political leaders in the mid-1970s, many of the newly established factories survived under the protection of local officials, especially in such provinces as Jiangsu and Guangdong (Ma Jiesan 1991).

The reform in 1978 marked the beginning of a new era of rapid growth of rural industry. Since the demise of the people's commune system in 1983, the township (*xiang zhen*) has emerged as the center of social and economic activities and the locus of government administration in the countryside.[6] Below the level of the township, clusters of households that used to be grouped as production brigades have reverted to villages, many of which are based on the traditional community boundaries before the collectivization movement in the mid-1950s. Accordingly, industrial concerns operating at the level of the former commune or brigade have been referred to as *xiangzhen qiye* or enterprises under township authorities since 1984 (ZGXZQYNJBJWYH 1989: 1). A significant number of them are categorized as collective enterprises,[7] because they are controlled by the township government directly or through a semi-official governing body called the village resident committee.[8] In 1998, rural collectives contributed 30% of China's gross industrial output,[9] and within the "collective sector," they accounted for

---

[6] The difference between *xiang* and *zhen* is that the former is defined as a rural administrative center with population predominantly engaged in farming activities, whereas the latter is defined as an urban administrative center with a high proportion of the population undertaking nonfarming activities (Zheng Yushuo and Xie Qingkui 1992: 338–41).

[7] *Xiangzhen qiye* should not be confused with *xiangcun qiye* or township and village enterprises (TVEs). According to the *Law on Enterprises under Township Authorities* (*Xiangzhen qiye fa*) enacted in 1996, *xiangzhen qiye* include both enterprises that are collectively owned (through township and village authorities) and enterprises that are owned by rural residents. *Xiangcun qiye*, on the other hand, refer to rural collectives only.

[8] The phenomenal rural industrialization since the early 1980s has been widely portrayed as being led by rural collectives. This image was largely true for the 1980s but it is inaccurate for the 1990s, which saw a growing role of rural private enterprises. From 1985 to 1998, for instance, the number of rural collectives (including those undertaking nonindustrial activities) declined from 1.57 to 1.07 million while that of rural private enterprises rose from 10.7 to 19 million. During the same period the share of the former in the work force, value-added, and sales of all rural enterprises dropped from 59%, 74% and 60% to 41%, 45%, and 43%, respectively (ZGXZQYNJBJWYH 1996: 102–9; 1999, 112–17).

[9] Before 1984 output from village-level industries was categorized as part of agricultural output. Since then it has been counted as part of industrial output (GJTJJb 1995: 401).

78% of the gross industrial output and 60% of the total number of enterprises (GJTJJa 1999: 421–3; ZGXZQYNJBJWYH 1999: 111).

In most places, rural collectives are placed under the supervision of a unified economic authority at the township or village level. Among the names commonly adopted for this type of authority are township or village economic development company, township or village economic cooperative, and township or village general company for agricultural, industrial, and commercial development. As the representative body of the "collective" to oversee its assets, it appoints enterprise leaders, authorizes major decisions, coordinates the activities of different enterprises, and collects a management fee from the enterprises.

Private economic organizations were eliminated after the socialist transformation movement in 1956 (Pan Shi 1991).[10] They did not make a comeback until the early 1980s. Since then enterprises owned by Chinese citizens have been classified as private enterprises. They include three categories: private sole proprietorships, partnerships,[11] and private limited liability companies.[12] In addition, private enterprises have also been further distinguished between private firms (*siying qiye*) employing more than seven employees, and self-employed individuals (*getihu*) involving the employment of one to two "assistants" and three to five "apprentices."[13] Unlike state enterprises and most collective enterprises, private enterprises do not have a specialized government supervising agency to oversee their major decisions. Their chief regulator is the State Industrial and Commercial Administration (*guojia gongshang ju*), the state agency that issues industrial and commercial licenses, regulates market transactions and economic contracts, and enforces trademark and other economic laws and regulations. In 1997 private enterprises contributed 17% of China's gross industrial output (GJTJJa 1999: 421).

---

[10] In urban areas, however, there were a very small number of "self-employed individuals" even before the reform. Their self-employment, which was temporary and unstable, was allowed because the government was unable to provide employment for them. Their activities were concentrated in the service sector (e.g., the repairing of bicycles, shoes, timepieces, etc.) and closely regulated by the government. In 1978 there were 150,000 people in this category. See Zhang Xuwu, Li Ding, and Xie Minggan (1996: 136).

[11] This includes those that are called *lianhu* (joint household) enterprises in rural areas.

[12] Such classification was spelled out in the *Provisional Ordinance on Private Enterprises* adopted in 1988. However, it was not until 1993 and 1997 that the *Company Law* and the *Partnership Law* were enacted, respectively, to clearly define the latter two categories. There has yet to be a law on private sole proprietorships.

[13] The reason why there is such a distinction between private firms and self-employed individuals is that in *Das Kapital* Karl Marx discussed a case where a concern employing more than seven employees was considered to have led to the exploitation of employees. As an extension of this rationale, those that employ only a few helpers are considered to be self-employed (Zhang Xuwu et al. 1994: 79).

The reappearance of foreign capital enterprises in China started in 1979, when the *Sino-Foreign Joint Venture Law* was enacted. They are organized in three forms: joint equity venture, contractual joint venture, and wholly foreign-owned venture.[14] In joint equity ventures foreign partners are required to invest a certain amount of capital (no less than 25%) and share profit and risk on the basis of their equity shares; in contractual joint ventures Chinese partners provide land, factory building, and labor, whereas foreign partners supply capital, materials, and equipment, share the profit according to mutually agreed formulas, and bear the risk for losses (Li 1993: 422–3). Foreign managers make all the decisions in wholly foreign-owned ventures, whereas decision making is shared between foreign and Chinese managers in joint ventures. In official statistics, the foreign capital involved in these enterprises is categorized as foreign direct investment (FDI).[15] In 1998 there were 62,500 FDI enterprises in the industrial sector, accounting for 15% of gross industrial output (GJTJJa 1999: 421).[16]

Joint ownership enterprises are also creations of the reform era. In the late 1970s shareholding was ushered in by Sino-foreign joint ventures. In the following decade, there emerged various domestic enterprises with mixed ownership arrangements, known as *lianying qiye*, among state enterprises, collective enterprises, and private enterprises. But their significance has been very limited.[17] Since the late 1980s, some rural collectives have been turned into employee shareholding cooperatives.[18] This arrangement has also been adopted by some urban collectives and state enterprises in their organizational restructuring since the early 1990s. By 1995 there were 3 million and 0.14 million such cooperatives in rural and urban areas respectively (*RMRB*, July 8, 1999). In government statistics, however, their output has been combined with that of collective enterprises. The most important type of joint ownership enterprise consists of shareholding companies organized

---

[14] There is a special form of joint venture – i.e., joint offshore oil exploration projects – where foreign partners provide technology and equipment and share in the gains from resultant output (if any) (Shi Lin 1989: 363–4).

[15] It should be noted that investment from Hong Kong and Macao has been categorized as "foreign investment" in official statistics despite the transfer of sovereignty over these territories in 1997 and 1999 respectively.

[16] These enterprises are different from subcontracting agreements between Chinese factories and foreign manufacturers, where the latter pay a processing fee for the delivery of output subcontracted to the former. Activities carried out under such agreements involve four major forms known in Chinese as *san lai yi bu* – i.e., processing supplied materials, assembling supplied parts, processing in accordance with supplied samples, and compensatory trade (Li 1993: 281).

[17] In 1998, they only accounted for 0.2% of gross industrial output (GJTJJa 1999: 421).

[18] Such cooperatives differ from private partnerships, which are owned by a few owners rather than by all or the majority of their employees.

according to the *Company Law* enacted in 1993. They include two forms: limited liability companies and limited liability stock companies.[19] Portions of the shares of some limited liability stock companies have been issued to the public and traded in the stock exchanges in Shanghai and Shenzhen, where a total of 920 companies were listed by the end of August 1999; in addition 45 were listed on the stock exchanges in Hong Kong, New York, London, and Singapore (*RMRB*, September 20, 1999).[20] In 1997 there were 12,522 shareholding companies in the industrial sector, accounting for 7% of gross industrial output and 10% of total industrial assets (GJTJJa 1998: 444–5; GJTJJb 1994: 102). In 1998, those where the state did not hold controlling shares totalled 9,262, contributing 7.8% of gross industrial output (GJTJJa 1999: 421).

In Chinese economic literature, state enterprises and urban and rural collective enterprises are referred to as *gongyouzhi qiye* or "public enterprises." Almost all the factory directors in these enterprises are appointed by their supervising agencies in the government. The majority of the laborers in state enterprises have been tenured workers (*guding gong*) whose employment started before the reform.[21] They are supplemented with contract workers (*hetong gong*) and temporary workers (*linshi gong*) employed during the reform.[22] Workers in other types of enterprises mainly fall into the latter two categories. The composition of factory workers reflects an urban-rural divide: Those employed in urban factories are mostly urban residents and those in rural factories are from peasant families,[23] though since 1978 the number of rural laborers in the urban industrial work force has been on the increase (Solinger 1999). A

---

[19] According to the *Company Law*, the main differences between limited liability companies and limited liability stock companies lie in the following: (i) the threshold of equity capital (0.5 million vs. 10 million yuan), (ii) the level of approving authority (sub-provincial vs. provincial or central authority), (iii) the number of shareholders (between 2 and 49 vs. between 5 and a higher number without an upper limit), and (iv) the liquidity of shares (only the shares of limited liability stock companies can be traded on stock exchanges). The shares of both companies are classified into five categories: state-owned, institution-owned, individual-owned, collective-owned, and foreign-owned. The first two categories cannot be traded on stock exchanges, and their transfer requires special approval from the government (*RMRB*, August 3, 1998).

[20] Sixty percent of the listed companies are industrial organizations (*RMRB*, September 27, 1999).

[21] In 1997, 56% of the employees in state enterprises (including nonindustrial enterprises) were classified as "long-term employees," 42% as "contract employees," and the remaining 2% as "temporary employees" (GJTJJd 1998: 296).

[22] In the reform, some of those employed before the reform as *guding gong* in state enterprises were also turned into *hetong gong* (He Guang 1990).

[23] A report prepared by the Research Office of the CCP Secretariat in 1982 revealed that in 1957 about 30% of the urban industrial work force consisted of members of workers' families, whereas 80% of those who entered factories from 1966 to 1981 were from workers' families (SJCYJS 1982: 172–3).

unique feature of Chinese factories has been the existence of a communist party cell in virtually all state enterprises and urban collectives and its involvement in decision making. Political functionaries of the Party cell, headed by the Party secretary, are normally members of the management team, but their paramount authority in decision making has declined during the reform, as shown below.

Institutional Change: Reform and the Rise of Markets

Because of the greater organizational complexity, stronger resistance from vested bureaucratic interests, and hence higher perceived risk and cost for changing the status quo in the urban industrial sector (Shirk 1993), it was in the rural sector and in foreign economic relations that major steps were first taken by central leaders to reform the old economic system. Nevertheless, immediately after the landmark decision on economic reform at the Third Plenum of the Eleventh Central Committee of the CCP in 1978, pilot industrial reform programs were developed and carried out in selected factories and limited localities. This paved the way for full-scale reform to start in the industrial sector in 1984,[24] when its centerpiece, the "factory director responsibility system" (*changzhang zeren zhi*), was introduced (Liu Guoguang and Zhou Guiying 1992: 42–3). Although the reform since then has been gradual, partial, and haphazard, the structural changes that it has brought about are significant and have had profound impact on the decision making of firms. A synopsis of these changes is sketched in Table 1.2.[25]

The common theme of these changes is marketization – an expansion of exchange relations in economic activities and a concurrent decline of central planning based on the state's administrative commands. First, economic activities undertaken by new forms of industrial organization – i.e., rural collectives, private enterprises, foreign capital enterprises, and various shareholding enterprises – have drastically expanded. Their

---

[24] Industrial reform was initiated in 1978 (Naughton 1995a). But except for the "loan for grant" scheme and the "tax for profit" scheme started in 1980 and 1983 respectively, the reform programs introduced before 1984 were implemented as pilot measures (*shidian*). At the Third Plenum of the Twelfth Central Party Committee in October 1984, the CCP *Central Party Committee Resolution on Economic System Reform* was adopted, calling for an expansion of the reform from the rural to the urban sector and placing enterprise reform at the center of Party work. After that meeting, reform was fully unfolded in the industrial sector. See Wang Shiyuan (1993: 28–9).

[25] Various accounts have been offered on the reform process in the industrial sector (e.g., Bell et al. 1993; Byrd 1992; Byrd and Lin 1990; Granick 1990; Keun Lee 1991; Peter Lee 1987; Ma Rong et al. 1994; Naughton 1995a; Shirk 1993; Tidrick and Chen 1987). The reader is referred to these materials for more details.

Table 1.2. *A synopsis of major organizational changes brought about by reforms in the industrial sector, 1979–99[a]*

Organizational type	1979–84	1985–92	1993–9
State enterprises	Pilot reform programs to increase decision-making autonomy and link reward to performance in selected enterprises Replacement of fiscal grants with interest-bearing bank loans Replacement of profit hand-over with taxes	"Factory director responsibility system" aimed at introducing pilot measures to all enterprises Reduction of plan-allocated input and output "Dual-track price system" Adoption of contract employment system Decline of CCP's role in the workplace	Adoption of various forms of shareholding Privatization of some enterprises Debt restructuring Shift of enterprise-based welfare provisions to socialized funds Reduction of labor redundancy
Nonstate enterprises	Departure of urban collectives from the plan Rise of market-oriented rural collectives Entry of foreign direct investment Re-emergence of private entities	Full market orientation of urban collectives Rapid growth of rural collectives Managerial incentive schemes in collectives Expansion of foreign direct investment Legalization of private enterprises	Privatization of urban and rural collectives Rapid growth of private enterprises

[a] For detailed accounts of these changes, see Jefferson and Singh (1999), Lin and Zhu (2001), Naughton (1995a), Wang Shiyuan (1993), and Chapter 3.

actions have been oriented toward profit making and driven by independent decisions of their leaders instead of being subjected to the central plan. In 1998, their combined output made up 65.2% of China's gross industrial output (GJTJJa 1999: 423; ZGXZQYNJBJWYH 1999: 111).

Second, the influence of central planning has steadily declined among enterprises in the traditional public sector – state enterprises and urban collectives.[26] Under the "factory director responsibility system" and its variants,[27] the superior-subordinate relationship between government supervising bodies and state and collective enterprises has been redefined as being bound by an economic contract specifying the obligations (i.e., output and revenue targets) and decision and income rights of enterprises. Over time, output produced and sold according to government plan has decreased relative to that produced and marketed by enterprises themselves. According to one report, by the end of 1992 state price control was imposed on the production of only 5.9% of the total retail value and 18.7% of the output of producer goods; by the end of 1994 the state production plan covered only 10% of consumer goods output and 20% of capital goods output (BSBXZ 1995: 68, 257). Within the remaining scope of plan-bound activities, production has been increasingly shifted from restrictive "mandatory plans" to flexible "guidance plans" (Liu Guoguang and Zhou Guiying 1992). After fulfilling the output targets specified in their contracts with the government and paying taxes (in lieu of total profit hand-over), public enterprises now have great autonomy in the disposal of their retained profits and a wide range of other decisions. Such increased autonomy in decision making is indicated by survey findings in Table 1.3.

Third, transactions outside the confines of the state plan have significantly expanded and competition for customers and resources has intensified. With the expansion of self-arranged production, self-arranged exchanges have proliferated between parties that were not allowed to transact with each other under the central planning system (Liu Guoguang and Zhou Guiying 1992: 56–7). In the meanwhile, various forms of vertical and horizontal integration have emerged (ibid.), including mergers, institutional cross-holding of ownership, holding companies (known as *qiye jituan* or enterprise groups), and loosely coupled economic collaboration networks known as *hengxiang jingji lianhe ti* across regional, sectoral, and traditional administrative boundaries.[28]

---

[26] There are, however, variations in this change among firms in the state sector. Large and capital goods producers tend to be more tightly bound by the state plan than small and consumer goods producers, though the scope of state planning has been decreasing among both types of enterprises (Gui Shiyong 1994: 7–19).

[27] By the end of 1988, the system was adopted by 95% of state enterprises (*RMRB*, January 5, 1999).

[28] According to a government report, by the end of 1991 there were over 1,600 enterprise groups; in 1992 *hengxiang jingji lianhe ti* totaled 40,000 (Wang Shiyuan 1993: 101, 104).

Table 1.3. *Decision-making autonomy of firm leaders*

	% of those claiming to have autonomy[a]			
Decision issue	CESS 1993 survey (*n* = 2,620)	CESS 1994 survey (*n* = 2,756)	CESS 1995 survey (*n* = 2,752)	CESS 1997 survey (*n* = 2,415)
Production	88.7	94.0	97.3	98.3
Pricing	75.9	73.6	85.4	92.0
Sales	88.5	90.5	95.9	96.8
Sourcing	90.9	95.0	97.8	98.8
Import & export	15.3	25.8	41.3	54.0
Investment	38.9	61.2	72.8	82.5
Disposal of after-tax profit	63.7	73.8	88.3	90.6
Disposal of assets	29.4	46.6	68.2	76.5
Lateral collaboration & merger	23.3	39.7	59.7	61.4
Hiring & firing	43.5	61.0	74.8	84.3
Personnel	54.7	73.3	83.5	90.3
Wage & bonus	70.2	86.0	93.1	96.0
Internal organization	79.3	90.5	94.4	97.3
Resisting ad hoc levies (*tanpai*)	7.0	10.3	17.4	35.1

[a] Of the respondents surveyed in 1993, 1994, 1995, and 1997, 75%, 74.2%, 72.9%, and 64.4% respectively were directors of state enterprises.
Source: CESS (1993, 1994, 1995, 1997).

On the other hand, both new and old enterprises have been facing increasingly intense competition, as shown by the figures in Table 1.4. A major driving force of such competition comes from the entry of large numbers of new enterprises from the nonstate sector.[29] Another source of growing competition lies within the state sector, where the prereform policy known as *xiao er quan* or "small but complete" that encouraged local (especially provincial) industrial self-reliance resulted in parallel construction of similar industrial facilities, ranging from raw material extraction to end product manufacturing within different localities (Naughton 1988; Riskin 1987). With the expansion of self-arranged, market-oriented transactions undertaken by state enterprises during the reform, the preexisting duplications of industrial facilities have become a major factor that augments peer competition in input and output markets.[30]

---

[29] From 1978 to 1993, the total number of industrial enterprises increased from 1.2 million to 10 million, most of which were formed outside the state sector; during the same period of time the total number of state-owned industrial enterprises increased only from 83,700 to 104,700 (GJTJJa 1985: 16; GJTJJa 1995: 375; ZGXZQYNJBJWYH 1989: 573).

[30] For example, most of those categorized as "large and medium" enterprises are in the state sector and enjoy some form of protection (against entry) by the state. Between

Table 1.4. *Managers' assessment of the intensity of competition faced by their firms*

Data set	Intensity of competition (% of respondents)		
	Strong	Moderate	Weak
1986 CASS-World Bank survey ($n = 111$)	21.6	14.4	34.2
1992 CASS-World Bank survey			
state enterprises ($n = 871$)	66.4	32.4	1.3
urban collectives ($n = 340$)	67.4	29.7	2.9
TVEs ($n = 263$)	65.0	31.2	3.8
1993 CESS survey ($n = 2,620$)	64.9	29.5	2.8

Source: 1986 and 1992 CASS-World Bank survey data sets; CESS (1993: 14).

Fourth, within enterprises the once dominant role of political control and ideological indoctrination (Walder 1986) has drastically declined (if not totally disappeared) in decision making, which is now driven primarily by profit making. Most new enterprises do not even contain a functional unit of the CCP (Wang Jingsong 1995),[31] whereas Party cells in traditional public enterprises have become increasingly inactive and their activities have been re-oriented toward facilitating the implementation of the economic agenda.[32] Although most public enterprise leaders are still appointed by the government,[33] their qualifications pertain primarily to economic decision making,[34] and their financial rewards are

1980 and 1994, their share in the total sales of independent accounting industrial enterprises at and above the level of township (*xiang*) only changed slightly from 57.9% to 55.3%, but the number of enterprises in this category increased from 4,700 to 20,400 (GJTJJa 1993: 24, 129–32; GJTJJb 1995: 79, 109, 112). See also Rawski (1994c).

[31] In 1994, for example, only 24% of the rural collectives had formed CCP branches, whereas only 0.16% of rural private enterprises had CCP branches (ZGXZQYNJB-JWYH 1995: 338).

[32] A 1998 survey conducted by the State Statistical Bureau on state enterprises ($n = 2,558$) undergoing organizational restructuring found that only 37% of the Party secretaries performed their political functions on a full-time basis (data set). For a detailed discussion of the survey data, see Lin and Zhu (2001).

[33] A 1992 Chinese Academy of Social Sciences-World Bank survey found that the percentages of government-appointed enterprise directors were 93.3% for state enterprises ($n = 967$), 94.3% for urban collective enterprises ($n = 366$), and 78.4% for township enterprises ($n = 282$) (figures computed from data set). Two surveys conducted by the China's Entrepreneurs Survey System under the State Council in 1993 ($n = 2,620$) and 1994 ($n = 2,756$) found the figures to be 92.2% and 86% for state enterprises and 75.3% and 58.4% for urban and rural collective enterprises respectively (CESS 1993, 1994).

[34] The 1993 survey by the China's Entrepreneurs Survey System mentioned above and a 1995 Beijing University survey of published biographical accounts of 5,249 enterprise directors show that over 70% of the directors held technical or managerial positions before their appointments, whereas less than 25% were former political functionaries (CESS 1993; Wang Hansheng and Liu Shiding 1995).

directly tied to the economic performance of their enterprises.[35] More important, the focal concerns of enterprise leaders have steadily gravitated toward economic outcomes of their enterprises.[36]

In view of the significant decline of the plan both in and beyond the industrial sector, the 14th Congress of the CCP in 1992 dropped the emphasis on the centrality of the plan in economic activities and proclaimed that China was in the process of building a "socialist market economy" based on diverse forms of public ownership.[37] This opened the way for another wave of reform, especially in the state sector. Its central measure is to turn state enterprises and other public enterprises from sole proprietorships under the exclusive purview of their supervising authorities into shareholding companies that are truly independent and self-responsible in decision making, diverse in ownership structure, and fully guided by markets. The basic institutional framework was laid out in the *Company Law* enacted in 1993 and a growing number of related laws and regulations that were introduced concurrently or subsequently to form what the Chinese leadership has called a "modern enterprise system."[38] According to a survey conducted by the State Statistical Bureau in 1998, 17.1% of the state enterprises in the sample

---

[35] Since the salary scales of top leaders (i.e., director, Party secretary, and deputy directors) in state and collective enterprises are fixed within certain limits, their main formal source of additional income lies in what is called *chengbao jiang* (contract bonus).

[36] A survey of 20 state enterprises conducted by the World Bank and the Chinese Academy of Social Sciences (CASS) on the eve of the full implementation of the industrial reform found that family and compliance to superiors were the predominant motives of top factory managers (Tidrick and Chen 1987: 62–5). But a follow-up study of seven enterprises in the same sample during the late 1980s showed a strong re-orientation toward profits of managers' focal concerns in decision making (Byrd 1992: 14). In a 1986 CASS-World Bank survey of TVEs (*n* = 115) in four counties, 61.7% of the enterprise leaders chose "long-term growth of the firm" (33%), "maximization of profit" (16.5%), or "enhancement of firm reputation" (12.2%) as the most important goals of their operations. In another CASS-World Bank survey of urban and rural public enterprises (*n* = 1,633) conducted in 1992, a question was asked about the most important goals of the factory directors. 95.6% of the 919 state enterprise leaders who provided valid answers chose "increase of profit" (41.5%), "expansion of output and operation scale" (30.9%), or "fulfillment of the objectives in the economic contract with the government" (23.2%). (The percentages reported above are computed from the data sets of the two surveys.) Although to my knowledge no systematic survey results have been reported on this issue for private and foreign capital enterprises, it is not implausible to assume that their profit orientation is at least as strong as that of public enterprises.

[37] This view was reiterated at the 15th Congress of the CCP in 1997, when the leadership explicitly highlighted the centrality of market in economic activities and stressed the importance of nonconventional forms of public ownership. In the spring of 1999, the National People's Congress adopted a constitutional amendment to legitimize the growing private sector as "an important integral part" of the new Chinese economy.

[38] Among these are *Accounting Law* in 1993, *Partnership Law* in 1997, *Provisional Guidelines for the Development of Urban Employee Shareholding Cooperatives* in 1997, *Contract Law* in 1999, and *Securities Law* in 1999.

(n = 40,246) had completed organizational restructuring under the new system, 4.2% had their restructuring plans approved, 7.7% had completed restructuring plans pending approval, and 19% were in the process of designing their restructuring plans.[39]

Uneven Pace of Marketization

Although there has been a common trend toward markets among all forms of enterprises (see Table 1.4), the ability to participate and compete in market-oriented economic activities has varied. Such variation is particularly noticeable between state enterprises and nonstate enterprises,[40] especially in the 1980s and early 1990s. Findings from the above-mentioned 1992 World Bank-CASS survey, for example, show that more than a decade after the start of the reform, state enterprises still faced greater constraints in a wide range of major decisions than urban and rural collectives. This can be seen from the statistics reported in Table 1.5.[41]

A common feature of enterprises in the nonstate sector is that they were mostly formed in the reform and have not been bound by the plan from the very beginning of their operations. But there is a complicating factor for the comparison between state and nonstate enterprises: The latter category includes urban collectives. Some of these enterprises were formed before the reform and their operations, like those of state enterprises, were subject to the plan. The effect of this complication is limited, however.

First, the significance of urban collectives in the nonstate sector has drastically declined with the rise of other forms of economic organization in this category. Their share in the gross industrial output of the nonstate sector was 73% in 1980; but it decreased to 29% in 1990 and further to 8.5% in 1998 (GYPCBGS 1987: vol. 3, 88; GJTJJa 1993: 409; GJTJJa 1999: 421–3; ZGXZQYNJBJWYH 1999: 111). Second, about half of the urban collectives were formed in the reform era (GJTJJa 1998: 431; GJTJJb 1988: 25), and their operations were not subject to central

---

[39] See Lin and Zhu (2001) for more details about the survey as well as discussions about the new reform measure.

[40] As noted in the introductory chapter, this distinction by no means implies a distinction between public and private ownership. Rather, it is used as an indication of the variations in the pace and outcome of marketization.

[41] The Wilcoxon test measures the statistical difference between the responses of two groups to the same ordinal variable. The p-value indicates the probability (<0.05, <0.01, <0.001, etc.) of the opposite situation (i.e., no difference between the two groups) being true.

Table 1.5. *Differences in major decision issues: State vs. nonstate enterprises (1992 World Bank-CASS questionnaire survey)*

	Average score		
Issue	State (coded 1)	Nonstate (coded 0)	z score for Wilcoxon test
1. Who makes the following decisions?			
(1 = supervising body alone; 2 = firm together with supervising body; 3 = firm alone)			
Production plan	2.01	2.18	4.29*[a]
Appointment of major factory leaders	1.21	1.40	5.43*
Recruitment of new employees	1.95	2.45	13.38*
Dismissal of employees	2.52	2.57	0.97
Setting bonus level	2.44	2.40	−1.52
Setting employees' wage difference	2.07	2.41	7.43*
Investment & capacity expansion	1.87	2.11	7.06*
Allocation & use of retained profit	2.43	2.54	2.79*
2. How strong are government restrictions on the following issues?			
(1 = not restrictive; 2 = somewhat restrictive; 3 = highly restrictive)			
Setting product price	2.07	1.57	−13.64*
Adopting sales strategy	1.29	1.15	−6.53*
Identifying customers	1.27	1.13	−6.39*
Specifying sales market	1.40	1.24	−5.72*
Determining material input prices	1.39	1.34	−2.62*
Determining quantity & quality of material inputs	1.33	1.16	−7.26*
Selecting material input providers	1.25	1.13	−5.57*

[a] * $p < 0.01$.
Source: Data set.

planning. Third, those formed before the reform had broken away from the plan by the mid-1980s,[42] ahead of most state enterprises.

Obviously, the slow pace and constrained ability of state enterprises to compete during the process of marketization are related to the fact that they have had to undo the institutional legacies carried over from the central planning era. Such unevenness with most nonstate enterprises has posed an extra obstacle for state enterprises to overcome. Despite the advantageous initial position of nonstate enterprises in this regard, however, entering and expanding the formative space outside the plan is by no means a hurdle-free undertaking. I leave the discussion of this issue

---

[42] See, e.g., discussions in Ji Long (1991). A major contributing factor is the low status given to urban collectives in resource allocation under the central planning system. The peripheral administrative attention and weak resource commitment to these enterprises paved the way for their early departure from the plan. See also discussions in the next two chapters.

to the ensuing chapters. Here, it is important to take note of another disparity in the process of marketization – the variations in financial performance between state and nonstate enterprises.

Performance Variation

With the marketization of the industrial economy, the pattern of performance variation among firms has been markedly reshaped. The most salient change is the deterioration of the performances of many state enterprises. In fact, Chinese industry has been portrayed by press accounts in a black-and-white picture. It consists of two sharply different segments: a lethargic, inefficient, and loss-making state sector that is incapable of or slow in adapting to the sea change of marketization, and a dynamic, entrepreneurial, and productive nonstate sector that comprises rapidly expanding private or de facto private enterprises.[43] This view is at least in part shared by some academic researchers, who consider property rights arrangements as a key determinant of economic performance variation in the reform era (e.g., Lee 1991; Shan 1992; Xiao 1991; Woo 1999). While recognizing the vitality and even superiority of the nonstate sector, others caution against this dichotomized view and point to evidence that, despite its many problems, the state sector has on balance performed adequately to support a virtuous cycle of reform (e.g., Jefferson and Rawski 1994a, 1994b; Naughton 1995a; Rawski 1994b, 1999).

Various indicators have been used to assess the performance of industrial firms, such as rate of return or profit rate (ratio of profit to assets), profit margin (ratio of profit to sales revenue), labor productivity (ratio of value-added to number of employees), capital productivity (ratio of value-added to assets), and total factor productivity (ratio of output to joint inputs – capital, labor, and, in the case of gross output being used, intermediate inputs). In different ways, they measure the ratio between input and output. None of these indicators, however, is without drawbacks.[44]

---

[43] For a sample of such reports, see *Far Eastern Economic Review*, March 1, 1990, March 7, 1991, February 23, 1995; *Newsweek*, March 24, 1994, September 12, 1994.

[44] Total factor productivity, for example, is an indicator widely used by economists to measure the efficiency in resource use. Its estimation often entails certain strong assumptions that are questionable in the context of China's transforming economy, such as perfect competition and disembodiment of technical change from capital or labor (Samuelson and Nordhaus 1985: 796–9). Also, the selection of a functional form for estimating total factor productivity is arbitrary and the results derived from the use of different methods may vary significantly. Moreover, because labor and capital inputs are measured in different units (i.e., number of employees or work hours versus capital expressed in monetary terms), the resultant ratio of output to joint inputs does not have a clear meaning and is subject to different interpretations.

In the discussion below, I focus on one of these indicators – the ratio of profit to total assets or profit rate.[45] It is widely used and easy to understand. Despite its limitations,[46] it still provides a useful indication of the effectiveness with which assets are used to generate financial gains.[47] To avoid distraction, I leave the discussion on data sources to Appendix A and concentrate here on the results of data analysis, which indicate three major patterns of performance variation.[48]

First, on average and as a group state enterprises have had a lower profit rate than nonstate enterprises, especially since the late 1980s. This can be seen from the figures in Table 1.6.[49] The results derived from aggregate data and firm-level data point to a similar pattern, which is consistent with that revealed by existing findings (e.g., Naughton 1988, 1995a).

Second, the figures in Table 1.6 also show a clear trend toward a declining profit rate among both state and nonstate enterprises. Although this has been noted by some existing studies (e.g., Naughton 1994b,

---

[45] Due to the lack of consistent data on net profit, profit before income tax is used for this estimation. Assets consist of current assets and net value of fixed assets. The definitions of these indicators on assets were revised in 1993 (Holz and Lin 2000). Such change may cause some inaccuracy in the comparison between the profit rates for the years through 1992 and those thereafter. This problem, however, does not affect the comparisons between the years within each period.

[46] A major problem is that profit figures may be distorted by industrial firms for various purposes, such as tax evasion, exaggeration of performance, creation of slush funds, etc. But the same can happen to other output data, such as value-added, thus indicators using value-added as the numerator in the calculation of output-input ratios do not necessarily provide better alternatives.

[47] Since profit is the last accounting item in the distribution of value-added (i.e., the surplus after deduction of input cost from sales revenue) among factor providers, a firm with a high profit rate is likely to be able to generate adequate value-added to accommodate all those that have an immediate interest in its operation, including owner(s), creditor(s), employees, and the tax authority. A below-average (especially negative) profit rate, on the other hand, suggests a weaker ability of the firm concerned to create value, a calculated effort by management to distort the gains accruing to some interested parties, or a combination of both. The agents of interested parties, such as firm owners, creditors, and the tax authority, for example, may collude with each other for private gains at the cost of their principals. (In the case of public enterprises, these agents are enterprise managers and government officials, and the principal whose interests are at stake is the state.) These different possibilities reflect variations in the institutional incentives and constraints faced by management and other relevant actors. An examination of the pattern of performance variation in terms of profit rate, therefore, may provide useful signposts for investigating the forces that shape the behavior of firms under different structural conditions. It should be noted, though, that I do not assume a consistent correlation between profitability and what economists define as "technical efficiency" (Shim and Siegel 1995: 119), as the gains from output sales are not necessarily derived primarily from productive use of resources in economic activities.

[48] All the data analyzed in this section are about independent accounting industrial enterprises at and above the township level.

[49] Except for that based on aggregate data, each pair of comparisons is subject to a *t*-test. In all the cases, the differences in the mean values are found to be statistically significant at the level of $p < 0.001$.

Table 1.6. *Profit rate (%): State vs. nonstate enterprises*

Year	National aggregate		National average		Average of province A (coastal)		Average of province B (inland)	
	State	Nonstate	State	Nonstate	State	Nonstate	State	Nonstate
1978	15.5							
1979	16.1							
1980	16.0	18.8						
1981	15.0							
1982	14.4							
1983	14.4							
1984	14.9							
1985	13.2	15.9						
1986	10.6	11.4						
1987	10.6	10.7			13.2	16.3		
1988	10.4	11.7			14.6	15.7	9.6	11.3
1989	7.2	8.0			14.2	15.3	9.2	10.9
1990	3.2	4.4			9.9	14.2	6.4	8.8
1991	2.9	5.0			7.2	10.5	6.7	8.1
1992	2.7	5.3	6.9	8.8	7.1	10.4	4.2	7.6
1993	3.2	6.2	5.7	7.9	6.6	11.2	5.1	8.0
1994	2.6	5.1	4.2	7.1	5.3	9.2	3.9	7.7
1995	1.7	3.9	2.1	6.4	4.4	8.0	2.5	5.1
1996	1.0	3.5	1.9	5.7	3.1	6.2	2.4	3.9
1997	0.9	3.5	2.0	5.4	1.6	4.3	0.8	2.1

Source: GJTJJb (1993: 116, 129; 1998: 76–81); data sets.

1995a),[50] there is a concurrent trend, shown in Table 1.7, that merits attention – i.e., the proportion of loss-making enterprises has steadily increased. Although the state sector has had a higher proportion of such enterprises, the nonstate sector has also experienced a significant increase in such a proportion. In fact, before the 1990s, the two groups had similar proportions of loss-making enterprises. It is also worth noting that the nonstate sector has gradually increased its share in the total

[50] In a comprehensive review of existing findings on industrial performance during the 1980s and early 1990s Jefferson and Singh (1999: Chapter 6) report three additional pieces of evidence. First, both state and nonstate enterprises experienced declining profitability but improving productivity. Second, state enterprises had slower improvement in productivity and faster decline of profitability than nonstate enterprises. Third, from the mid-1980s to the early 1990s labor productivity increased but capital productivity declined among both state and nonstate enterprises. On the other hand, they both demonstrated some improvement in total factor productivity in the first decade of reform; however, there are no data on the trend since 1992. It appears that the picture of productivity change is much less clear than that of profitability, and more extensive research is needed to bring greater light to it.

Table 1.7. *Losses incurred by industrial enterprises: State vs. nonstate sectors*

Year	% of loss-making enterprises		Share in total losses incurred (%)	
	State	Nonstate	State	Nonstate
1978			93.3	6.7
1979			90.5	9.5
1980			88.4	11.6
1981			85.9	14.1
1982			85.3	14.7
1983			85.4	14.6
1984			77.8	22.2
1985	9.6	11.7	80.1	19.9
1986	13.1	13.2	75.3	24.7
1987	13.0	14.7	72.1	27.9
1988	10.9	11.8	76.9	23.1
1989	16.0	15.9	77.0	23.0
1990	27.6	19.7	76.9	23.1
1991	25.8	17.2	77.2	22.8
1992	23.4	14.3	78.7	21.3
1993	28.8	17.3	70.8	29.2
1994	30.9	17.7	62.5	37.5
1995	33.8	23.3	53.4	46.6
1996	33.6	19.6	55.2	44.8
1997	38.2	20.9	52.4	47.6

Source: GJTJJb (1993, 90; 1998, 51–2, 76).

losses incurred by industrial enterprises, especially in the 1990s when the gap in the percentage of loss-making enterprises widened between the two groups.

Third, although there are differences in the aggregate and average levels of performance between the state and the nonstate sectors, the differences have been exaggerated in many existing accounts. This is shown by the two bell-shaped distribution curves in the illustration to the right in Figure 1.1. Table 1.8 shows the total size of the overlapping points connected under the two curves in Figure 1.1.[51] They indicate that a sig-

---

[51] The horizontal axis in Figure 1.1 represents profit rate, and the vertical axis represents the percentage of enterprises at various levels of profit rate in each group. What the figures in Table 1.8 indicate is the sum of the overlapping points under both curves. It ranges from 0%, when the two curves do not overlap at all, to 100%, when the two curves totally overlap. These figures are derived with the following formula:

$$S = \frac{200 - \sum |A_i - B_i|}{2}$$

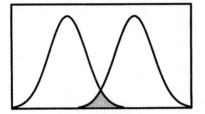
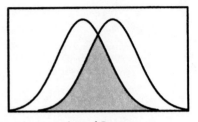

Perceived Pattern   Actual Pattern

Figure 1.1: Comparison of performance distribution between state and nonstate enterprises. [*Note:* The horizontal axis indicates the range of performance (from low to high); the vertical axis indicates the percentages of enterprises in each group that achieve different levels of performance. The curve to the left represents the distribution of state enterprises; the curve to the right represents the distribution of nonstate enterprises.]

Table 1.8. *Percentage of enterprises in the same range of performance: State vs nonstate enterprises*[a]

Year	National	Province A (coastal)	Province B (inland)
1987		70.5	
1988		68.0	76.7
1989		69.2	76.5
1990		71.9	74.2
1991		73.6	72.1
1992	80.5	72.7	66.1
1993	77.9	70.1	60.2
1994	71.4	65.0	65.4
1995	74.0	65.1	67.8
1996	66.5	60.0	68.3
1997	66.4	59.0	64.9

[a] The scope of coverage for 1996–7 differs from that for 1987–95. See Appendix A.
Source: Data sets.

nificant proportion of enterprises from each group fell in the same range of performance, though there was some decrease in the degree of overlapping after 1992. What this finding suggests is that the difference in average profit rate between the two groups, shown in Table 1.6, may be in large part due to the significantly above or below average performances of a limited number of enterprises, especially those in the two tails where state and nonstate enterprises are more heavily represented in the low and high performance ranges respectively. This does not mean that state enterprises have achieved better financial results than those that have been widely portrayed.[52] Rather, the proportion of nonstate enterprises with lackluster performance is greater than that portrayed in the widely perceived image of the performance difference between the two groups, which resembles the first pattern illustrated in Figure 1.1.[53]

These findings point to three interesting questions. First, what accounts for the performance variation between state and nonstate enterprises in the reform era? Although some explanations, such as the economic competition thesis noted in the preceding chapter, have been developed, there remains a need to investigate further how such variation has been related to the above-mentioned uneven paces and varying strategies between enterprises in the two groups, and to explore what has defined their different trajectories of marketization. Second, what accounts for the similar performances between large numbers of state and nonstate enterprises? Little has been said about this important issue, which has largely been masked by the widely held view that the two groups are distinctively different, especially in the pace of marketization. A probe in this direction may well shed additional light on the mechanisms of economic institutional change. Third, why has there been a trend toward declining profit rate in both groups of enterprises? This question looks particularly intriguing if one takes into account a concurrent economic change in the reform era, i.e., sustained output growth for two decades.

To address these questions, it is important to go beyond the black-and-white image of state and nonstate enterprises to examine the diverse forces that have shaped the behavior and performance of industrial enterprises in concrete organizational and institutional contexts. I argue that

---

where S is the sum of the overlapping percentage points (which, in the case of a total overlap, amounts to 100%), and A_i and B_i stand for the values on the vertical axis that correspond to the same point on the horizontal axis.

[52] Some studies, though, emphasize that the performance of the state sector has been underestimated (Jefferson and Rawski 1994a, 1994b; Naughton 1995a; Rawski 1994b).

[53] A factor that may further reduce the performance gap between state and nonstate enterprises is the cost of enterprise-provided social services for employees, such as housing, child care, and other communal facilities. State enterprises, especially large and medium ones, tend to spend much more on these on a per capita as well as per unit capital basis than nonstate enterprises. Although such spending falls into the category of fringe benefits for employees, a large part of it has been counted as added capital stock in China's enterprise accounting system. To a certain degree this distorts the ratio between profit and assets, though the precise magnitude of such a problem is difficult to measure. An adjustment in input figures to address this problem would further strengthen the argument made here. See Chen, Jefferson, Rawski, Wang, and Zheng (1988a) for a thorough discussion of this issue.

marketization in both the economic and political processes holds a key to understanding these issues. In the next five chapters I explore various aspects of such a dual process. Since the central planning system was where the evolution of the economic and political markets set off, it is logical to start the journey from there.

2

Central Planning and Its Decline

In the ideal-typical market economy envisioned by Adam Smith, markets operate under a relatively neutral state and direct resource allocation by providing self-interested economic actors with a nexus of trade, a locus of information and incentives, and a screen through which winners are selected and losers sifted out. Such a mechanism, however, would be hampered if the assumption of state action as being relatively neutral breaks down. In some economies, the breakdown may be short-lived or limited to certain market niches, whereas in others it may be widespread and sustained despite the existence of a few oases resembling the Smithian vision. The post-Mao Chinese economy, I argue, is akin to the latter.[1] Although concrete markets for products and factors have emerged to become the main motivating and mediating force of economic activities, they often fall short of playing the dominant role in shaping the distribution of relative payoffs among firms, where particularistic state action holds enormous sway. Nevertheless, the post-Mao era has seen a shift of the locus of such action from centralized institutional authority to decentralized, increasingly individualized bases of power.

To set up a backdrop for discussing these changes in the reform, I provide a sketch, based on the experiences of several firms,[2] of the institutional change from the plan to markets. I first illustrate the essential features of the centrally defined, highly institutionalized particularism in the state's treatment of different firms under central planning. Then I highlight two forms of marketization that have combined to weaken such a practice, i.e., the expansion of economic activities carried out by new

---

[1] It should be emphasized that economic marketization (i.e., expansion of exchange relations among economic actors) seen in the light of this conception differs from that seen in the Smithian vision, which is the frame of reference of the economic competition thesis, as discussed in the introductory chapter.

[2] See Appendix B for a discussion of the method used in the case studies.

firms outside the plan and the adaptive responses by old firms to the push-and-pull effects created by this expansion. Unlike the accounts sharing the economic competition thesis, however, my story does not end here, as the reader will soon find out.

The Hierarchy of Differential Treatment: Cases in Point

Northern Machinery Factory

The Northern Machinery Factory (Northern Machinery hereinafter) was one of China's largest milling machine producers in 1978. Established as a state enterprise in a centrally administered municipality in 1949, it was drastically expanded during the first five-year plan (1953–7). The central government identified the factory as an enterprise of strategic importance and invested 19 million yuan to expand and upgrade its facilities, primarily with Soviet technology. In the following two decades, the factory continued to grow with a steady injection of resources from the state. A milling machine research institute was set up in the factory in 1959. After the ideological dispute between Chinese and Soviet leaders in the early 1960s and the subsequent withdrawal of Soviet aid, the institute became the main R&D base of the factory and designed a series of improved products in the late 1960s and early 1970s. It also served as a major center of technical support for other milling machine factories in the country. In 1978, the factory had a total of 1 billion yuan in net fixed assets and a workforce of over 7,000, of which 80% had an education of junior high school level or above. Twenty percent of the employees were categorized as managerial and technical personnel, including several Soviet-trained senior engineers and dozens of graduates from the nation's top engineering universities. A vocational school was set up in the 1950s to provide training to junior workers and to improve their skills.

Administratively, the locus of the supervising authority over the factory shifted between the central government (1949–57 and 1963–71) and the municipal government (1958–62 and from 1972 onward). Largely because of the city's special status as one of the three centrally administered municipalities with provincial rank, such changes in jurisdiction level during different periods of time did not have much effect on the treatment that the factory received in resource allocation. Like other Chinese factories at the time, it operated under the leadership of a CCP committee, obtained inputs from state-specified sources at state-set prices, manufactured products according to state plans, sold its products to state-designated parties (mostly in northern and eastern China) at state-set prices, and carried out various political indoctrination activities assigned by Party-state authorities. But unlike many enterprises with lower status, it never encountered any major difficulty in obtaining inputs and selling its output, and always fulfilled state plans. As a star enterprise frequently featured in the news media, it was a major site of work inspection visits by important leaders of the city and the central government. According to a chronology compiled by the factory's propaganda office, Zhu De, Deng Xiaoping, Li Fuchun, Yang Shangkun, and Wang Zhen were among the prominent central leaders who had visited the factory before 1978.

The factory occupied an area of over 400,000 square meters in the eastern suburb of the city, about one-sixth of which was used for living facilities for its employees. Although the basic wages for workers were on the same scale as those for other state enterprises in the same industrial sector, the fringe benefits provided by the factory were rather wide-ranging. About 70% of the employees were housed in apartments and dormitories constructed by the factory, the remaining 30% lived with their relatives in the city and went to work by bicycle or factory shuttle bus. The factory ran several canteens to provide subsidized meals that, according to old timers (Informants no. 82/1989, no. 91/1989), were of a more substantial quantity, better quality, and greater variety than those in neighboring small factories. The factory had to ration meal tickets to its employees to prevent outsiders from sharing in the goodies. Younger children of factory employees went to the day-care center or primary school run by the factory. In 1977, the day-care center was turned into a kindergarten, which occupied a whole building with room space totaling 3,000 square meters. There were several auditoriums, the largest of which usually showed movies once or twice a week. The factory also ran a clinic housed in a two-story building, a retail outlet, a barber shop, and several bathhouses. It maintained its own gardening team, security team, motor vehicle fleet, sports facilities, and an amateur orchestra with a full set of Western and Chinese musical instruments. Many of the resources needed for all these facilities and the auxiliary personnel came from the factory's employee welfare fund, set aside with the ad hoc approval of its supervising authority owing to the "importance and significant contribution of the factory to the country" (Informant no. 76/1989).

No. 2 Polyester Fiber Factory

A dozen kilometers away from Northern Machinery lay the No. 2 Polyester Fiber Factory (Polyester Fiber hereinafter). It was established as a large collective enterprise in 1973 when the economy was recovering from the chaos created in the early years of the Cultural Revolution. The initial capital of 1.5 million yuan was allocated by the Textile Industry Department of the city, which was instructed by higher level authorities to expand the production of textile products in order to narrow the consumer goods supply gap that had widened during the preceding years of disorder. The main products of the factory were various types of polyester fiber, a synthetic material that can be blended with wool or cotton. The fiber was sold primarily to weaving factories under the jurisdiction of the city government, which, like many other local governments in China at the time, aimed at achieving a certain degree of self-sufficiency in industrial production. By 1978 the factory had accumulated 8.9 million yuan in fixed assets and employed a workforce of 680. About 10% of the employees were categorized as managerial and technical personnel.

From its very beginning, the factory was faced with difficulties. The main input that it needed – polyester chips – was a centrally allocated industrial material (a petrochemical product). Because of an imbalance between the expansion of the city's two polyester fiber producers and the increase of its annual allocation quota from the central planning authority, the Textile Industry Department had to address the needs of the other factory – the No. 1 Polyester Factory (a state enterprise) – first. As a result, it could only allocate the barest amount of polyester chips to Polyester Fiber, which had a lower priority ranking in resource allocation. In order to fulfill the output target set by the Department, the factory had to make up a 10 to 20% gap in input supply through other channels. Every year it sent out sourcing agents (known as *caigou yuan*) to large petrochemical enterprises throughout the country to explore sources of slack inventory of polyester chips. If these agents were lucky, they could find some small pockets of surplus. Because under the central planning system industrial material producers were normally not authorized to sell their output to parties other than those specified by the plan, producers of the polyester chips had to re-categorize the surplus as "defective products" and then dispose of them to the factory at a discount as waste. To make up the price difference and get around the accounting restrictions on self-arranged transactions, the factory compensated the providers with items in kind – mostly consumer goods – that could be distributed by them to their employees as fringe benefits. To set a buffer against uncertainty, the factory often had to purchase more than it needed at the time when the supply was available. This costly exercise put a serious strain on its already very tight budget.

Related to this was a problem in the supply of utilities. Although the factory was under the direct supervision of a city government department, it was physically located in one of the city's satellite counties. The county government was responsible for the provision of power and water to the factory. But it had many enterprises under its own jurisdiction and tended to take better care of them than other enterprises. Because of the limited transforming capacity at the local power station, partial shutdowns were often needed for maintenance work. In its initial years of operation, Polyester Fiber and a few other small "outsiders" were always the first to be hit by such power outages. Also, the county is situated in an arid area of the North China Plain where water shortages often occur during dry seasons. Moreover, huge quantities of water were consumed by a large chemical factory directly supervised by the Ministry of Chemical Industry and located in the county. Because of the clout of that factory in the central government and the influence exerted by its supervising agency over the county government, it was guaranteed a stable supply of water by the county water authority. Short on such influence, Polyester Fiber had to face periodic cuts in water supply and long delays in pipe repair work. Because of the sensitivity of its production process to a stable supply of water and power, the factory had to find other means to cope with the unfavorable situation. It struggled for five years to squeeze out the necessary resources and to obtain bureaucratic approval for drilling three deep wells within the factory compound and installing a backup power line directly linked, through a self-maintained transforming substation, to the Northern China Power Grid.

The problems in input supply faced by the factory and its low status in resource allocation directly affected what it could provide to its employees in addition to their basic wages, which were structured on a slightly lower scale than that for state enterprises in the same sector. The majority of the workers were recruited from among urban residents in the county. Only 45% of the employees were accommodated in housing units constructed by the factory. Other social services offered by the factory were limited to a canteen, a bathhouse, and a one-doctor clinic, all of which were overcrowded. As the number of employees grew, so did the pressure on the factory leaders to keep the level of basic services and workers' morale from falling. The difficulty of management under such conditions was further exacerbated by the frequent commands from above to organize and carry out political indoctrination activities. During its first six years of operation, the factory could barely fulfill annual state plans; and the positions of Party secretary and factory director changed hands four times.

Red Star Cotton Weaving Plant

As compared to Polyester Fiber, some other collective enterprises, especially those at the bottom of the resource allocation hierarchy, faced even more difficult situations. Take the example of the Red Star Cotton Weaving Plant (Red Star Weaving hereafter), an industrial enterprise run by the Sun Flower People's Commune near a medium industrial city in the lower reaches of the Yangtze River. It was first established as a brick-making factory in 1972, with 25 workers, a small piece of land, a walking-tractor, and some basic equipment and tools. The workers were initially drafted from nearby production teams to construct a new building for the commune headquarters. When the construction was completed, they were retained to work in the newly formed enterprise – the commune leaders discovered a potential source of extra revenue after selling all the unused bricks made for the building and making a small profit of 930 yuan. Du Yongsheng, the Party secretary of a production brigade, was assigned to run the factory. Both he and the workers continued to be paid as peasants according to the work point system,[3] which in their production teams carried an average daily wage of 0.3 yuan or an equivalent of one-third of the average daily wage for workers in urban collective enterprises in the nearby city. The commune, on the other hand, kept all the revenue after reimbursing the factory workers' home production teams for their agricultural wages.

The brick-making operation lasted for only about 6 months, partly because of poor earnings, and partly because of the emergence of an alternative. Du's uncle was then the director of a medium-sized cotton weaving factory – a state enterprise – in the nearby city. In early 1973, the factory needed to scrap 50 sets of old cotton weaving machines from its main workshop to make room for the addition of two new production lines. Du persuaded the commune Party secretary to help remove the old machines and to store them in the auditorium of the new commune building. A makeshift workshop was quickly set up on the grounds of the brick factory. Technicians were invited from the state enterprise to put the equipment in working order and show the peasants how to operate it. After two months of preparation, Du started to take in a small amount of work farmed out from his uncle's factory. The factory paid the commune a small processing fee, in the name of "technical collaboration in support of agriculture," for the delivery of sub-contracted products.

This arrangement encountered problems, however, when the two new production lines at the state enterprise became fully operational after installation and initial testing – much of the state-allocated cotton yarn had to be used for the factory's own production. To keep his production going, Du had to search for other sources of supply. What he did was similar to what the sourcing agents of Polyester Fiber did – he went up and down in the neighboring areas to locate pockets of surplus materials. But he faced greater difficulties. Rural enterprises like Red Star

---

[3] See Crook (1975) for a discussion of the work point system.

Weaving could not obtain quota capital from state banks. All the funds used in sourcing, production, and sales had to come from the enterprise itself. Despite their interest in seeing the enterprise grow, the commune leaders could provide little help in this regard due to a lack of resources. Moreover, the sales of output from this factory were not part of the state plan and had to be self-arranged. Given the poor quality of the cloth produced by the enterprise, that was a difficult task. Du had to rely primarily on his uncle's factory to resell his product through its channels. Because of the shortage of capital and uncertainty in input supply and output sales, production in the enterprise was unstable, and the number of workers fluctuated between 30 and 60 during 1974–8. Although the factory had virtually no social service obligations for its employees and political activities were rarely organized in the workplace, operating outside the state plan at that time gave little economic advantage to Du's enterprise.

Structure and Choice

The differences among the above three factories represent a main feature of the industrial economy before the reform, that is, a centrally stratified hierarchy of enterprises of different status and treatment in resource allocation and economic regulation. The central leadership's ideological commitment to public ownership and self-reliance excluded alternative domestic and international sources of resources. This, coupled with inefficiencies in the use of state-allocated resources, posed a serious constraint on output growth. To cope with the problem of shortages, the state had to prioritize the allocation of limited resources such that the factories deemed as most critical to China's socialist industrialization would be accommodated first and foremost. As a result, some factories were more favored than others in resource allocation and in the rules governing the organization of economic activities and the determination and distribution of the resultant gains. The preferential treatment granted to the more favored factories mainly took the form of a guaranteed supply of capital and human and physical resources of good quality, a practice known as *baozheng zhongdian* or guaranteed support for the key enterprises (Zhou Taihe 1984). In addition to an abundant and secure supply of inputs, they were also allowed to provide better fringe benefits to their employees.

The most favored factories were mainly large capital goods producers like Northern Machinery that were placed under the direct purview of central ministries or provincial governments. They were regarded by the leadership as vital to the formation of a solid domestic industrial foundation and thus key to China's self-reliant industrialization (Riskin 1987; Zhu Rongji 1985). On the other hand, small and locally controlled enterprises (such as Polyester Fiber), especially those producing consumer goods (e.g., Red Star Weaving and its like), had to cope with limited means of production and settle for meager benefits for their employees. Table 2.1, constructed with statistics from the 1985 industrial census, illustrates the variations in resource allocation among different types of firms at a time when the landscape of the industrial economy was just beginning to undergo drastic transformation. As can be seen from the statistics, up to the mid-1980s enterprises were stratified along three lines, with state-owned, large, and centrally controlled enterprises at the top and collective, small, and locally controlled enterprises at the bottom. The more advantaged enterprises had a greater share in the allocation of human and financial resources, better financial and material rewards for employees, and a more politicized workforce.

It should be noted, however, that factory leaders did not necessarily take an entirely passive attitude toward this highly stratified organizational and institutional environment. Indeed, many of them pursued strategies to sustain or enhance their advantages or to contain or reduce their disadvantages. Maintaining a certain degree of organizational slack and limiting the extent to which state plans were overfulfilled, for example, were tactics used by the leaders of Northern Machinery as a way to keep its supervising agency from following a "ratchet rule" to raise output targets without increasing input supplies (Informant no. 171/1993). Facilitating political education and propaganda was cited as the reason why it expanded and upgraded its main auditorium and added other recreational facilities in the early 1970s (ibid.). Leaders of Polyester Fiber used the allocation gap in input supplies as an excuse to bargain with the Textile Industry Department for a lower output target and more discretion in self-arranged sourcing activities (Informant no. 66/1988). By emphasizing the importance and sensitivity of relationship building with the state enterprise led by his uncle, the head of Red Star Weaving gained from the commune a certain autonomy in decision making concerning external affairs; and the constant threat to organizational survival posed by the lack of stability in input supplies and output sales also provided him with grounds of justification for ignoring the factory's social service functions and political activities (Informant no. 189/1993).

But the room for these maneuverings was rather small and their effects were limited mainly to providing more breathing space for the actors concerned, rather than being strong enough to alter the overall pattern of decision making and allocation of resources and benefits. They could do little, for example, to change the important fact that the financial

Table 2.1. *Comparison of selected indicators among enterprises of different ownerships, administrative levels, and sizes*

Indicator	State enterprises	Collective enterprises	Central state enterprises	Local state enterprises	Large & medium enterprises	Small enterprises
% in total number of employees						
1980	65.1	34.5	23.6	76.4		
1985	58.8	40.3	22.6	77.4	33.4	66.6
% in total gross industrial output						
1980	80.8	18.5	25.7	74.3	51.0	49.0
1985	73.1	25.5	26.8	73.2	43.1	56.9
% in total sales revenue						
1980	81.5	17.9	26.8	73.2	57.9	42.1
1985	73.9	24.7	26.5	73.5	50.5	49.5
% in total net value of fixed assets						
1980	90.3	8.6	39.6	60.4	68.4	31.6
1985	85.2	14.0	40.4	59.6	64.4	35.6
% in total net quota working capital						
1980	81.2	18.1	28.9	71.2	56.9	43.1
1985	71.7	26.8	26.2	73.8	48.0	52.0
Number of engineers & technicians per 100 employees						
1985	4.0	0.9	5.9	3.5	5.1	1.6
Number of college graduates per 10,000 employees						
1985	399	54	628	342	532	120
Number of vocational/high school graduates per 10,000 employees						
1985	2,045	1,605	2,265	2,035	2,254	1,164
Number of communist party members per 100 employees						
1985	15.8	5.8	18.3	15.0	16.4	7.6
Average wage (yuan)						
1980	859	629	942	834	912	698
1985	1,195	900	1,357	1,147	1,292	967
Spending on fringe benefits per employee (yuan)						
1980	167		174	165		
1985	332		371	329	372	
Nonproduction fixed assets per employee (yuan)						
1980	1,181	257	3,000	1,539	2,397	644
1985	2,760	449	4,727	2,248	3,680	916
In-house medical personnel per 10,000 employees						
1985	119		192	100	156	
Size of indoor recreational facilities per 10,000 employees (square meter)						
1985	3,182		4,758	2,798	4,016	

Source: GYPCBGS (1987, volume 1: 132–46; volume 3: 375–87).

rewards of enterprise leaders were not tied to the level of efficiency of their enterprises. This in turn tended to limit or even weaken the incentive for extensive favor-seeking efforts aimed at improving enterprise performance. Although it was not entirely impossible for the status of some enterprises to be upgraded from collective to state-owned or from a lower to a higher level of supervision, this was mainly a matter of bargaining between different levels or agencies of the state administration rather than a result of the vertical bargaining between enterprises and their supervising departments. Moreover, under the central planning system, decision chains were long-stretched, intertwined, and teemed with interpersonal rivalries and factional politics (Harding 1981; Lampton 1987; Lieberthal and Oksenberg 1988; Walder 1986), making it extremely difficult for enterprise decision makers to rely on a few contacts in the government for a drastic change in their current status and treatment.

In short, particularistic state action was key to how enterprises fared in the distribution of the means and the gains of economic activities, and its path was centrally defined and highly institutionalized. Shrewd strategies to manipulate state action might help certain enterprises carry out their activities more smoothly along this path, but they could hardly be potent enough to turn particularistic state action into a force to help those enterprises to blaze a new trail of success. This, however, was to change in the course of the reform.

Marketization Led by Newcomers

A major driving force of the marketization of Chinese industry is the entry of new industrial firms, which started in the late 1970s and accelerated in the mid- to late 1980s (Naughton 1995a). As noted in Chapter 1, these new enterprises carried out their activities entirely outside the scope of the state plan and made largely independent decisions on production, exchange, and distribution according to their own calculations of profitability. In other words, they both produced for and transacted in markets. Many of them were run by innovative and risk-taking entrepreneurs in search of new economic opportunities. Their growth increased the share of products and resources allocated through exchange relations instead of authority relations. This not only led to a rapid development of product markets and a slower, uneven yet sustained emergence of factor markets (Naughton 1995a; Wu 1995), but more important, it changed the pattern of performance variation. Many of the new players were able to mobilize financial, physical, and human resources and make economic gains at or even above levels that had been attainable only for a small number of privileged state enterprises. Consider the following firms.

Flying Horse Motors Company

The Flying Horse Motors Company (Flying Horse Motors hereinafter) grew out of a small enterprise in Lakeside Village, a few hundred kilometers from a very large industrial city in East China. In 1979, the production brigade in Lakeside allocated a few thousand yuan from its collective fund to finance a sideline operation producing wooden barges for transport use in the Grand Canal. Kang Long, a carpenter who provided the design, was put in charge of the project. Because of limited demand and growing competition in the coastal region of East China in the early 1980s, the factory had to explore markets in other parts of China where waterways were used for transportation. During one of his exploration trips in 1984, Kang discovered a different opportunity at Victory Motorcycle Factory, a state enterprise located in a southwestern province. The factory was eager to increase its extra-plan output in the burgeoning consumer market for motorcycles but faced constraints in plant space and manpower. Kang offered to process and assemble certain parts for the factory at low cost. The subcontract arrangement went through within a few weeks. In 1985, the village enterprise abandoned the barge-making operation to concentrate on the work farmed out from the motorcycle factory.

In the process of subcontracting, Kang's technicians gradually gained the know-how to make motorcycle engines and built up the necessary facilities and technical personnel to manufacture them. In 1988, the subcontracting relationship was brought to an end and Kang started to manufacture motorcycles of his own brand – Flying Horse – and renamed the factory after it. While competing with his former partner and other manufacturers, he also embarked on the development of a related product, a stand-alone, multipurpose diesel generator, which went into batch production in 1992. In 1994, the enterprise was further expanded with the creation of an automobile assembly line, where Flying Horse Motors, operating as a subcontractor of one of China's largest automakers, assembled full-scale subcompact cars with imported Izuzu engines and chassis made by an automobile plant in Northeast China.

What governed its relationship with the village as a collective was a managerial contract that specified the tax and profit targets and Kang's salary and bonus for each year. Within the enterprise, Kang had total authority in decision making. His son was one of the deputy directors and his daughter worked as the accountant. Part of the after-tax profit was contributed to the village as a collective fund and part of it was retained as a development fund for the enterprise. To address its deficiency in human resources, the factory drew heavily on the expertise of "Sunday engineers" – moonlighting technical personnel from state enterprises in urban areas, especially a nearby industrial city. Most of the workers were villagers. They lived at home and used their after-hours to tend the crops in the farmland that their families contracted from the village. During planting and harvest seasons, some of them took short leaves from the factory to concentrate on farm work. When the enterprise was first established, it contributed only a small fraction of the village's revenue. But in 1994 it accounted for 80% of the village's economic output. In 1993, Kang was appointed the head of the village economic development company – the administrative body that oversaw economic activities in the entire village, making him a key decision maker in village affairs (along with the Party secretary and the village chief).

Peak Construction Equipment Factory

The Peak Construction Equipment Factory (Peak Equipment hereinafter) was among the first private industrial enterprises that reemerged in the post-Mao era. Its owner, Ma Li, was an ex-officer of the People's Liberation Army. In 1983, after 17 years of service in the army, Ma returned to his hometown, a large industrial city in North China. He turned down an offer by the local Civil Administration Department to assign him as the director of a state enterprise, and instead started a business of his own. Equipped with his experience as an electrician in the army, he used his demobilization allowance as seed capital and hired several unemployed urban youths to start a small service shop to install and repair electric circuits and other electric control devices for local factories. In 1984, he learned from his contacts in a nearby large city that researchers at the Institute of Construction Technology there had designed a new water supply system for high-rise buildings that could be more efficient than the conventional water tower design but had yet to be mass-produced for commercial use. He immediately went to the Institute to seek the technology, but his request was rejected. Seeing great potential in the application of the technology, he approached several researchers at the provincial institute of construction technology and commissioned them to develop a modified design. In mid-1984, the prototype was rolled out and passed the test of government technical inspection authorities. Production began in 1985, and sales and profits rose steadily.

The land occupied by the factory was rented from the government of the district where it was located. All the equipment, machinery, and material inputs used for the factory's operations were purchased at market prices from state and collective enterprises that sold part of their output outside the state plan. The backbone of the factory consisted of two dozen "Sunday engineers" from state enterprises and research institutes. They played a critical role in product design and development, and for this they were offered much higher pay than that received from their regular work units. Some of them eventually quit their state jobs and joined the factory permanently. Another key group of employees was the sales representatives who were responsible for marketing the factory's products to construction companies. Their role was especially important in the early years of the factory when its products were little known to users and a fall in sales would have created a serious cash flow problem for the factory. Their commission was directly tied to sales, and they were given full autonomy in carrying out their activities. By 1988 the factory had expanded its work force to 410 and amassed nearly 10 million yuan in fixed assets. In 1991, the factory joined hands with a Hong Kong manufacturer to start a new line of product – loading frames for heavy trucks, and the number of workers and fixed assets increased to 580 and 15 million yuan respectively.

Modern Housewares Company

The Modern Housewares Company (Modern Housewares hereinafter) was founded in 1983 as a contractual joint venture between a Hong Kong manufacturer, Dennis Cheung, and a collective enterprise in Golden Field, a rural township in the Pearl River Delta of Guangdong province. Cheung was a native of Golden Field. In 1968 when the Cultural Revolution was in full force, he sneaked into the border town Shenzhen and from there swam to Hong Kong to escape the turmoil. In the mid-1970s, he started a small factory to produce cooking utensils. Like many Hong Kong residents, after 1978 he paid visits to his hometown where his parents and many relatives still resided. During one of the visits, he met a former middle school classmate who was then the head of the industrial and sideline office of the Golden Field People's Commune and who invited Cheung to make an investment in their hometown. In 1983, when the commune was turned into a township and his former classmate became a deputy township director, Cheung entered the joint venture agreement. His local partner was a 15-person agricultural equipment repair center run by the township government. The township allocated a piece of land (about 1,000 square meters) as part of its contribution to the joint venture. Cheung shipped in equipment and materials and brought over three technicians from Hong Kong. At first, production replicated that of the Hong Kong shop. But starting from 1986, it was expanded to include a whole range of metal kitchenware. By the end of 1993 the firm had a total of 460 employees (mostly peasants from nearby villages) and fixed assets of approximately 35 million yuan.

Although the enterprise was a joint venture, the township government did not take an active part in decision making. Cheung chose all the managers and exerted full control over issues of employment, sourcing, production, and sales. According to the agreement, at least 70% of the output would be exported and the two parties would equally share the profit. But in reality export never exceeded 40% of the total output and the remaining portion was sold in China. The main clients of the enterprise were organizations with catering facilities. Since the demand for Modern Housewares' products was very broad and only a small number of factories in China manufactured similar products before the late 1980s, the joint venture made substantial profits in the first few years of its operation. Also, it profited greatly from a sideline transaction – the trading of aluminum, which was the main metal used in its production and an industrial material tightly regulated by the government before the early 1990s. Importing more than it needed for actual production, the company saved the extra amount for arbitrage, selling it to factories that could not obtain sufficient supply from state allocation. In the early 1990s, competition from other joint ventures and domestic firms drove down the margin of gains from both activities and consequently the trading sideline shrank considerably. But the firm continued to be profitable and expanded its operations into the manufacturing of building materials (such as window frames).

Everbright Heating Device Coompany

The Everbright Heating Device Company (Everbright Heating hereinafter) was spun off from a warehouse under an industrial bureau of a northern city. It was a manufacturer of heat converters used in water heating devices. The technology, which has a much higher energy conservation level than those used in conventional heat converters, was jointly developed by a professor at a local engineering university and a professor at an Australian university where the former was a visiting scholar in the early 1980s. It was patented in Australia and won several international awards. After returning from Australia in 1984, the professor approached several factories to promote the technology and manufacture products for industrial and household use, but failed to convince them of its commercial value. In 1985, Wang Jianguo, an employee of the warehouse of the industrial bureau and a part-time student attending vocational training courses in the professor's department, learned about the technology. He persuaded his supervisor to give it a try. Wang was assigned to lead the project, with a loan of 30,000 yuan from the warehouse and ten unemployed children of its employees. Under the guidance of the professor, the first batch of heat converters was manufactured in 1986. Connected to a water tank, they could be turned into a water heating system for industrial or household use. Wang started to market the products; they sold well and the enterprise flourished. In the same year, Wang's operation was separated from the warehouse and registered as an independent urban collective enterprise.

The factory's facilities were built in the compound of the warehouse, for which an annual land-use fee was paid. The key components needed by the factory, vacuum glass tubes, were tailor-made by a state enterprise in a northern province, which until being approached by Everbright Heating had underused capacity. As the initial success of Everbright Heating became known to the local university, it also set up a workshop to produce the same product, which soon became the chief competitor of Everbright Heating. In 1990, the output of the university plant exceeded that of Everbright Heating, whose profit margin began to narrow. In 1991, the status of Everbright Heating was changed from a collective enterprise to a joint venture with a company from a Southeast Asian country, which injected additional capital into the enterprise and earned it a three-year tax holiday.

Rainbow Joint Pipe Factory

The Rainbow Joint Pipe Factory (Rainbow Pipe hereinafter) was an enterprise specializing in the manufacture of elbow-shaped joint pipes for use in radiators. It was started in 1989 as a private enterprise in Lotus Pond Township near the eastern end of the North China Plain. Its owner, Zhu Linan, was a former physics and mathematics teacher in a local school. From the mid-1970s, he had been invited by various agricultural equipment repair centers in the county to help improve casting techniques. In the mid-1980s, he found a new way to reduce the amount of coal needed for casting elbow-shaped joint pipes, which were key components in heating systems. Confident of its potential for commercial application, he quit his teaching job and raised money from relatives to start a small manufacturing shop. After repeated experiments, he perfected and built a new type of furnace that could reduce the heating time and energy consumption for casting large batches of joint pipes. Also, he used a mixture of scrap steel and iron to replace pure iron (which was more expensive) as the input material. Together, these measures could save up to 30% of the cost for making the same product using conventional methods. This gave him an edge in price competition with other manufacturers. Because of the relatively low price and reliability of his products, sales expanded quickly. By the end of 1993, the factory became one of the largest producers of elbow-shaped joint pipes in North China.

Like Peak Equipment, Rainbow Pipe rented its land from the local authority – that of a village within Lotus Pond Township. When it first started, there were only eight workers. In 1994, the number increased to over 250. Most of them were peasants from nearby villages. They worked in the factory and attended to their farmland as did the workers at Flying Horse Motors, but they were provided with virtually no fringe benefits. The intensity of work was rather high and working conditions were very poor, in part because of the high temperature and heavy dust in the casting operation. Most of the technical personnel were part-timers, including some consultants from research institutes in two adjacent large cities. In 1994, the township government offered to become a partner in the enterprise by investing 2 million yuan in one of its major workshops, making it a joint-ownership enterprise. In the same year, the factory contributed one-third of the gross economic output produced in the township and, partly because of this, Zhu was appointed a pro bono deputy township director and invited to participate in the making of important decisions.

Adaptations by Old Enterprises

The expansion of the activities of new firms like the ones just described had an important impact on old enterprises: They stimulated institutional change in the traditional public sector by creating a push-and-pull effect. On the one hand, these newcomers intensified the competition in product sales and the supply of resources (e.g., by "stealing" human resources from state enterprises in the form of "Sunday engineers"),[4] crowding the economic space occupied by existing public enterprises and forcing them to search for alternative ways to generate revenue and profit. On the other hand, the self-arranged transactions initially dominated by the new players demonstrated the potential gains to be made in the marketplace, thereby providing a clear frame of reference in which the opportunity cost of the rigid institutional arrangement of traditional public enterprises could be gauged. At the same time, new firms also created opportunities for traditional public enterprises to search for profits beyond the plan (e.g., Flying Horse Motors' subcontracting arrangement with the motorcycle manufacturer in the state sector and

---

[4] From 1980 to 1993, the share of state enterprises in total net fixed asset value decreased from 90.3% to 72% and that in total working capital from 79% to 62.7% (GJTJJb 1995: 81–95; GYPCBGS 1987, volume 3: 580–1), which indicates a rise in the financial resources attracted to nonstate enterprises.

Everbright Heating's sourcing from the state enterprise manufacturing glass). The adaptations made by old firms to engage in self-arranged production and transactions inevitably deepened the marketization of the economy, whereas the uneven pace and effectiveness of their adaptations directly affected the pattern of performance variation among industrial firms.

At Northern Machinery, the certainty that existed under the central planning system gradually slipped away as the reform progressed. The scope of mandatory planning in production and pricing declined from 95% of its output in 1980 to 40% in 1985 and further to less than 10% in 1990. Increasingly, the orders that the factory received or solicited from users became the main guide for its production. The shrinking scope of the plan was also accompanied by a reduction of inputs supplied at state-set prices, and the factory had to make up the widening gap in input supplies with industrial materials purchased at higher market prices. In 1983, state banks started to charge and increase interest on capital borrowed by the factory. Furthermore, sales were no longer guaranteed and the factory confronted stiff competition from other major producers of milling machines and from foreign companies. Its main domestic competitors were also state enterprises, especially a milling machine factory in South China (a former branch plant of Northern Machinery in the 1960s) and another one in Northeast China. From the mid-1980s, with the growth of international pressure for China to open its markets and the weakening of state protection under a regime of decentralized foreign trade regulation (Shirk 1994), imports from Germany, South Korea, Russia, and Japan increased, posing a major threat to the factory's market dominance in North and East China. In 1993, for example, Northern Machinery signed an RMB 10 million preliminary agreement with a factory in Jiangsu to manufacture a milling system within 20 months. But that deal was subsequently snapped away by a German firm that offered a shorter delivery period of 15 months for a similar set of machines. In 1994, for the first time in its history, Northern Machinery's profit rate dropped below 10%.

On the other hand, marketization also created opportunities and stimulated changes in the decision making of the firm. With the focus of activities in the factory shifting toward profit making, political mobilization and ideological indoctrination gradually lost their significance. In 1984, the factory adopted the contract responsibility system, which tied the wage bill of the factory to its profitability and expanded the autonomy of factory leaders in decisions regarding production, sourcing, sales, and personnel. In 1987, it was the first enterprise in the milling machine sector to win from its supervising agency a contractual arrangement under which it had the obligation to achieve a fixed annual increment of

5% in output value and gross profit for a period of five years and, in return, was permitted to keep all the above-target surplus. The same arrangement was modified and renewed for the period of 1992–6. In 1989, Northern Machinery succeeded in lobbying for the right of direct import and export without the mediation of state foreign trade agencies. In 1994, the factory was again the first among its peers to adopt a measure to trim off over 1,000 redundant workers through early retirement, transfer to service auxiliaries, and voluntary resignation with compensation.

Polyester Fiber was exposed to the emerging markets earlier than Northern Machinery. In 1979, a reduction in the centrally allocated quota for polyester chips led the city's Textile Industry Department to cut – on top of the usual gap of 10–20% – the input supply to the factory by 40%, forcing the factory to intensify its efforts to search for material input from self-arranged sources. As an incentive for the factory to keep output from falling, the Department also lowered the mandatory output target to 50% of the original requirement. Polyester Fiber could sell the remaining output to self-arranged parties at mutually agreed prices. In the ensuing years, the share of centrally allocated input further decreased, as did that of the output required by the mandatory state plan. By 1985, the factory was virtually on its own in sourcing and sales. In 1984, it adopted the contract responsibility system, under which it was given enhanced decision-making autonomy on the condition that it would be subject to an annual assessment by the Textile Industry Department to determine the level of its profit retention.

From the early to the mid-1980s, the demand for polyester fiber was rather high because of the rise of large numbers of newly formed textile enterprises – driven by the pent-up demand for textile products – outside of the traditional public sector. In the meantime, large state enterprises producing polyester fiber were still under tight state planning in production, input supplies, and output sales. This opened up an opportunity for Polyester Fiber to capitalize on shortages in supply and its relative autonomy. Although it had to source polyester chips from self-arranged channels at prices higher than the state-allocation price, it could now manufacture products in short supply and sell them at higher prices. Seizing the opportunity, it expanded its production and sales. From 1983 to 1988, its gross profit rose steadily at an average annual growth rate of 6%, rivaling the performances of many state enterprises. During the same period, the factory's work force was increased from less than 800 to over 1,300, and more communal facilities, especially housing, were built with retained profit. In 1989 and 1990, the factory undertook a major technological upgrading project, involving borrowing 14 million yuan from state banks to import new production lines from Italy. But at the same time, the state's control over large petrochemical enterprises was relaxed, making it possible for them to integrate the production of polyester chips with that of polyester fiber and sell their products at much more competitive prices. The increase of market competition, plus the saturation of the demand from textile enterprises, made it difficult for Polyester Fiber to make a profit, not to mention achieve its expected level of return. Interest payments for the huge debt suddenly became unbearable. It started to incur heavy losses in the early 1990s, and eventually was dissolved in 1995.

At Red Star Weaving, the first decade of reform was filled with ups and downs. It was among the first to benefit from rural industrialization in the post-Mao era. The rise and growth of textile and garment enterprises run by townships and villages in the coastal region of East China created a huge demand for its product and thus a good profit-making opportunity. From 1979 to 1984, it increased its work force from 50 to 250, tripled its production capacity, and quadrupled its profit. But the good time did not last long. In the mid-1980s, the market space Red Star Weaving benefited from was crowded by newly established cotton weaving factories as well as state and urban collective enterprises that had gained more autonomy in decision making under the contract responsibility system introduced in 1984. In the nearby city alone, there were 17 pre-existing and new cotton weaving operations in 1987. Faced with growing competition and dwindling profit, the factory resorted to an extension of its production process downstream by setting up a workshop for garment making, which turned out to be a failure. It also tried integration upstream into spinning, but failed again. By the end of 1988 the factory had reduced its workforce by half and could barely break even.

In the spring of 1989, Du's brother, the sales chief of the factory, learned about the heating devices produced by Everbright Heating (described above) during a business trip to the city where Everbright Heating was located. He approached Director Wang and offered to help sell the product in East China. Wang agreed. After initial sales, the Du brothers discovered that the product had great market potential. They went back to Wang to request a subcontracting arrangement for assembling water heaters. At that time, Everbright Heating had more orders for water heaters than it could produce. So Wang decided to farm out part of its work to the Du brothers and to concentrate its own resources on making the core components – heat converters. After the agreement, Du vacated a workshop from the cotton weaving factory, transferred some workers, and registered a new township enterprise under the name of Red Star Heating Devices (Red Star Heating hereinafter).

For two years, it purchased heat converters from Everbright Heating and made various water heaters. Sales went well in several coastal provinces, such as Jiangsu, Zhejiang, and Shandong. While assembling water heaters, Du hired researchers and engineers in Shanghai and Nanjing to experiment with ways to make heat converters, which eventually succeeded. In 1993, the factory started to produce both heat converters and water heaters. Du handed over the lackluster cotton weaving factory to a deputy factory director, moved the heating device operation to a different location, and devoted himself fully to the new venture. In 1994, the sales of Red Star Heating exceeded those of Everbright Heating.

Driving Forces of Marketization: Questions

As markets emerge as the center of transactions, information, and incentives, and as economic life becomes more competitive, the flow of resources and the distribution of economic rewards no longer closely follow the traditional pecking order of status differentiation under central planning. Financial, human, and physical resources are attracted to increasing numbers of traditionally disadvantaged enterprises and newly established enterprises in the nonstate sector, instead of following the hierarchy of administrative commands under the central plan. Many newcomers have joined the ranks of winners while large numbers of state firms (including star enterprises like Northern Machinery) have experienced slippage in performance, as indicated by the case studies presented above and more broadly by the statistics in Chapter 1.

To explain these changes, one needs to address two important questions. First, what accounts for the uneven paces and effectiveness in the efforts of firms to tackle the barriers to free market activities? Second, has the expansion of markets led the interplay between demand and supply, as embodied in the exchange relations among economic actors, to become the predominant force shaping performance variation among firms? In the next chapter, I will show that the expansion of the economic space outside the plan has been conditioned by particularistic state action and interactions between economic actors and state agents. Also, the state's differential treatment of firms continues to exert an important influence on the selection of winners and losers in the new economic game, though the driving forces of such treatment have been recomposed.

3

The Rugged Terrain of Competition

In 1993 a research unit (China's Entrepreneurs Survey System, CESS hereafter) under the State Council conducted a survey of 2,620 industrial enterprise leaders. Most of the respondents indicated that the economic environments that they faced were either competitive (29.5%) or highly competitive (64.5%), but 74.2% regarded the competition as "unfair" (CESS 1993: 15). The main reasons given by those choosing this last answer included "preferential treatment enjoyed by some firms" (42%), "uneven income tax rates" (17.4%), "local protectionism" (12.9%), and "overly restrictive accounting procedures for state enterprises" (12.8%).[1]

What this finding suggests is that opportunities in the new economic game are not equally distributed among competing firms and the state is largely responsible. There is little surprise in this. Despite the enormous economic change since the late 1970s, China is nowhere close to Milton Friedman's ideal of a free market economy where the government plays a minimal role except in order keeping and enforcement of property rights and social justice. Even those who see the Chinese economy as increasingly "marketlike" regard the slow progress in the reform of laws, regulations, and property right institutions as major obstacles to China's completing the transition to a market economy (e.g., Naughton 1995a; Rawski 1994a, 1995). But the above finding does point to an important question that needs to be closely examined: Is the problem revealed by the survey mainly the result of lapses and gaps in policy and regulation amidst rapid and wide-ranging economic change or is it largely driven

---

[1] A survey of 2,561 enterprise leaders conducted by the same unit in 1994 revealed similar results: 67.8% of the respondents regarded the competition that they faced as "unfair," and the main reasons cited were "preferential treatment enjoyed by certain firms" (36.8%), "use of illicit means by competitors" (24.9%), and "imperfection of market regulations" (17.4%). See CESS (1994: 16).

by deliberate efforts to manipulate state action for competitive advantage in the economic game?

I hypothesize that the latter is the main contributing factor. In this chapter, I explore how economic actors' efforts to expand the boundary of markets and seek profits have been accommodated or adversely affected by ad hoc actions of the state. Such an interplay between economic action and state action has taken place in the context of a decentralization of the state's decision-making authority. I first highlight major changes brought about by decentralization in three areas of state action: resource allocation, regulation, and distribution of state-engendered liabilities. Then I return to the case studies, mostly introduced in the preceding chapter, to examine the effects of these changes on firms' behavior and performance.

Decentralization: An Overview[2]

Resource Allocation

Before the reform, resource allocation was directed by the state's integrated plans. Although the degree of centralization and coherence of the plan in China might not be as high as that in the former Soviet Union (Granick 1990; Shirk 1993), local authorities faced great rigidities imposed by various "cannot do" regulations on allocation decisions (Zhu Rongji 1985). This is an area where major changes have taken place in the reform.

Capital. In the allocation of capital, the fiscal authority was the center of control and coordination under central planning. Funds for the addition of fixed assets were appropriated free of charge, and working capital was either appropriated to factories on a recurrent basis without interest or lent at low interest rates (less than 4%) (Zhao Haikuan 1993). Since the reform, however, the locus of authority has shifted from the fiscal system to the banking system, where decisions have become increasingly profit-oriented and localized. Also, various government departments have amassed large sums of off-budget funds that they can allocate with great discretion.

In 1980 a measure called *bo gai dai* (substitution of loans for fiscal appropriations) was introduced to turn fixed asset investment in state and urban collective enterprises into bank loans. This was followed by

---

[2] In this section I only highlight the changes in the decentralization process that have had most immediate effects on the behavior and performance of firms. For detailed accounts of the background, process, and dynamics of various aspects of decentralization in the reform, see Bell et al. (1993), Huang (1996), Jia and Lin (1994), Oksenberg and Tong (1991), Shirk (1993), Wong (1991, 1997), Wong et al. (1995), and World Bank (1994).

a central government decision in 1983 to reduce the role of the fiscal authority in the allocation of working capital and to make state banks the main source of supply and supervision.[3] In the ensuing years, the banking system itself underwent a major change from serving as a sheer policy instrument to profit making. From 1979 to 1993 the base rates of interest for working capital and medium- to long-term fixed asset loans were increased from 5.08% and 2.16% to 8.10%–10.98% and 8.46–14.04% respectively (ZGJRXH 1994: 491). In 1994, the magnitude of low-interest "policy loans" was reduced from the mainstay to 25% of the lending by state banks (Mao Hongjun 1994: 31). Under a bank branch director responsibility system started in the mid-1980s, the rewards for bank branch officials have been tied to the performance of their lending activities (Zhang Yichun 1994; Zhao Haikuan 1993). Within the annual lending ceiling set by the central bank (the People's Bank),[4] local branch offices have been given increasing latitude in determining the recipient, amount, and duration of loans, adjusting interest rates within or even beyond a centrally authorized 20–30% range above the official rates, and assessing the qualifications for preferential interest rates that amounted to more than 30 categories in the early 1990s (ZGRMYHJRTZGGS 1991: 61).

Although the budgets and personnel of all the state banks have been vertically administered within the purview of each bank, their branch offices have operated under the shadow of local governments. Local governments may influence the selection by local public enterprises of bank branches for opening and maintaining their accounts; they also control or regulate the supply of various local social services to bank agents, including housing, health care, children's education, and utilities. This provides a basis on which they can act on behalf of their favored firms to press state bank branches for capital on favorable terms (Chen Yuan 1994: 29–30). The role of local governments in the allocation of credit has been further enhanced by their provision of loan guarantees for many nonstate enterprises, especially TVEs, which have been required by state banks since 1985 to secure guarantors as a precondition for borrowing (Shang Ming 1989).[5]

---

[3] There are four major state banks: the Bank of China, the Industrial and Commercial Bank, the Agricultural Bank, and the Construction Bank. Each state enterprise or urban collective has been required to maintain its main account at one of these banks (principally, the Industrial and Commercial Bank), known as its *kaihu yinhang* (bank for an enterprise's primary account).

[4] Starting from 1998, the binding limit has been changed to a quarterly "guidance plan" for lending extended by state-owned commercial banks, including the four mentioned above (ZGJRXH 1998: 12–13).

[5] In February 1985, the State Council issued a document called *jiekuan hetong tiaoli* (borrowing contract regulation). It required that in order to qualify for a bank loan an orga-

Outside the fiscal and banking authorities, various state agencies have built up large pools of "extra-budgetary funds" in the reform (Wong et al. 1995). Such funds are revenues generated from channels other than those for budgetary revenues – mainly taxes[6] – and controlled and used by the state agencies that generate them (Li 1993: 408). In official statistics, they are further divided into three categories: (i) various surcharges levied or controlled by the finance departments of local governments; (ii) various fees collected by other state agencies; and (iii) retained profits and depreciation and maintenance funds of state enterprises, which are partially controlled by the supervising agencies of these enterprises. Since 1994 (iii) has been excluded from official statistics on extra-budgetary revenue, reflecting an increase of enterprise autonomy over retained profits.

In 1996, the total size of (i) and (ii) was equivalent to 45% of government budgetary revenue (GJTJJa 1998: 281–2). The bulk of them has been generated and controlled by local governments, which accounted for 76% of extra-budgetary funds in 1996 (GJTJJa 1998: 282). Although there have been regulations regarding how and where such funds should be used, monitoring has become increasingly difficult as the source of such funds expands and diversifies (Deng Yingtao et al. 1990; see also Oi 1999: 162–6). As a result, they have become an important pool of resources that can be flexibly spent for various self-defined purposes, including industrial financing.

Land. All the land in China has been publicly owned.[7] Before the reform, the assignment of land use rights was controlled by the planning authority. Farmland use was subject to an agricultural tax, but land use for commercial and industrial activities was free of charge. The expenses for land requisition and reallocation (e.g., relocation costs incurred by existing users) were shouldered by the government instead of the receiving enterprises (Zhang Xiaohua 1993). Several important changes have taken place since the late 1970s.[8]

nizational borrower must show evidence of adequate self-owned funds and collateral. If the borrower could not meet this condition, it would have to find a third party to serve as loan repayment guarantor. Since most TVEs could not meet this condition, especially in the initial stage of their operations, they had to rely on local governments for the provision of guarantee. It was not until 1995, when the *Guarantee Law* was enacted, that local governments were effectively banned from acting as guarantors.

[6] In 1997, for example, 95% of government budgetary revenue came from taxes (GJTJJa 1998: 282).

[7] According to the Constitution enacted in 1982, all the urban land is owned by the state; except for certain segments specified by law as state-owned, all the rural land is collectively owned by rural residents.

[8] See IFTE & IPA (1994), Xu Mu and Zhang Xiaohua (1995), Zhang Xiaohua (1993), and Zou Yuchuan (1998) for detailed discussions of these changes.

First, defining the purpose of land use and assigning land use rights have become primarily local government decisions. With the expansion of economic activities outside the plan – especially in the countryside – the once dominant role of the planning authority in land allocation has declined. Although a national land administration agency was established in 1982, its role has been centered on the coordination rather than the allocation of use rights. The demarcation of jurisdiction over different pieces of land was based on the pattern of administrative affiliation of existing users at the start of the reform; but it has since been subject to renegotiations between different levels (provincial, city, county, township, and village) of local authority. Since the demise of the people's commune in 1983, rural land has been divided between townships and villages, where local public authorities have acted as representatives of "collectively owned" land. In the village, land has been divided into small pieces, with their use rights contracted to peasant households for farming. In return, peasants have been required to pay a prorated agricultural tax on the output from their contracted farmland, sell part of their output (mostly grain) to state procurement stations at state-set prices, and in some places pay a fee to their village. Without prior approval from the village or in some cases the township, farmland cannot be changed to other uses. In urban areas, any change in land use purpose requires the approval of the local government, but it is the end users instead of the government that now bear the pertinent costs.

Second, industrial and commercial land use has been subject to various newly imposed levies, which constitute a major source of local government revenue. These include a fee, introduced in 1980, for the land used by economic entities with foreign investment,[9] an urban real estate tax (1986), an urban land use tax (1988), and a capital gains tax on land appreciation (1994). Tax rates are based on the location and the quality and commercial value of the land, both of which are assessed and determined by local governments. But the criteria used in different localities may vary considerably.

Third, land use rights have become saleable items and local governments exert predominant influence on the pricing and transfer of land use rights. In 1988 the Constitution was amended with a clause that legalized the sale of land use rights. Local governments have since held the authority to approve or disapprove the change in land use purpose resulting from such a transfer, and played a key role in selecting the receiving party and determining the terms of transfer. They have done so either by acting as the arbitrator between the buyer and the seller

---

[9] Such a fee is waived, however, if land is evaluated and included as part of the equity capital of the Chinese partners of joint ventures.

(existing use right holder), or by first acquiring parcels of land from existing users (at low prices) and then reselling them to other users (at higher prices).

Capital Goods. Under central planning the supply of capital goods (known as *wuzi* in Chinese) was subject to centralized control by the State Planning Commission (SPC) and various industry-specific ministries. This involved three related areas: production planning, pricing, and output sales. In the reform, central control has declined in all these areas, whereas control by local authorities has been relaxed at uneven paces (Ma Kai 1992).

In 1978, the SPC had mandatory plans for the production of 120 types of industrial products (most of which were capital goods), accounting for 40% of gross industrial output. The number of such products declined to 60 in 1988 and 33 in 1994, which accounted for 17% and 4.4% of gross industrial output respectively (Gui Shiyong 1994: 8). In 1984, there were 1,900 products subject to mandatory plans by various ministry-level supervising bodies of the central government; in 1988, they declined to 380 (Wang Shiyuan 1993: 173–4).

Related to this is the decline of central control over pricing. Before the reform, the central authority exerted tight control – mainly through the State Price Control Bureau (*guojia wujia ju*) – over the prices of various products, especially capital goods. Before 1979 authorities at or above the provincial level directly set 248 procurement prices and 225 sales prices for different types of agricultural products, and 1,127 ex-factory prices and 339 sales prices for different types of industrial products (Tong Wansheng and Zou Xiangqun 1992: 7). Since 1978, the control over the prices for consumer goods has been gradually relaxed and the scope of centrally controlled prices for capital goods significantly reduced.[10] In 1978, products sold at state-set prices made up 97% of retail values, 94.4% of the total output procured from the agricultural sector, and 100% of capital goods (Ma Kai 1992: 31). By the end of 1992, only 5.9% of the retail values, 12.5% of the sales of agricultural products, and 18.7% of the sales of capital goods came from products priced by the state. At the same time, of the 89 capital goods and 9 agricultural

---

[10] In 1983 the central authority started to allow certain oil producers to sell their extra-plan output with reference to international market prices. In 1984, some coal mines were allowed to mark up the prices of their extra-plan output, and the State Council stipulated that capital goods producers could sell their extra-plan output at prices higher than state-set prices by up to 20%. In 1985, the 20% upper limit was removed. This resulted in the adoption of the so-called "dual-track" price system – coexistence of prices for planned and extra-plan output of capital goods. See Ma Kai (1992) and Tong Wansheng and Zou Xiangqun (1992).

products still subject to central price control, 33 and 4, respectively, had prices directly set by the central authority; the remaining products were subject to the more flexible "guidance prices" (*zhidao jiage*) enforced primarily by local authorities (Gui Shiyong 1994: 10).

In the distribution of capital goods, the State Materials Allocation Bureau (SMAB) (*guojia wuzi zongju*) was the main instrument of centralized control before the reform.[11] The central planning system required that industrial enterprises sell or obtain capital goods at state-set prices through a capital goods distribution network coordinated by the SMAB. Such products were classified into three categories, those directly allocated by the SMAB according to the plans from the SPC (category one), those allocated by central ministries (category two), and those allocated by local authorities (category three). From 1980 to 1990 the total number of category one and category two products declined from over 800 to 72 (Liu Suinian 1993: 120). In 1979, there were 256 category one products; the figure decreased to 19 in 1990 and 12 in 1992 (Gui Shiyong 1994: 8), whereas category three products were gradually decontrolled by provincial and subprovincial authorities at varying paces (Shao Zunting, Zhang Shengshu, and Xie Minggan 1992: 35). In the production of category one products remaining under central control, extra-plan output has significantly increased. From 1979 to 1993, the output of steel, timber, cement, and coal (all category one products) that was actually centrally allocated decreased from 77.1% (steel), 85% (timber), 35.7% (cement), and 58.9% (coal) to 19.9%, 9.9%, 4.5%, and 49.2% respectively (Gui Shiyong 1994: 9). In fact, local subsidiaries of the SMAB have been increasingly oriented toward organizing and regulating sales activities for capital goods outside the central plan. In 1981, 77.2% of the capital goods sales arranged by such agencies was guided by the central plan; in 1991 the figure dropped to 17% (Liu Suinian 1993: 667).

Regulation

Entry. Under central planning, the use of the "material balances" method to arrange and coordinate the production, supply, and consumption of goods and services in physical terms made it crucial for the state to monitor closely the size, location, and sectoral distribution of industrial enterprises (Chow 1994; Riskin 1987). The planning organs and the various industry-specific ministries and departments at different

---

[11] The agency was closely associated with the State Planning Commission, where it was a subsidiary organization in the late 1950s and the early 1970s. In 1988 it was elevated to a ministry. In 1993, it was merged with the Ministry of Commerce to become the newly formed Ministry of Domestic Trade.

administrative levels played a key role in authorizing and regulating the establishment of new enterprises. Although there were enterprises formed on the periphery of the central planning system, such as commune and brigade enterprises like Red Star Weaving (described in Chapter 2), they were limited in magnitude,[12] and faced great uncertainties in input supplies, production, and sales (Ma Jiesan 1991).

A major change in the reform is a decline of the centrally integrated planning authority in access control. Concurrent with this are the decentralization of the authority to approve the establishment of new industrial enterprises and the ascendance of the State Industrial and Commercial Administration (SICA) (*guojia gongshang ju*) as the main agency to regulate entry.[13] Although the agency has a vertical command chain running from the national headquarters to its branch offices in urban and rural townships, the budgets and personnel of most local *gongshang* offices are controlled by local governments, as are their decisions.[14]

Although there are national policies regarding where, how, and in what form a new enterprise can be registered, such policies have gradually lost coherence due to a shrinking of the scope of the central plan and a parallel growth of market-oriented economic activities. More important, they have become increasingly difficult to enforce – even in the sectors that used to be closely guarded by the state as areas of strategic importance. The interpretation of these policies lies in the hands of various local authorities, and it is mainly the locally based *gongshang* branch offices that now determine what level of approval a new enterprise needs to obtain and what procedures it needs to go

---

[12] In 1978 the gross industrial output from commune and brigade enterprises, which was then included as part of agricultural output, was equivalent to 9.1% of the gross industrial output from state enterprises and urban collectives (GJTJJa 1999: 423; ZGXZQYNJBJWYH 1988: 572).

[13] The SICA is the government's licensing authority for industrial and commercial enterprises. Under the central planning system, enterprise registration was only a matter of formality in that all the major decisions on the organization of new enterprises, such as ownership form, capital, number of workers, products, location, etc., were made or authorized by the planning authority. During the Cultural Revolution, except for those in a few localities, local offices of the SICA were closed down and merged into the administrative system under the Ministry of Commerce (Fei Kailong and Zuo Ping 1991). It was not until 1978 that the national headquarters were restored under the State Council. Since then it has re-established its local branch offices and taken on administrative functions in such areas as industrial and commercial licensing, market regulation, regulation of private economic entities, enforcement of economic contracts, and implementation of laws and regulations on trademark and advertising (Wang Shiyuan 1993).

[14] In the reform, the expansion of the personnel in local *gongshang* offices has been in large part financed with retained fees generated from regulation-related activities (such as management of merchandise markets, fines, registration fees, etc.), which may be enhanced or restricted by the top authority of local government (Fei Kailong and Zuo Ping 1991).

through in order to register as a particular type of enterprise in a particular sector.

Figures in Table 3.1 show that from the mid-1980s to the mid-1990s most industrial sectors, including upstream, capital goods industries where state control had been very tight, experienced a significant increase in the number of newly formed firms, and the penetration came from both state and nonstate enterprises.[15] Most of the new enterprises are under the jurisdiction of local governments. From 1985 to 1997, for example, the number of centrally controlled state enterprises increased from 3,825 to 4,692, whereas that of enterprises regulated by local authorities at or above the township level rose from 0.36 million to 0.53 million (GYPCBGS 1987, volume 3: 88; GJTJJa 1998: 434; GJTJJb 1998: 84).

Procedures and Standards. Before the reform, both state and urban collective enterprises were required to abide by similar, centrally defined procedures and standards. Their accounting methods and transaction formalities were guided by strict rules on the use, verification, and record keeping of receipts. Bank transfer was designated as the main form of payment in transactions. The use of cash was restricted to three areas: wage and other remuneration payment, expenses for pre-authorized travel, and small purchases from self-employed individuals (Shang Ming 1989). Moreover, they were required to follow a practice called *zhuankuan zhuanyong* or "use of purpose-specific funds only for their designated purposes." This practice prohibited the funds specified for one type of activity from being used for another, as characterized in the saying "the money for buying soy sauce cannot be used for buying vinegar and vice versa" (ZGGLKXYCJS 1994: 81). Industrial enterprises also adopted similar employment practices to recruit employees within the quotas authorized by labor and planning authorities, paid wages according to centrally determined pay scales, and shared broad common ground in personnel policies on such issues as work hours, leave, transfer, retirement, etc. Because of the rigidities in the rules laid out by the central authority on the above issues, the role of local governments was mainly confined to enforcement.

Despite the increase of decision-making autonomy in the reform, most urban public enterprises (especially state enterprises) have had to follow many established rules of operation, such as the restrictions on cash use in transactions, the division of funds into mutually exclusive categories,[16]

---

[15] The Pearson correlation for the last two columns of the table is 0.87 (p < 0.01), indicating a persistence of the shares of state and nonstate firms in the various sectors being compared in the analysis.

[16] This practice was brought to an end in July 1993 when a new accounting system was adopted.

Table 3.1. *Changes in the number of firms in different industrial sectors*

Industrial sector	Number in 1985	Number in 1994	1994 # as % of 1985 #	% of state firms in 1986	% of state firms in 1994
Ordinary machinery	37,352	26,360	71	21	14
Furniture	10,597	8,171	77	4	6
Beverage	13,197	13,161	100	21	25
Logging	1,090	1,103	101	58	59
Garment	18,196	18,439	101	.	5
Power, steam, hot water	10,406	11,203	108	29	38
Food	39,202	43,130	110	29	34
Metal products	26,097	29,311	112	5	7
Nonmetal mineral products	48,291	56,762	118	12	13
Tobacco	313	382	122	78	78
Coal mining & processing	8,633	10,689	124	18	19
Textiles	18,846	24,774	132	17	17
Rubber products	3,184	4,242	133	16	14
Nonmetal mineral mining & processing	8,220	11,561	141	8	10
Printing	9,280	13,576	146	.	22
Timber	9,139	13,486	148	7	8
Paper making & paper products	8,296	12,282	149	.	8
Leather, furs, & down	6,580	9,773	149	.	8
Plastic products	10,798	16,826	156	5	7
Electric equipment & machinery	11,379	17,755	156	14	13
Stationary, educational, & sports	3,082	5,001	162	.	8
Instruments	3,091	5,165	167	.	20
Transportation equipment	9,300	16,411	177	23	20
Water supply	2,262	4,182	185	61	51
Raw chemicals	13,131	24,866	189	27	21
Electronics and telecommunications	3,522	6,877	195	.	22
Medical & pharmaceutical products	2,273	4,453	196	.	42
Nonferrous metal mining & processing	1,436	3,094	216	29	27
Ferrous metal mining & processing	936	2,035	217	16	13
Smelting & processing of nonferrous metals	1,326	3,609	272	22	17
Petroleum processing & coking products	790	2,176	275	22	16
Smelting & processing of ferrous metals	2,192	6,400	292	24	15

Industrial sector	Number in 1985	Number in 1994	1994 # as % of 1985 #	% of state firms in 1986	% of state firms in 1994
Petroleum & natural gas extraction	23	85	370	84	81
Other manufacturing	4,400	17,308	393	.	6
Chemical fiber	284	1,154	406	35	20
Gas production & supply	64	371	580	21	71
Other mineral mining & processing	16	109	681	.	21
Special equipment	470	18,828	4,006	.	23

Source: GYPCBGS (1987, volume 3: 10–24); GJTJJa (1995: 388, 392); GJTJJb (1987: 310, 314).

and the regulation of employment practices. In contrast, new forms of industrial organizations have had more room for maneuvering in these regards, partly because of the lack of precedents and consistent regulations and partly because of the latitude of local governments in making and interpreting new rules governing these enterprises. For example, they were initially not required to follow the *zhuankuan zhuanyong* procedure and thus could freely switch funds between different uses. In 1984 local governments were instructed to extend the restrictions on cash use to TVEs, and in 1988 the rule was further extended to private and foreign capital enterprises (Zhao Haikuan 1993). But it was up to local governments to work out the details and implement them (ZGGLKXY-CJS 1994). In labor-related matters, before the enactment of the *Labor Law* in 1994 there was a lack of uniformity in labor regulations for new forms of enterprises (Yuan Shouqi 1993). Again, it was up to local authorities to decide what rules to adopt and apply (Zhang Zuoji 1994).

Redistribution of Opportunities and Property Rights. In October 1994, the Beijing municipal government made a decision to terminate a 20-year lease held by the fast food chain McDonald's for a prime site on Beijing's Wangfujing Street and to make the site available for the Oriental Plaza, a potentially more lucrative commercial complex to be constructed by Hong Kong billionaire Li Ka-shing's Cheung Kong group (*South China Morning Post*, November 27, 1994; *Far Eastern Economic Review*, January 5, 1995). McDonald's fought back through legal channels to protect its right to the site, occupied by the then world's largest McDonald's restaurant. Information about the dispute was leaked to foreign reporters and the case was highly publicized. Partly because of the publicity and perhaps more important and luckily because of the downfall of Mayor Chen Xitong and a number of other top leaders of the Beijing municipal government in the wake of the Wang Baosen affair in early 1995,[17] the demolition of the restaurant was put on hold for three years, after which a settlement was reached. What this case signifies is an important fact of economic life in post-Mao China: Existing opportunities enjoyed by certain economic actors may be redistributed arbitrarily by state agents.

Before the reform, because the state exerted tight control over all major decisions on production and exchange and dictated the use of all the surplus, firms were left with little autonomy in the organization of their activities and the disposal of their output. Thus, there was not much in the rights of firms that could be taken away by redistributive state action. Although there were periodic waves of decentralization that resulted in a downgrading of the status of certain industrial firms from higher to lower administrative levels, this did not change the opportunity structure of the affected firms: No matter what status was assigned to a firm, it tended to face similar constraints on decision making.[18] Moreover, long and complex decision chains, limited individual authority, and entrenched departmental interests all made it difficult for local officials to unilaterally redraw the boundaries of resource and opportunity distribution.

A major change during the reform is that increasing numbers of firms have gained de jure or de facto revenue right and decision right over the resources that they own or use. In the meanwhile, decentralization in many aspects of resource allocation has increased and consolidated the authority of local governments, which have acted as representatives of the state to enter into and enforce contracts with economic organizations for the use of state-owned resources. Since there is more to be taken away and since there exist the means and incentives for local officials to act in this direction, redistributive state action has assumed greater relevance to the well-being of industrial enterprises. The driving force may come from the attraction of greater gains (e.g., tax revenue and fees) accruing to officials from an alternative arrangement of the resources or

---

[17] Wang Baosen was a vice-mayor of Beijing and a close associate of former mayor Chen Xitong. He was in charge of the planning of the city's real estate development projects and allegedly responsible for the decision on the McDonald's. In early April 1995, he committed suicide after learning about an investigation into his connections with several corruption cases. Further investigation after his death revealed extensive involvement by other top leaders of the city in corrupt dealings and brought down Mayor Chen in late April 1995. See *RMRB*, July 5, 6 1995; *QS*), June 1995, 21–3.

[18] Such downgrading, though, could reduce the entitlements (especially those in the form of employee fringe benefits) to the firms concerned and thus have a negative, albeit limited (especially when the downgrading did not go beyond the next lower level), effect on the resources available to them.

accesses that they control or can lay some claims on, as illustrated by the McDonald's case. It may also come from a high or increased time discount rate in the calculation by officials of their gains from such resources and accesses (Levi 1988). A realization that their individual or collective gains from an existing source are slipping away or a heightened need to increase short-term gains during the tenure of certain officials, for example, may drive pertinent officials to use their authority to redraw to their own advantage the boundaries of existing property right arrangements, as will be shown below.

Distribution of Liabilities

Formal Obligations. Taxes are the most important obligation of industrial firms to the state. The significance of this issue was rather limited before the reform in that the state defined – mainly through the centralized pricing mechanism – and extracted virtually all the surplus of enterprises by requiring them to hand over their profits to the state. The fiscal system featured a practice called *tongshou tongzhi* or "unified control over revenue and spending," which deprived enterprises of financial independence and subjected the collection and use of revenue by every level of state administration to the control and close monitoring by the authority of the next higher level. This centralized fiscal control has been weakened in the reform by two concurrent developments, namely, the substitution of taxes for total profit remission (known as *li gai shui*), and the adoption of various revenue-sharing arrangements between different levels of government.

The change from profit handover to payment of taxes was started in 1981 and completed in the mid-1980s. It substituted an enterprise income tax for the old arrangement under which state enterprises had to hand over all their profits to the government. Its main purpose was to provide an incentive for enterprises to improve productivity by allowing them to keep and make independent use of part of their profits. Likewise, weak incentive for local governments to increase revenue collection under centralized fiscal control was the main factor leading to the adoption of various fiscal contracts in place of the *tongshou tongzhi* system.[19] The contracts, formed through negotiations between different levels of government, gave local authorities a certain share in the tax revenue collected under their jurisdiction and granted them a certain degree of autonomy in the use of this revenue – especially the amounts exceeding the targets specified in the contracts.

---

[19] For detailed discussions on this issue, see Jia and Lin (1994), Shirk (1993), Wong (1997), and Wong et al. (1995).

Before 1994 when a uniform enterprise income tax rate (33%) was adopted and a value-added tax (17%) was imposed on all industrial and commercial enterprises, the official income tax rates varied among different types of enterprises. State enterprises faced higher rates (up to 55%) than other enterprises (no more than 35%). This undoubtedly posed a constraint on the former. However, the constraint was not cast in stone nor was the official rate necessarily the one at which a particular firm paid its income tax. According to an estimate by the State Tax Bureau (GWYYJSKTZ 1994: 17), in 1991 the actual average rates at which state enterprises were taxed was 33.39%, and those for urban collectives and private enterprises were 28% and around 29.7% respectively, all lower than the official rates.

How much tax a firm actually pays depends on the decision of the pertinent tax collection authority, which used to serve simply as a relay point for the transfer of funds of limited categories under the central planning system but now plays a much enhanced role under the reformed tax system.[20] Like those of local branches of state banks, the personnel and budgets of local tax authorities are not controlled by local governments. But their decisions are subject to the influence of local governments, which not only control and regulate the economic activities that constitute the revenue bases of the tax offices, but also oversee the provision of social services for tax office employees. As the authority of local governments in revenue generation and spending expands, cooperation between the local tax authority and local government in tax-related matters becomes a critical issue for mutual benefit. Under the revenue-sharing system, although local governments would have more budgetary funds to spend if they could generate more tax revenue, they still must share with higher authority the above-target portion of their revenue. Moreover, the spending of both the funds from the regular budget and the additional amounts of taxes resulting from above-target collection were subject to the review and close scrutiny of the fiscal authority. In contrast, there was greater latitude in the use of extra-budgetary funds from nontax sources (such as local fees, surcharges). Thus many local governments, especially local government agencies in charge of enterprises, tended to contain, with the consent from local tax authorities, the level of over-fulfillment of the fiscal contract so as to retain under their belt more resources which, when needed, could be activated and collected as fees for self-defined purposes. Although the new tax system adopted since 1994 may have contained the magnitude of this tendency

---

[20] During the Cultural Revolution, the only taxes that the tax bureau collected from industrial enterprises were a transaction tax called industrial and commercial tax and an income tax for urban collective enterprises (Xiang Huaicheng 1994).

with a reduction and clearer specification of the scope of shared tax revenue, its effect is mainly confined to the fiscal relations between central and provincial governments; the fiscal relations between jurisdictions below the provincial level have not been fundamentally changed (Wang 1997).

Granting tax breaks has also been facilitated by the existence of various preferential policies or grounds on which such policies can be invented and justified by local authorities. Foreign capital enterprises, for example, are generally given a two-year income tax holiday and two or three additional years of tax reduction (up to 50% of the official rate) (Liu Kegu and Wang Zheng 1995). Factories employing large numbers of handicapped persons and school-run factories are given tax exempt status. According to a handbook on tax reduction and exemption policies used by a district tax bureau in a northeastern provincial capital in 1993 (see Chapter 5 for more on this district), there were 26 broad categories under which various tax breaks could be offered to enterprises, with grounds of justification ranging from investing in new technology to providing jobs for unemployed urban youths. Also, the use of a tax agent system under which each tax agent is assigned to assess and collect the taxes of a given number of industrial enterprises leaves open ground for taxpayers to seek ad hoc favorable treatment from the responsible agents by offering them personal benefits.

Tanpai and Other Locally Imposed Fees. Tanpai, which means spreading burdens, refers to irregular levies and obligations arbitrarily imposed by state agencies on economic organizations. According to a study guide for implementing the *State-owned Enterprise Law* enacted in 1988 (Zhang Lingyuan and Zhu Weiping 1988: 122), the most common forms of *tanpai* include the following: (i) ad hoc charges for urban construction and maintenance, (ii) irregular charges imposed by cultural, educational, and health departments, (iii) extra levies for urban transport, public security, and environmental improvement, (iv) fund provision requests from neighborhood committees and other social service agencies of the government, and (v) demands from supervising bodies for various contributions from enterprises. Levies from such diverse sources are rarely coordinated among different state agencies at different levels. Nor is there much statutory or regulatory basis for the imposition of *tanpai*, which is largely sustained by an implicit threat of future retaliatory action against those who fail to accommodate the demands from state agencies (Zhang Delin 1993). In addition to *tanpai*, industrial firms also face various regular fees imposed by local authorities for the provision of government services. Provincial or central approval is required for creating such fees (*ZGCJB*, April 2, 1996), but who should pay and how much are often subject to interpretation by local officials, who have often contrived fees without proper authorization. Together with *tanpai*, they are a major source of off-budget funds for the agencies that levy them.

Before the reform, *tanpai* and other locally imposed fees were not a widely reported problem, perhaps largely because of the practice of total surplus extraction from enterprises, which left little to be taken away from them. Their magnitude was also contained by the weak financial incentive and limited fiscal power of local authorities under the *tongshou tongzhi* system. But there are signs that the categories and amount of arbitrarily imposed nontax levies have multiplied and become a widespread problem since the early 1980s,[21] when fiscal decentralization began and led to an increase in the power of local governments in revenue and spending. Starting from 1983 the central authority has issued circulars, directives, and stipulations each and every year to ban such arbitrary levies.[22] Despite such repeated efforts, the problem has persisted. According to one study (Fan Yongming 1992: 168), 53 types of levies were found to be arbitrarily imposed by various government agencies on firms with foreign investment in Fujian. An investigation conducted by the Finance Department of Liaoning province at 10 large and medium enterprises found that from 1985 to 1989 the total amount of *tanpai* imposed on these enterprises increased by 31 times (Luan Tao and Li Zhengzhi 1993: 4). Survey results reported in Table 1.3 indicate that many enterprises were unable to resist *tanpai*. According to a survey of private enterprises (n = 29,208) jointly conducted by the State Economic Reform Commission and the State Industrial and Commercial Administration in 1993, on average the respondents handed over 4–5% of their net profit to various government authorities as *tanpai* (GJTGW & GJGSJ 1993: 315).

Implications for Industrial Firms

With the locus of state authority shifting toward lower level governments and various agencies, the centralized differentiation of status along the lines of administrative level, ownership, sector, and size no longer provides a reliable indication of the allocative and regulatory treatment received by different firms. However, increasingly localized state action has continued to treat firms unevenly in the allocation of resources, opportunities, and liabilities. As a result, those that can obtain favorable treatment and contain or minimize unfavorable treatment from local state agents tend to have an edge in increasingly competitive economic

---

[21] See Chapter 7 for more discussion on this.
[22] For a sample of these documents, see SJSFGS (1995).

activities. To illustrate this development, I now turn to the experiences of a number of the enterprises where I did case studies, most of which have already been introduced in Chapter 2.

Particularism in Resource Allocation

When industrial firms entered the reform era, their starting points were not equal. At Northern Machinery, when state banks took on the role of regulating the use of working capital in 1983, about 75% of its recurrent working capital (30 million yuan) was in the form of fiscal appropriation. The factory leaders intensely lobbied their supervising body, the Department of Machinery Industry of the municipal government, not to turn the capital into interest-bearing loans. With the help of several senior leaders in the Department who had worked in the factory in the 1950s and 1960s (and some of whose children were employees of the factory), the effort succeeded. This saved the factory an enormous cost for the use of capital. Although the subsequent expansion of the factory led to a steady increase of borrowing from banks to cover its need for working capital (loans accounted for 50% of its working capital in 1989 and 80% in 1994), the inheritance from the central planning era provided the factory with a strong initial condition under which to compete with enterprises that did not have this advantage.

Southwestern Machinery Factory (Southwestern Machinery hereinafter),[23] one of Northern Machinery's competitors, was less fortunate in this regard. In 1983, fiscal appropriation accounted for only 35% of its recurrent working capital (in part because of its lower status under the central planning system). This was further reduced to 10% in the following year when the local financial authority was instructed by the provincial government to transfer a large part of the fiscally appropriated working capital to the local branch of the newly formed Industrial and Commercial Bank as seed funds. Polyester Fiber had a similar and even more unfavorable experience. Between 1983 and 1984 the share of fiscal appropriation in its working capital was reduced from a little over 20% to nearly zero.

For newly formed enterprises, inheriting a certain amount of cost-free capital was out of the question. But there are other sources of advantage. Obtaining a bank loan on favorable terms may make a big difference to a firm's competitiveness and personal ties can be valuable here. When Flying Horse Motors decided to start motorcycle production in the mid-

---

[23] A medium-sized state enterprise established in 1959, Southwestern Machinery operated under the government of the capital city of a southwestern province. In 1978, it had a work force of 1,950, less than one-third of Northern Machinery's.

1980s, it resorted to the local branch of the Agricultural Bank for a 400,000 yuan loan to purchase the necessary facilities. The request was turned down on the grounds that the new venture was too risky. With the help of the village Party secretary, Director Kang discovered that a resident in Lakeside (village) was the mother-in-law of a deputy division chief at the Construction Bank's branch in a nearby city, which then did not have lending activities in the rural sector but maintained a mutual borrowing relationship with the Agricultural Bank branch that turned down Kang's request. They contacted the old woman and through her enlisted the help of her son-in-law. In the end, Flying Horse Motors not only obtained a 650,000 yuan loan from the Agricultural Bank, but also got it at a preferential interest rate, which was offered in the name of "supporting technological innovation of TVEs." Among the benefits which later accrued to those who offered help were sales of Flying Horse motorcycles at a substantial discount and assignment of top priority to the old woman in the distribution of village welfare benefits (for example, she was among the first to be accommodated with village-built housing in 1994).

The situation at Peak Equipment was similar. In the initial years of its operation, Peak Equipment made extensive use of low-interest loans from the local Agricultural Bank branch. The daughter of the branch director, a middle school Chinese teacher, was hired by the factory as a part-time employee in its office for propaganda affairs. In 1988, her monthly "allowance" from the factory was four times as high as her monthly salary from the school. In 1989, she left for a job at a foreign trade company in the provincial capital. After her departure, the ties between the factory and the bank branch began to weaken, posing a major resource constraint (which was later alleviated through the formation of a joint venture with a Hong Kong investor). Rainbow Pipe was first formed in a neighboring township where Director Zhu could not obtain support from the township government for his request for a loan guarantee, which was required by the local Rural Credit Cooperative. After moving to his native Lotus Pond township where family ties were thick and deep-rooted, he not only obtained such support but also borrowed directly from a cooperative fund run by the township government (see Chapter 5 for more details about the fund) at interest rates lower than those offered by state banks.

Northern Machinery not only had the blessing of a huge inheritance from the fiscal authority, but was able to obtain special funds allocated by other city authorities. In 1985, it was granted a low-interest loan of 580,000 yuan by the Economic Commission of the city for technological upgrading. In the late 1980s, it obtained two medium-term loans (US\$ 760,000 and US\$ 1.1 million) at preferential interest rates from the Ministry of Machine-building and the Construction Bank to finance the importation of equipment from Japan and West Germany. For its regular loans from the Industrial and Commercial Bank, it managed to keep the interest charge at the official rate without the additional 20% markup usually charged by state banks.[24]

Not all the efforts made by firm leaders to obtain capital from the state and contain its costs are equally successful. Throughout the 1980s and early 1990s, for example, Southwestern Machinery (whose performance lagged behind that of Northern Machinery) had to borrow virtually all its working capital from state banks at regular interest rates plus the usual 20% or more markups. The same situation was faced by Polyester Fiber. From 1989 to 1990, it undertook a major technological upgrading project (described in the preceding chapter), but failed to obtain sufficient working capital at an affordable rate to sustain the expanded operation. The final blow came in the summer of 1993, when the austerity measures taken by the central authority led to a serious tightening of credit and closed off the remaining cash flow avenue for the factory.

In land use, particularistic actions of the local state have a direct bearing on the operating costs of industrial firms. When Modern Housewares was formed in 1983, the Golden Field township government provided a piece of land as its contribution to the joint venture. Because the township government was a partner in the joint venture, it did not require the enterprise to pay any land use fees or taxes. When Modern Housewares needed additional storage space for its output in 1989, the township government vacated an adjacent basketball court of a primary school and allocated the space to the enterprise free of charge. The nearby village was asked by the township government to donate a piece of reserve land (which was not contracted out to individual peasant households) to the school for a new sports ground.

At Red Star Heating, the land used for its initial operation came from the township government. In 1991, the township government moved out of its old office compound to a newly completed office building. The vacated space was subsequently granted to the newly formed Red Star Heating as a plant site, free of charge. That helped Red Star Heating to gain a foothold in competition when it switched from cotton weaving to the production of water heaters. But as the scale of its operation expanded, the factory needed additional space to assemble water heaters. This time, the township government did not have another piece of land

---

[24] Several factors might have contributed to its clout. Its star enterprise status gave it a high profile in the eyes of city leaders. Some of its former directors held important positions in the Department of Machinery Industry, the Economic Commission of the city, and the Ministry of Machine-building. From 1991 to 1994, the director of the factory was even appointed a deputy director of its own supervising agency, the Department of Machinery Industry.

to spare. The factory had to purchase from a nearby village the use right for 25 *mu* of farmland at the price of 10,000 yuan per *mu* (the township government did help, by offering to reduce the village's grain procurement quota slightly, to persuade the village to lower its initial asking price – 12,500 yuan per *mu*).[25]

With the increase of government levies on land use in the reform era, moreover, enterprises occupying a large space need to find ways to minimize such costs in order to be competitive. Northern Machinery had a large piece of land (400,000 square meters), which lies within the boundary of the city proper. After the introduction of the urban land use tax in 1988, it managed to pay the lowest possible amount required by the tax code. According to the tax code, the scale points for tax per square meter of land used by industrial facilities in large cities range from 0.5 to 10 yuan, whereas the range for counties, urban townships, and industrial and mining areas is between 0.2 and 4 yuan. It is up to local authorities to decide which scale point applies to which enterprise on the basis of an assessment of land value and quality. The amount that Northern Machinery paid was 0.3 yuan per square meter – on the grounds that the factory could be categorized as located in a "mining and industrial area" when it was formed back in 1949, and only about 60% of its land was taxed. Southwestern Machinery also sought to minimize this levy despite its location within the provincial capital. It obtained a one-year exemption for 1989 on the grounds of financial difficulties and afterward paid 0.7 yuan per square meter for about 90% of the land occupied by the factory. These terms were favorable, though not as favorable as those obtained by Northern Machinery.

In the supply of material inputs, an important factor affecting the competitiveness of firms in the early years of reform was the price disparity between state-allocated materials and those sold by capital goods producers outside the allocation channels of the plan. From the early 1980s, the share of planned output at Northern Machinery steadily declined, largely because of the adoption of the contract responsibility system that allowed the firm to produce beyond the plan and keep the surplus above the fixed output target. But the decline was faster than the decrease of inputs supplied at state-set (low) prices, which factory leaders sought to maintain with the help of allocating authorities. In 1985, for example, when the output under the mandatory state plan accounted for 65% of its total output, the factory managed to have about 80% of its need for steel – the main material input used by the factory – accommodated with quota supplies. Not until the early 1990s did the extra-plan production of the factory rely almost entirely on inputs obtained at market prices.

---

[25] 1 *mu* = 1/15 hectare.

At Southwestern Machinery, however, this parity took place several years earlier. In fact, in the mid-1980s an under-supply of quota supplies even forced the factory to use inputs at market prices for output under the mandatory state plan. This, of course, increased the cost of its output.

At Modern Housewares, the main input used by the joint venture was aluminum, which was a centrally controlled material input until the early 1990s. Not eligible for state quotas, the firm imported – duty free – all the input it needed for production. But very soon, Director Cheung discovered that there was enormous demand for aluminum in Guangdong's booming construction sector and a profit could be made from arbitrage. By importing more than it needed (with the tacit consent of the township government) and selling the surplus at prices higher than the state-set price, Modern Housewares ran a lucrative sideline business. Competition intensified in the late 1980s when domestic suppliers, especially small ones, managed to increase sales of extra-plan output at market prices. In the face of diminishing returns, Cheung moved upstream and started to manufacture aluminum window frames.

At Rainbow Pipe a major input was coke, the fuel that it needed in large quantities for use in casting. Until the decontrol over the price and distribution of this industrial material in the mid-1990s, the performance of the factory was directly correlated with its ability to obtain coke at prices lower than those in the extra-plan output markets. The main sources of this special supply were government agencies that oversaw the production or distribution of coke, where Director Zhu had developed close personal contacts. With the help of such contacts, plan-allocated coke was channeled from designated users to the factory, at below-market prices. But there was no guarantee that such favors could always be secured. Uncertainty in this regard, according to Director Zhu, accounted for a large part of the periodic fluctuations in the cost and profit of the factory.

Selective Enforcement of Regulations

For enterprises formed in the reform, entry was the first regulatory issue that they had to deal with. When Flying Horse Motors decided to switch its production from barges to motorcycles in the mid-1980s, it faced formidable licensing requirements. Manufacturing motorcycles required the approval by provincial-level authorities, and a series of safety, environmental protection, energy conservation, and other technical tests were needed before a license could be issued. Director Kang worked very hard, largely through personal contacts, to gain support from the township government, which in turn exerted influence on the local *gong-shang* branch. With the help of the latter (in the name of supporting

TVEs), it eventually obtained the necessary approvals from various city and provincial authorities. All the test requirements were waived – on the grounds that the prototype that it made was modeled on the motorcycle produced by its former partner, the state-owned enterprise in Southwest China, which had already passed all the tests. As a token of appreciation, Flying Horse Motors later sold motorcycles with a huge discount to those who helped in the registration process. At Peak Equipment, with the aid of some officials in the local government Director Ma first acquired, without the necessary technical proof for production capacity and product reliability, a license for the manufacturing of the water supply system. After that he started to develop the product, which did not pass technical tests until six months later. When Everbright Heating was set up by its parent organization, there was no evidence that it had the capacity to manufacture water heating devices. Accommodating unemployed urban youths was the only justification for approval. But Director Wang and his supervisor worked through their personal networks in the district government to turn their plan into reality.

Since the costs and benefits for firms seeking access to new or additional economic opportunities are associated not only with the height of entry barriers but also with the organizational forms in which economic activities are carried out, whether an enterprise can influence the licensing agency's decisions in the most favorable direction may matter a great deal to its competitiveness.

In 1991, for example, Everbright Heating was re-registered as a joint venture, mainly for the purpose of getting a tax holiday. To maximize the benefits, Wang used a fake address for Everbright Heating's head office, which was actually located in the Eastern District of the city. The address at which the joint venture was registered was a high school (where his former classmate was the principal) located in a high-tech development zone in the Western District, where high-tech joint ventures could get a three-year tax exemption and three-year tax reduction by 50% instead of the usual two-year tax free and three-year half tax arrangement for joint ventures. The foreign partner of the joint venture was a Southeast Asian company in which a subsidiary of one of China's largest trust investment companies owned the majority share. The daughter of Wang's former supervisor was an employee of the subsidiary company and helped make the arrangement. According to the agreement, the foreign company would inject US$ 56,000 into Everbright Heating in each of the first three years and Everbright Heating would export 25%, 50%, and 75% of its output respectively during those three years. The money was deposited into Everbright Heating's bank account so it could get the registration, though not a single penny was used and in fact the whole sum was later returned through covert channels. During the first three years, Everbright Heating operated as before and sold all its products in China. None of these arrangements could have been possible without laxity in enforcement by the local *gongshang* branch which, according to Wang, had a "very good relationship" with Everbright Heating.

In addition to *gongshang*, the supervising agencies of state and collective enterprises could also exert enormous influence on the efforts of firms to change their organizational forms or their boundaries. In 1989, Northern Machinery imported a new production line from West Germany. That required a large-scale expansion of the capacity of its casting workshops, which was not allowed by the fire regulations of the city. To address the need, the factory took over a casting factory of 1,300 employees under the jurisdiction of the Ministry of Geological Exploration and Mineral Resources. The process of integration could have been a protracted one because it involved the merger between an enterprise controlled by a centrally administered city and an enterprise controlled by a central government ministry but located in a county outside of the city. To make sure that the new production line be operational as quickly as possible, the Department of Machinery set up a task force to help streamline the complicated paperwork among the three jurisdictions. It took only three weeks for the deal to go through.

Polyester Fiber was not so fortunate in obtaining ad hoc support for a merger proposal from its supervising agency. In 1992 when the factory was already in the red, it was asked to become a member of one of China's largest petrochemical companies. Under the proposal, the petrochemical company would guarantee the supply of polyester chips at ex-factory prices while integrating Polyester Fiber's production into its own operations. Fearing a gradual loss of its control and revenue rights over Polyester Fiber, the Textile Industry Department vetoed the proposal. A year later, the financial crisis of the factory deepened. With the permission of its supervising agency, it approached the petrochemical company for a re-opening of the earlier offer, only to be rejected.

Another area where regulatory unevenness may affect the competitiveness of firms involves the various restrictions on fund use, discussed in the preceding section. To nonstate firms like Flying Horse Motors, Red Star Heating, Peak Equipment, and Rainbow Pipe, the regulation on "special funds for special purposes" (*zhuankuan zhuanyong*) was a nonissue. Also, despite the extension of the regulation on cash use to newly formed enterprises in the mid- and late 1980s, it had little binding power on these firms – largely because of the lack of action on the part of local authorities. *Da baitiao* or "reimbursement without receipts" was a common practice used by the top decision makers. This gave them great flexibility in fund deployment and in dealing with business partners and officials. In contrast, *da baitiao* was out of the question for traditional forms of public enterprises like Northern Machinery and Polyester Fiber, where established regulations on financial discipline remained intact. But in 1987, Northern Machinery was able to obtain, in the name of a reform experiment, a special waiver on the rule of *zhuankuan zhuanyong*. Southwestern Machinery had to wait until 1993 to have that rule removed under the new accounting regulation. This one step ahead taken by Northern Machinery gave it greater flexibility in fund use and therefore a slight edge over those behind it (Informants no. 89/1989, no. 137/1992).

Sometimes uneven treatment of firms in regulation may simply result from arbitrary interpretations of loosely defined rules by enforcement agents. At the end of 1990, Polyester Fiber was fined by the county environmental protection office for failing to pass a pollution inspection on two of its large chimneys. The fine was determined to be 23,000 yuan, a figure that just matched the remaining gap in the office's "fine quota" for the year. A county-owned food processing plant next door was inspected at the same time, and found to have similar problems in its chimneys (plus under-treated sewage water). But instead of being ordered to pay a fine, the food processor was given a written warning on the grounds that the plant was "newly formed" (in 1986) and should be given some time to adjust its facilities fully. The director of Polyester Fiber attributed such uneven treatment to the fact that Polyester Fiber was not under the jurisdiction of the county and its supervising agency had little sway over the local government.

To Everbright Heating, selective enforcement was not only helpful, but vital. The factory was built in the compound of the warehouse of the local industrial bureau. Its manufacturing involved a high-temperature operation – processing vacuum glass tubes – only 15 meters away from a row of storage towers for cotton, wool, and chemical fiber. Fire regulations strictly banned such an operation within close proximity of the storage of inflammable materials. It so happened that Director Wang's father-in-law was the head of the inspection division of the local Fire Department. Instead of ordering that the operation be closed down after the problem was discovered by a fire inspector, he asked Wang to chop off the trees between the main workshop and the storage towers, build a wall, and locate the high-temperature processing facilities toward the side of the workshop that did not face the storage towers. Wang followed the advice and kept the factory from being ordered to relocate or closed down.

High-temperature operation was also a major feature of the manufacturing process at Rainbow Pipe, where the harsh working conditions were further worsened by heavy dust in its closed-window, low-ceiling casting shops. The majority of the workers were peasants from nearby villages, plus some migrant laborers who were assigned to perform the most dangerous and dirtiest tasks. Summer was the peak season for production when workers often had to work for 10–13 hours a day. This was partly to make up the hours lost during a harvest season leave (about two weeks) given to most workers in June and partly because a large number of orders were normally due by early fall so that users of Rainbow Pipe's output (mostly producers of radiators) could turn out their products before the start of winter. Director Zhu installed no ventilation device and safety measures were limited to gloves and goggles. There was no health or safety insurance. All these practices were inconsistent with labor regulations. Despite the fact that in 1994 the township government became a partial partner of the factory, it left all labor-related decisions to Zhu.

But the ad hoc helping hand from local officials may not always stay that way. It may be withdrawn and even turned into an adverse force that wipes out the economic opportunities of a firm. After forming the joint venture in Golden Field, for example, Mr. Cheung of Modern Housewares set up another operation, a factory making beer cans, in the capital city of a southern province in 1987. It was a joint venture with an urban collective enterprise under the jurisdiction of the city's Second Light Industry Department. The factory was situated in the downtown area of the city. In 1988, the street where the factory was located was under redevelopment by a real estate company under the district Construction Commission. The land occupied by the factory was where a large shopping center was to be built, which was also one of the "10 Major Projects" that the Commission promised to complete for the celebration of the 40th anniversary of the PRC in 1989.[26] The district government imposed a drastically increased land use fee to force out the joint venture. In view of the fact that after paying the fee there would be little profit, Cheung decided to pull out in 1989. According to his estimate, the three-year operation in that city yielded a net loss of half a million yuan.

After Peak Equipment was set up in 1984, it out-sourced molds from a molding workshop of a machine tool factory – a collective enterprise – located in the New Town District of the city (Peak Equipment was located in the Southern District). In 1987, the central building of the machine tool factory burned down, though the molding workshop was

---

[26] The head of the Commission was subsequently promoted to a higher position in the city government because of good performance during his tenure in the district. His brother-in-law was the head of the real estate development company.

left intact. After the fire, the Industry Department of the District – the supervising authority of the factory – decided not to continue the production of machine tools. But it kept and reregistered as a separate enterprise the molding workshop which, aside from processing work for the factory, had also taken in orders from enterprises like Peak Equipment. Director Ma offered to become a partner of the new enterprise by compensating the Industry Department for the net fixed asset value (excluding land) of the factory and upgrading its facilities, which cumulatively cost him 1.4 million yuan in the following three years. In return, he shared 60% of the profit earned by the enterprise.

In 1991, Peak Equipment was turned into a joint venture with a Hong Kong manufacturer. Ma decided to consolidate the molding factory with Peak Equipment's expanded operations by moving it out of the New Town District. Although he promised to continue the 60–40% profit-sharing agreement with the Industry Department, the latter would not allow the move. It was concerned about the loss of management fees and other ad hoc charges it imposed on the factory, the relocation of the factory's tax payment to the Southern District, and a dwindling of shared profits due to possible transfer of real profit by Peak Equipment to its main profit center. In reaction to Ma's proposal, the Department first did a unilateral re-evaluation of factory assets by discounting existing equipment and facilities at a high depreciation rate and including and grading at above-market value the land that the factory occupied, which made the Department the majority owner of factory assets. Then it replaced the factory director appointed by Ma with its own appointee. Finally it demanded that Ma give up his share in the factory through compensation in kind: Ma's heavily discounted share of assets would be paid back with molds to be made and priced by the molding factory for Peak Equipment within five years. Seeing little chance of winning the battle, Ma withdrew from the molding factory.

Uneven Burdens

In the reform era, all industrial enterprises in China have been subject to government taxes. At Flying Horse Motors, Red Star Heating, Peak Equipment, and Rainbow Pipe actual tax rates varied from year to year, subject to negotiations between the enterprise and the township government, though they never paid their taxes at the official rates (for rural collectives and private enterprises). In fact, all of them had accumulated large sums of "owed" taxes – taxes that were not collected by the tax authority because the overall revenue targets of the local government had been over-fulfilled or fulfilled with taxes fully paid by other taxpayers. Although the resultant funds were subject to "recall" – often in the form of accommodating ad hoc spending needs of local governments (ranging from payment of banquet bills to purchase of office supplies) – the remaining balances were used by the enterprises to facilitate their own cash flows, thus in fact functioning as interest-free loans.

During the first three years of operation, Modern Housewares was granted tax exempt status. The additional year above the normal two-year exemption (for joint ventures) was added in the name of "supporting the development of TVEs" and "providing job opportunities to unemployed urban youths." In the ensuing three years, it paid income taxes at half the official rate for enterprises with foreign investment. The amount it paid was minimal, because much of the real profit from the sales of its products was used to import aluminum and thus counted as a "cost." A large part of the aluminum was then sold by its sideline profit center, which was registered as a joint venture (a trading company) in 1986 and had another three-year tax holiday. Since the township government was also a partner in that operation, and since the township government was able to fulfill its revenue target with taxes from other sources, it gave the green light to the arrangement.

At Everbright Heating, its three-year tax holiday (described above) was also extended. After reregistering the enterprise as a joint venture in the high-tech development zone in November 1991, Director Wang discovered that the whole year of 1991 would be counted as the first year of its three-year tax holiday. To benefit fully from the exemption that he worked so hard to obtain, he sought help from the tax agent in charge of Everbright Heating. The problem was "studied" and a compromise solution was found: Everbright Heating continued to pay tax as if it were still an urban collective until the end of 1991 and the tax holiday started from January 1, 1992.

Special treatment in tax-related matters, however, is rarely extended to every enterprise under the jurisdiction of a local government. Efforts have to be made to obtain it. When Northern Machinery first adopted the contract responsibility system in 1984, it was treated like other enterprises under the city's Department of Machinery Industry. An annual target was set for its gross profit, which was taxed according to the official rate. Any above-target profit was divided between the factory and the government according to a 60–40 formula. Three years later, however, it won a much more favorable arrangement, modeled on a special package granted by the central authority to the Capital Steel and Iron Co. (a star enterprise headed by a former head of the Metallurgical Industry Ministry), which required the factory to achieve a 5% annual growth rate for its output and gross profit (taxed according to the official rate) for five consecutive years while allowing it to keep all the above-target surplus. Northern Machinery was the only enterprise among all the enterprises under the Department of Machinery Industry, and the first in the milling machine sector, to get such an arrangement, wrapped (again) in the cover of "reform experiment." The deal that Southwestern Machinery worked very hard to obtain around the same time was good (also the first among local machinery industry enterprises) but not so favorable. It was allowed to keep 75% of the above-target profit, of which at least half had to be used as a reinvestment fund.

Another major burden on industrial firms is *tanpai*. As major providers of revenues (especially nontax revenues) for their local governments, Flying Horse Motors and Rainbow Pipe both maintained very close relationships with top local officials and did not encounter any *tanpai* from local government agencies. But Peak Equipment's clout was less far-reaching. It faced frequent ad hoc requests from various agencies, especially those at the district and city level. When asked to particularize such levies incurred in 1993, the accountant listed the factory's contributions as the following: road construction (three times), arts festival of the city, summer camps of local schools, expansion of the local power station, construction of new staff quarters of the local public security office, payment for miscellaneous items consumed or purchased by various government agencies (24 items in total, including meals and transportation expenses), tree planting in local parks, printing of new household registration cards for the local public security office, opening and closing ceremonies of government-sponsored conferences, renovation of the city stadium and procuratorate building, employment of two handicapped persons for the local Department of Civil Administration, whitewashing of the slogans painted (during the Cultural Revolution) on walls and buildings in nearby streets, and prize money for a provincial sporting event held in the city. The total amount incurred was 128,597 yuan, whereas the gross profit of the enterprise in that year was 478,000 yuan.

Although extracting contributions directly from enterprises is the most common form of *tanpai*, sometimes it may take the form of shedding responsibility by state agencies for their own mismanagement or miscalculation. After setting up the joint venture in 1991, for example, Director Wang planned to use the tax holiday to expand the operation of Everbright Heating to achieve economy of scale and improve its competitiveness. His proposal for expansion and space was approved by the local industrial bureau. But there was a string attached: He had to take in 280 workers from an enterprise with heavy losses under the bureau. After a careful cost-benefit analysis, Wang concluded that the gain from such an expansion would be outweighed by the cost, and consequently he withdrew the proposal. The failure to expand confined Everbright Heating to small batch production. As its competitors expanded their operations, its initial competitive edge became increasingly narrow, and its performance steadily declined.

During the seventh five-year plan period (1986–90), the Chemical Fiber Bureau of the former Ministry of Textiles, in an effort to raise its own profile in the Ministry and that of the Ministry within the central government, pushed through a proposal to expand the existing production capacity of short polyester fiber by 7,500 tons. Under the proposal, nine polyester producers would be allowed to borrow from state banks to import new production lines and the Ministry of Textiles would provide matching funds to finance the purchase of auxiliary facilities and material inputs for the expanded production capacity. Polyester Fiber was one of the nine enterprises chosen for the project. Like several other enterprises in the group, it questioned the feasibility of the proposal. But the Bureau insisted on its implementation. Polyester Fiber followed instructions and borrowed 14 million from the Industrial and Commercial Bank to import new production lines from Italy. But the promise by the Bureau to provide matching funds fell through. The main reason was the withdrawal of support by the Ministry of Finance in 1990 when the Ministry of Textiles failed to sustain a traditional division of labor that prevented large petrochemical enterprises under the Ministry of Petroleum from entering its traditional turf of chemical fiber production (the Ministry of Textiles was itself dissolved in 1993). To Polyester Fiber, the new production lines imposed on it became a nightmare. It had to find ways to pay back the bank loan while facing strong competition from newly entering petrochemical enterprises. After its supervising agency turned down the merger proposal from the petrochemical company in East China in 1992 (described above), the last chance of survival was gone.

Summary

If the experiences of the enterprises portrayed above have a common story to tell, it is that how they responded to the reform process and how well they performed cannot be adequately explained within a narrow view of market and economic efficiency. Although all of them were situated in increasingly competitive environments and sought to enhance their competitiveness through innovation and efficient use of resources, competition went beyond interactions between economic actors. Vital to their survival and growth was the relationship with the state agencies and agents that they encountered under a decentralizing authority structure of the state.

First, localized state authorities still directly control large amounts of resources and can vary, according to their own preferences, the terms of allocation to different parties in an ad hoc fashion. Second, localized state authorities command enormous regulatory power that can redistribute economic opportunities by selectively facilitating or restricting the activities carried out by different economic actors. Ad hoc relaxation or tightening of registration and licensing requirements, accounting procedures, regulations on land use and labor practice, for example, may greatly reduce or increase the operating costs of affected firms and alter the balance of relative payoffs to firms. Third, localized state authorities can selectively distribute liabilities to certain firms, especially those that are less favored by local state agents, thereby weakening or even hamstringing the ability of the affected parties to excel in economic activities.

Under the shadow of particularistic state action, both the expansion of markets and the distribution of competitive advantages and disadvantages among firms hinge greatly on ad hoc decisions and actions of various loci of state authority. The preceding section illustrates two types of ad hoc favorable and unfavorable state actions that firms need to deal with: those that were carried over or modified from the central planning system, and those that have been created, sustained, or enhanced in the reform. Some institutional arrangements, such as formal restrictions on decision making and centrally allocated low-cost resources (capital, land, and industrial materials), have declined in magnitude during the reform. But the decline has been a slow and gradual process in which enterprises that could overcome traditional constraints earlier and secure and/or maintain low-priced resources for longer periods of time tended to have a competitive edge over their peers. Newly developed sources of advantages and disadvantages, such as resources at the disposal of specific local authorities and agencies, localized gatekeeping and rule-making authorities, and intensified predatory state action, tend to be more tenacious and can hardly be ignored by competing firms.[27] It therefore can be hypothesized that, *ceteris paribus*, the more effective a firm's manipulation of state action in these regards, the stronger its ability to

---

[27] Since new enterprises were not bound by many pre-existing rules, they had greater freedom in decision making than old enterprises. Although expanding and competing in the formative economic space outside the plan have by no means been a hurdle-free undertaking, this disparity in initial constraints may have been a contributing factor for their more active participation in market-oriented economic activities and relatively higher rate of return, particularly in the first decade of reform. On the other hand, old enterprises, especially those in the state sector, have also made efforts to adapt to the changes in their environments. Some of them, such as Northern Machinery, have even managed to turn their traditional privileges (e.g., cost-free capital) into resources for market-oriented activities while gaining new ad hoc favorable treatment (e.g., favorable terms for managerial contract). These responses may have contained, to a certain extent, the overall performance gap between state and nonstate enterprises. See Chapter 7 for more discussion on this issue.

participate in and benefit from market-oriented economic activities, and vice versa.[28]

Although it cannot be ascertained from the limited case materials how intensely industrial firms were affected by particularistic state action, they do suggest that such influence was not trivial, which is consistent with what is indicated by the survey findings cited at the beginning. They also indicate that the ad hoc rule bending by state agents was driven by their calculation of self-interest, which could be tied to the mutual benefits cultivated by favor seekers. In the next chapter, I will further illustrate these with an account of another type of particularistic state action that affects the behavior and performance of firms, namely, direct pursuit of profits by state agents themselves.

[28] This hypothesis implies that effective manipulation of state action is a necessary condition for firms to excel. But it does not downplay the importance of productive use of resources in economic activities, which may well constitute a sufficient condition for the success of firms in the new economic game.

4

Referee as Player: Menaces and Opportunities for Industrial Firms

Differential treatment of firms is only a partial feature of state action in the new economic game. An important development in the reform is that increasing numbers of state agents have directly engaged in profit-seeking activities. In other words, the referees have not only bent the rules according to their own preferences but have also become active players themselves. The intensification of this entrepreneurial pursuit in the reform has led to a reprioritization of the allocative and regulatory decisions of state agents, which has had an important impact on the ability of industrial firms to compete and on economic institutional change.

In this chapter, I examine how industrial firms' profit-seeking activities have been affected by those of state agents. My focus centers on the interaction between regular industrial firms and front organizations used by state agents in pursuit of profits. The latter have been set up, run, or facilitated by state agencies outside the scope of their regular administrative functions and budgets since the mid-1980s. Mostly registered as independent public enterprises in the tertiary sector, such economic entities are managed by former or incumbent officials or the persons they trust. They receive funding and favorable regulatory treatment from, or with the help of, their government sponsors, and contribute a significant part of their revenue to the slush funds of the latter. In view of their close ties with the private interests of the individuals in their sponsoring state agencies, I call these economic entities the backyard profit centers of state agencies.

I first highlight the main features of backyard profit centers. Then I explore how the behavior and performance of industrial firms have been affected by their interactions with these economic entities in three aspects: competition, transaction, and collusion. It seems clear from this account that the industrial firms that are able to minimize the menaces and capture the opportunities in such interactions have an edge over those extensively exposed to the downside. The findings add further evidence to the argument that the forces that shape the economic space outside the plan cannot be adequately defined within the ideal-typical notion of "the market." They also indicate that the decline of the plan is due not only to the push-and-pull effects from interactions among different economic actors (Chapter 2), but to the corrosive effects of state agents' self-seeking behavior.

Main Features of Backyard Profit Centers[1]

In Chinese literature, the profit-seeking entities sponsored by state agencies are referred to as (*jingji*) *shiti* (economic subsidiaries), *gongsi* (companies), or *sanchan* (tertiary sector undertakings) under the auspices of state agencies.[2] Most such organizations undertake activities in the tertiary sector (*ZGGSB*, September 11, 1989), and the majority of them are registered as independent, for-profit public enterprises.[3] But there are important differences between these and other public enterprises.[4]

First, they are not part of the vertically integrated command chains of the government and have enormous autonomy and flexibility in decision making. Unlike conventional public enterprises placed under the jurisdiction of various functional departments in charge of economic affairs (such as bureaus of textiles, machine building, chemicals, and commerce), these entities can be affiliated with any state agencies, including those not in charge of economic affairs, such as the Public Security Office, the local Communist Party Committee, and the Bureau of Cultural Affairs. The activities that they carry out often fall outside

---

[1] This section is based on Lin and Zhang (1999).

[2] State agencies in China fall into two categories: *jiguan danwei* and *shiye danwei* (Song Defu 1994, vol. 2: 430–3). The former consists of Party organizations and functional departments of the government, whereas the latter includes nonprofit units that have no administrative, allocative, or regulatory authority beyond their own organizational boundaries, such as newspapers, research institutes, and hospitals. In this chapter, I focus on the profit-seeking entities sponsored by *jiguan danwei*. For a discussion of the profit-seeking entities sponsored by organizationally independent *shiye danwei*, see Francis (1999).

[3] Of the 27,000 such organizations investigated by the State Industrial and Commercial Administration in 1984–5, for example, 23% were classified as "state-owned," 67% "collective," and 10% "jointly owned by the state and collectives" (Fei Kailong and Zuo Ping 1991: 64). This "public" image remained unchanged five years later. According to a 1989 report presented by the director of the agency to the Standing Committee of the National People's Congress (*ZGGSB* September 11, 1989), of the 23,913 such entities investigated by the central authority in 1988–9, 43% were registered as "state-owned" enterprises and 53% as "collective enterprises."

[4] A more detailed account of the origins and growth of backyard profit centers is offered in Lin and Zhang (1999).

the regular administrative and regulatory functions of their sponsoring agencies.[5]

Second, most of these economic entities are affiliated with state agencies at administrative levels higher than the township. Township-owned economic organizations are normally placed under the control of a unified economic authority which assumes different names in different localities (such as township economic development corporation, township economic cooperative, township enterprise corporation, to name a few) and are subject to close monitoring by the heads of the local government. The taxes on their proceeds constitute a major revenue obligation of township governments to higher level authorities. In contrast, although the revenue of the backyard profit centers is subject to taxation, their sponsoring agencies are not obligated to achieve any tax target based on such revenue. On the other hand, these entities are not eligible for the allocation of budgetary funds and other economic resources (such as policy loans and industrial materials at state-controlled prices) earmarked for enterprises under the state budget, nor are they subject to close monitoring by the fiscal authority of the government. They receive allocative and regulatory favors from their sponsoring agencies, to which in return they contribute part of their gains. Since their entire operation lies outside the scope of the budgetary process, they are sometimes referred to as "extra-budgetary" units.

Third, perhaps the most important difference between these entities and other public enterprises is that, despite an initial orientation toward tackling some imperative problems faced by the state after the Cultural Revolution,[6] their operations have been increasingly aimed at generating profits that benefit, individually or collectively, the state functionaries in

[5] According to a Beijing University study on a northeastern district government (Wang Sibin and Wang Hansheng 1998), for example, the district headquarters of the Youth League ran thirty economic entities in 1993, among which were one hotel, one kindergarten, one barber shop, one beauty parlor, eleven retail outlets, four trading companies, three repairing centers, one applied research institute, and five factories. None of them had anything to do with the political functions of the Youth League.

[6] The origins of backyard profit centers can be traced to the late 1970s and early 1980s when limited numbers of state agencies were allowed to run profit-seeking entities as an expedient measure to tackle several imperative problems faced by the state. Those problems included a severe shortage of budgetary funds, a pressing need to provide jobs for large numbers of unemployed urban youths, inadequate accommodation for redundant government personnel resulting from massive retirement of old cadres and administrative restructuring, and huge gaps in the financing of newly added regulatory functions (Lin and Zhang 1999). The backyard profit centers have since been greatly expanded in scope and scale and turned from a tentative arrangement into an entrenched fixture serving the private interests of state agents. But their initial problem-solving mission has been continuously projected as their main agenda and used as a legitimate cover to justify their expansion (ibid.).

their sponsoring agencies. The contributions from these entities end up in the pool of discretionary resources of the agencies, which takes two major forms: extra-budgetary funds, discussed in Chapter 3 (cf. section 1), and *xiao jinku* or "little coffers" – illicit funds generated and hidden by various state agencies for their own private or parochial uses. Since the early 1980s, the financial authorities have launched repeated inspection campaigns to curb the growth of *xiao jinku,* but the funds in this category have remained widespread and elusive.[7] Because of the flexibility in the disposal of these funds (especially illicit funds), they are widely used to bring various personal or group benefits, in such forms as bonuses, income supplements in kind, housing, and communal and office facilities, to the state functionaries in the agencies and departments that generate and control them.

Although the backyard profit centers are not identifiable from official statistics and detailed accounts of their operations are sparse, there are indications that they have been pervasive and difficult to eradicate despite repeated efforts by the central authority. The first cleanup campaign was carried out in 1984–5, when 27,000 backyard profit centers were investigated and severed from their sponsoring agencies. In 1988–9, an additional 24,187 were screened out in a second nationwide cleanup campaign, which also uncovered extensive involvement of large numbers of state agencies and senior Party and government officials in profit-making activities (*ZGGSB,* September 11, 1989). In 1993, a third nationwide campaign was launched by the central authority to tackle the same problem.[8] There is no sign that any of these campaigns has been successful, as indicated by the large numbers of surviving and additional backyard profit centers uncovered in each subsequent campaign.[9] In 1998, the central leadership started a fourth cleanup campaign, which for the first time included profit-seeking entities run by the military (*RMRB,* July 14, 16, 23, 1998). It remains to be seen whether this latest effort can achieve significantly different results.

[7] In the directives issued by the State Council to investigate and clean up *xiao jinku* in 1989 and 1995, for example, the same phrase *lujin buzhi* ("never stopped despite repeated bans") was used in the introductory sections to describe the tenacity of the phenomenon (Guowu yuan, November 14, 1989; May 4, 1995).
[8] According to one report, 50,000 backyard profit centers were formed during 1992–3 (Xu Weiguo 1993). Another report claimed that a total of 304,000 such entities were in existence before the 1993 campaign (*ZGCJB,* April 13, 1993).
[9] Less than two years after the 1993 campaign, for example, the Beijing Municipal Government conducted another investigation into the profit-seeking activities of state agencies. According to the concluding report on the investigation (BJSRMZF 1995), 42 of the 56 department-level agencies were found to have had backyard profit centers (169 in total, plus 309 subsidiaries), 78% of which had been set up before or during 1993 and apparently survived the cleanup campaign carried out in that year.

The existence and growth of backyard profit centers have had important implications for industrial firms. Although most of them do not operate in the industrial sector, they have extensive interactions with many industrial firms as well as with the supervising agencies of industrial firms. In the following three sections, I examine how such interactions affect the behavior and performance of industrial firms.

Competition

Competition between backyard profit centers and industrial firms takes place on two major fronts: the supply of input and the production and sales of output. Using their special connections with resource allocation agencies, many backyard profit centers have diverted resources designated for regular industrial firms and used them for arbitrage. Some backyard profit centers have also taken advantage of the regulatory power of their sponsoring agencies to cut into the gains of regular industrial firms that produce similar products.

Input Supplies

Arbitrage, known as *daomai daomai* in Chinese, has been a most important source of profit making by backyard profit centers during the marketization process of the economy, especially in the 1980s and early 1990s. State control of the prices of products and factors and the unevenness in the pace, scope, and degree of relaxation of such control across different boundaries (e.g., sector, ownership, and locality) of economic activities have spawned opportunities for profit making from price discrepancies. From the early 1980s, these opportunities have been extensively pursued by many backyard profit centers. The dwindling of plan-allocated resources due to diversion by backyard profit centers has weakened the ability of many traditional public enterprises (especially state enterprises) to meet their output targets. This has led to an intensification of bargaining by these enterprises with their supervising agencies for greater autonomy, adding to the pressures to bring down the plan.

As mentioned above, the majority of backyard profit centers operate in the tertiary sector.[10] The underdevelopment of this sector under the central planning system resulted in imbalances between demand

---

[10] According to the State Industrial and Commercial Administration (Fei Kailong and Zuo Ping 1991: 164; *ZGGSB*, September 11, 1989), the percentages of backyard profit centers operating in the tertiary sector during 1984–5 and 1988–9 were 85 and 75 respectively.

and supply and created abundant profit-making opportunities. This sector also includes many lines of activities where the costs for setup, management, diversification, and exit tend to be lower than those for production activities. But perhaps a more important reason for the concentration of backyard profit centers in the tertiary sector is that many of them are well positioned to make significant gains from the discrepancies between state-set prices and market prices for resources under state allocation during the change from the plan to markets. Reports about the extensive engagement of backyard profit centers in arbitrage activities abound.[11] In an apparent move to show its resolve to curb "unhealthy trends," for example, immediately after the Tiananmen Incident in 1989 the central authority publicized limited findings from an investigation into five large profit-seeking entities sponsored by central government ministries (*RMRB*, August 17, 1989). A common feature of their operations is that arbitrage constituted the most important means of their profit making. Among the major items that they brokered were foreign currency, bank loans, imported automobiles, minerals, and industrial materials.

Since a large part of the resources obtained by backyard profit centers for arbitrage came from supplies originally destined for existing public enterprises – especially state enterprises – operating under state plan, the diversion of the resources inevitably affected the ability of the designated users to carry out their activities. Under the central plan, industrial enterprises were required to produce output using inputs priced at state-controlled levels and to sell their output according to state-set prices (Liu Guoguang and Zhou Guiying 1992). A shortage of plan-supplied inputs would force the affected enterprises to obtain inputs at higher prices or reduce output. Either way, their performances would be undercut. Take the example of industrial materials.

The main state agency overseeing the allocation of industrial materials has been the State Materials Allocation Bureau (SMAB). But quite a number of other state agencies have also had varying degrees of control over the allocation of industrial materials. They include, among others, the supervising departments (and their subsidiary distribution companies) of industrial material producers, the supervising departments of industrial and other enterprises that make use of industrial materials, the Plan-

---

[11] The first major effort by the central authority to crack down on "speculative activities" undertaken by backyard profit centers was launched in 1984 (Fei Kailong and Zuo Ping 1991: 163–6). But it did not have much long-lasting effect. For reports about the continuation and expansion of such activities in the subsequent decade, see Fei Kailong and Zuo Ping (1991: 371–5), Liu Suinian (1991: 103–5), and *RMRB*, March 2, 1985, June 23, 1986, May 8, 1987, September 22, 1988, August 1, 1989, July 28, 1990, August 9, 1991, August 4, 1993, August 2, 1994.

ning Commission, the Economic Commission, the Ministry of Foreign Economic Relations and Trade, and the local subsidiaries or counterparts of these agencies (Liu Suinian 1993). Since the early 1980s these agencies have formed and run large numbers of backyard profit centers, which have benefited greatly from selling plan-allocated industrial materials diverted by, or with the help of, their government sponsors.[12]

Accounts of the growing difficulties of industrial enterprises in obtaining sufficient industrial materials under state quota began to surface in the mid-1980s and became regular features in media reports toward the end of the decade (e.g., Liu Guoguang and Zhou Guiying 1992; Ma Kai 1992; Luan Tao and Li Zhengzhi 1993; see also note 14), when activities carried out by backyard profit centers expanded and intensified. The initial brunt was borne mostly by urban collectives and small state enterprises.[13] These enterprises had low status in the pecking order of resource allocation under the central plan and were deemed by many pertinent government agencies as less important to the accumulation of their political capital. But large enterprises were also hit hard, especially in the late 1980s, when the opportunity cost of refraining from resource diversion became apparent to allocating agencies and when interagency coordination was made more difficult by increasing inconsistencies in the policy process.[14]

This development led to two parallel behavioral changes among industrial enterprises operating under state plan. First, those that faced a shortage in the supply of plan-allocated inputs intensified their bargaining with their supervising agencies to lower the targets for state-planned output or to gain greater freedom to produce and dispose of extra-plan output to compensate for the losses that they suffered.[15] Second, the profits that backyard profit centers derived from arbitrage provided a

---

[12] See, for example, BJSRMZF (1994, 1995); *JJRB*, September 24, 1988; *JRSB*, November 18, 1989; Liu Suinian (1991); Lin and Zhang (1999).

[13] A 1984 survey of 427 industrial enterprises, for example, found that the gap in plan-allocated industrial materials was wider and growing faster among small enterprises than among large enterprises (Zhang Shaojie 1986).

[14] Southwestern Machinery, for example, faced a sharp drop in the supply of plan-allocated inputs in the second half of the 1980s. Starting from 1987, it had to send back increasing amounts of steel (its main input) of poor quality to industrial material distribution centers under the supervising agencies of its suppliers. Then it had to buy, at higher prices, steel of the grades it needed from the backyard profit centers under the same distribution centers. The substandard steel was apparently delivered to keep up an appearance of still implementing the plan while the distribution centers diverted high-quality, plan-allocated steel for arbitrage. For examples of similar experiences in other state enterprises, see *RMRB*, May 17, 1987, August 13, 1987, August 31, 1987, December 13, 1988, August 14, 1989; and *WZGL*, No. 3, 1988, 11, No. 10, 1988, 7–8.

[15] Facing serious shortages of plan-allocated industrial materials and working capital in the mid-1980s, for example, Southwestern Machinery made strong appeals to its supervising agency for concessions. Fearing that growing financial problems in the enterprise

clear indication of the opportunity cost incurred by producers of capital goods (especially industrial materials) for adhering to the plan. They wanted to make the profits themselves instead of letting backyard profit centers get all the extra gains.[16]

As it became increasingly apparent that the old mode of operation could hardly be sustained due to the growing leakage of plan-allocated resources through backyard profit centers, supervising agencies gradually gave in to the mounting pressure from their subordinate industrial enterprises. During 1981–3, administrative control over pricing and sales of consumer goods produced by most small and medium enterprises was relaxed – first from mandatory plan to directive plan, and then at last to no plan at all (Ma Kai 1992; Tong Wansheng and Zou Xiangqun 1992; Wang Shiyuan 1993). In 1984, producers of capital goods were allowed to sell their extra-plan output under a cap of no more than 20% higher than the prices for state-planned output (Ma Kai 1992). In 1985, the cap was removed, resulting in the so-called "dual-track price system" (ibid.). Since then, the proportion of extra-plan output has steadily increased for both consumer and capital goods. Urban collectives and small state enterprises, which were hardest hit by the diversions through backyard profit centers, led the way to move out of the plan. Large enterprises soon followed suit. By the mid-1990s, outputs allocated by state plan had shrunk to a small part of total industrial output, as discussed in the preceding chapter (see also Naughton 1995a).

With the breakaway of more and more industrial firms from the plan in the 1990s, the significance of the competitive pressures generated by backyard profit centers in the supply of industrial materials may have gradually lessened (Xu Weiguo 1993). But what this signifies seems to be a shift in the focus of their arbitrage activities rather than a dissipation of such activities in general. According to Wu Jinglian (Wu 1995), an influential Chinese economist, in the reform era the center of arbitrage gravitated toward consumer goods in the late 1970s and early 1980s, shifted to industrial materials in the mid- and late 1980s, and subsequently moved to land and capital in the early 1990s when the markets for real estate and securities were gradually opened up. This view is consistent with findings from numerous studies about the plight of traditional public enterprises (especially those in the state sector) in the reform era, which is shown to have been exacerbated by a serious

---

would eventually become a serious administrative burden for it to deal with, the latter gradually increased the factory's autonomy in the produdction, sales, and pricing of extra-plan output. For similar examples, see Fang Weizhong and Wu Jiajun (1989), Ma Kai (1992), and Wu Jinglian (1993).

[16] See, for example, Liu Suinian (1991), Liu Suinian and Cai Ninglin (1993), and *WZGL*, No. 1, 1986, 13–16, No. 12, 1987, 29–31, No. 10, 1988, 7–8, No. 3, 1989, 12–13.

shortage of industrial materials in the mid- and late 1980s and by a serious shortage of capital, especially loans at government-set rates, in the early 1990s.[17]

Output Production and Sales

Although the tertiary sector is where the activities of most backyard profit centers take place, some of them operate in the industrial sector. Many of these latter are affiliated with their sponsoring agencies through an arrangement called *guakao* or mooring (Lin and Zhang 1999; Xu Weiguo 1993; Wang Sibin and Wang Hansheng 1998), which is one of the major methods by which backyard profit centers are formed.[18] What *guakao* means is a provision of patronage by state agencies to for-profit organizations that are already in existence but undergo a reorganization.[19] The agencies involved serve as their *zhuguan danwei* (supervising bodies), a regulatory requirement for all organizations registered as public (i.e., state or collective) enterprises (Fei Kailong and Zuo Ping 1991). They provide the adopted enterprises with various "services," such as acquirement of resources, protection against predatory actions by other agencies, facilitation of entry and expansion, creation of monopoly positions, ad hoc relaxation of restrictions, exemption from taxes or other levies, and defusing of punitive actions by law enforcement authorities. In return, the enterprises contribute part of their revenue to their patrons. Decisions on the personnel, operation, and finance of these enterprises are left to their leaders. They are thus de facto private enterprises maintaining a stable "fee-for-service" relationship with their government patrons.

The products of these enterprises compete directly with those produced by regular industrial firms. Because of their special ties with the interests of officials in their sponsoring agencies, they tend to be in a more advantageous position in the competition. Not only can they gain an upper hand over regular industrial firms in interacting with the state apparatus in the three important aspects illustrated in the preceding chapter – i.e., allocation of resources, regulatory treatment, and distribution of various government levies – but they can also directly squeeze the economic space of their rivals by using their sponsoring agencies'

---

[17] See, e.g., CESS (1993–8), Liu Guoguang and Zhou Guiying (1992), and Luan Tao and Li Zhengzhi (1993).

[18] There are two other methods: "conversion" (converting existing administrative or service units of state agencies into profit-seeking entities) and "creation" (establishing new profit-seeking entities under state agencies). See Lin and Zhang (1999) for more discussion on this.

[19] Reorganization in this context means a reregistration of an existing private enterprise as a public enterprise or the transfer to new owner(s) of an existing public enterprise from its previous government supervising agency.

authority to seize output contracts from their rivals and to impose ad hoc restrictions on the activities of their rivals. Consider the experiences of Elegance Furniture Company (a regular industrial enterprise) and Guardian Work-wear Supplies Company (a backyard profit center undertaking industrial production).[20]

Elegance Furniture Company (Elegance Furniture hereafter) is a collective enterprise in a northeastern provincial capital. Established in 1979 as a furniture toolmaker in the Gate Tower District (see Chapter 5 for more discussion on the district) of the city, it was unprofitable during the initial years of its operation. That situation was changed with the appointment of a new and innovative factory director, Liu Ping, in 1983. Under Liu, the operation of Elegance Furniture was changed from tool making to furniture manufacturing. He developed novel furniture designs, used less expensive materials as substitutes for wood, adopted a strategy of tailoring a wide range of its products to customers' preferences, and expanded into interior decoration. Within two years the firm began to make a profit.

With the decline of the state plan in the second half of the 1980s, competition intensified in the furniture sector. In Gate Tower alone, there were 19 furniture makers and interior decoration companies in 1990; Elegance Furniture was still the leader in sales. In 1992, however, two of its competitors (both of which had been private enterprises) became (via *guakao* arrangements) backyard profit centers of powerful local government agencies – the Finance Department and the Labor Department. Through their clout, they gained and divided between themselves lucrative contracts for the supply of furniture and interior decoration for all the major hotels and new office buildings in the district. In two separate cases, Elegance Furniture even lost contracts it had gained from two local hotels, which were pressured by the Labor Department (the local authority that issued the work permits for the migrant workers hired by hotels to do cleaning) to choose its own furniture company as the vendor. The Finance Department blocked a proposal from the Industry Department to let Elegance Furniture expand by taking over a state-owned plastics factory located in the district. A top official in the Finance Department even went so far as to "suggest" that the district Education Department disapprove a request from Elegance Furniture to acquire an unused parking lot from an adjacent middle school to build a warehouse. The

---

[20] The following account is based on information from the author's interviews (Informants no. 329/1995, no. 337/1995, no. 338/1995, no. 347/1995, no. 398/1996, no. 422/1996, no. 424/1996, no. 427/1996). For similar examples, see GPJYJ (1996: 32–63), Liu Bing and Deng Yizhi (1999: 74–93), and *RMRB*, January 6, 1995, May 28, 1997, July 9, 1997.

hostile environment in which Elegance Furniture operated slowed down its growth and led to a significant narrowing of its profit margin.

Guardian Work-wear Supplies Company (Guardian Work-wear hereafter) was established in 1988 in a southern provincial capital. It was a joint equity venture between a Hong Kong wholesaler and a garment factory set up by his cousin, a retired official from the State Industrial and Commercial Administration office in the city's main industrial district. Its main products were aprons, oven mittens, and pot holders. With the help of the former SICA official's contacts in the government, the joint venture obtained low-interest loans, power supply at subsidized rates, permission to sell a large part of its products domestically, simplified customs procedures for imports and exports, and an extended period of tax exemption (five years). The enterprise was quite profitable, but it faced a limited demand in highly competitive domestic and international markets.

In 1992, Guardian Work-wear was reorganized when the joint venture added a new partner, a five-person retail outlet under a labor service company run by the Office of Production Safety Inspection of the District Labor Department. The reorganization (and hence reregistration) brought the firm another tax holiday (three years). But the most important gain was the new business that the new partner's parent agency brought in – i.e., an exclusive contract to produce gloves and face masks used by construction companies, manufacturers of heavy machinery and equipment, and chemical factories in the district. At the time the contract was granted, 183 enterprises in the district were required by the Labor Department to use these protective items. Their supplies had been sourced from seven different manufacturers, five of which were state and collective enterprises located in the district. After its reorganization, Guardian Work-wear was designated by the Office of Production Safety Inspection as the sole supplier.[21] To ensure continued business for Guardian Work-wear, the Office also required that the depreciation period for each batch of supplies purchased by the enterprises in the district should be no more than six months. Within a year, Guardian Work-wear increased its workforce fivefold and sales sevenfold. Two of the five former suppliers in the district filed complaints through their supervising agencies, but to no avail. Another one offered to become a subcontractor of Guardian Work-wear. The other two simply closed their

---

[21] Three reasons were cited by the Office as the basis of its decision: (i) none of the seven existing suppliers specialized in the production of these products; (ii) Guardian Work-wear had the most advanced facility – two production lines yet to be imported from Germany with a low-interest loan arranged by the Office; and (iii) concentration of production in one enterprise would aid quality control.

production lines for gloves and face masks and focused on their other products.

The practices used by the backyard profit centers and their sponsors in the above two cases fall into the category of "unfair competition" defined by the Chinese government. In view of a surge of such practices in the reform, in 1987 the government began to draft laws and regulations to curb their spread. In the *Law against Unfair Competition* enacted in 1993, for example, it was clearly stipulated (under Article 6) that government agencies were not allowed to use their administrative power to restrict buyers to certain supplier(s) or to constrain the activities of rival supplier(s), which was exactly what the Labor Department had done in the above case. But it seems that the problem has persisted. In a series of annual questionnaire surveys conducted by China's Entrepreneurs Survey System (CESS) under the State Council during 1993–7, "unfair competition" consistently ranked first among the most serious problems identified by the enterprise leaders surveyed. Claiming that they faced or were affected by "unfair competition" were 74.2% of the respondents in 1993 (n = 2,620), 67.8% in 1994 (n = 2,756), 76.4% in 1995 (n = 2,752), 40.8% in 1996 (n = 3,154),[22] and 55.8% in 1997 (n = 2,415) (CESS 1993: 14; 1994: 16; 1995: 21; 1996: 11; 1997: 28).

Transaction

Backyard profit centers not only compete but transact with industrial firms. For the latter, such transactions may be voluntary or coerced. The items involved in voluntary transactions include resources that backyard profit centers divert from the plan, access to economic opportunities, and services that help simplify existing bureaucratic procedures or reduce the transaction cost for dealing with state authorities. In contrast, involuntary transactions involve products and services that industrial firms otherwise would not purchase from or sell to backyard profit centers in the absence of a threat of punitive action by their sponsoring agencies.

Voluntary Transactions

It is important to note that, although backyard profit centers' arbitrage activities have exacerbated the shortage in the supply of input to tradi-

---

[22] In that year's survey, the question was phrased rather differently and did not include such issues as "protectionism by government agencies and local jurisdictions" (which was marked by 13.9% of the respondents) and "sectoral monopoly" (which was marked by 3% of the respondents).

tional public enterprises, there is another side of the coin. That is, when backyard profit centers diverted resources from the plan, they had the explicit goal of selling such resources to parties that were willing to buy them at higher prices, especially those operating outside the plan – i.e., rural collectives, private enterprises, and foreign capital enterprises. These enterprises concentrated on the production of consumer goods (Liu Guoguang and Zhou Guiying 1992). In the early years of reform, they needed as input the capital goods produced by enterprises operating under state plan, but had difficulty addressing this need through the formal resource allocation channels of the state. Thus many of them became clients of backyard profit centers.[23] Although the prices charged were higher than state-set prices, their effect on production costs tended to be contained by the price competition among backyard profit centers and by the gains from the greater decision-making autonomy and flexibility enjoyed by those operating outside the plan.[24] As the number of these enterprises multiplied in the mid- and late 1980s, the interplay between their demand and the backyard profit centers' supply intensified, further contributing to the decline of the plan.[25]

In addition to securing resources in short supply through backyard profit centers, industrial firms also have transacted extensively with them for other purposes. Many sponsoring agencies of backyard profit centers have regulatory responsibilities. Since the mid-1980s, increasing numbers of state agencies have turned part of their public service functions into private services through their backyard profit centers. To industrial firms, this has offered an opportunity to bypass existing bureaucratic red tape and restrictions. Consider the following examples from some of the firms that I studied.[26]

---

[23] Of the 46 industrial enterprises where I conducted case studies during 1988–96, 29 operated outside the state plan. During the 1980s and early 1990s, all of them had transacted with backyard profit centers for state-allocated resources, especially industrial materials and loans.

[24] This was particularly true when their rival state enterprises were forced to obtain input from outside the plan while still lacking adequate autonomy in decision making on production and sales of their products.

[25] Throughout the 1980s TVEs were criticized by some Chinese economists and state enterprise leaders for "cutting into the cornerstone" (*wa qiang jiao*) of the traditional public sector economy (Fan Xiumin and Ma Qingqiang 1994; Ma Jiesan 1991; Li Peilin and Wang Chunguang 1993; Zhang Yi 1990), which in part reflected the competitive pressures generated by such enterprises through various ad hoc supply arrangements with allocating authorities through their backyard profit centers.

[26] For accounts and reports about similar transactions, see Gong Xikui and Jin Hongwei (1995), Huang Weiding (1992), *RMRB*, November 17, 1997, Xia Xingguo (1994), Xu Weiguo (1993).

When Everbright Heating was reorganized as a joint venture in 1991, its application needed the approval of, among others, the Foreign Economic Relations and Trade Commission of the city government. The review process involved a verification, through the commercial affairs office of a Chinese embassy or consulate, of the information about the organizational profile and assets of the foreign partner(s). This ordinarily took four to eight weeks. In case of further questions or requirements for clarification from the Commission, the process could be longer or truly bogged down. In order to speed up the process and, more important, to make sure that the deal was not blocked by the Commission,[27] Director Wang hired an accounting and consultancy firm under the Commission to process the paperwork. Within a week after Everbright Heating sent in 50% of the total charge (3,000 yuan) as nonrefundable advance payment, approval was obtained.

In 1993 Director Kang of Flying Horse Motors planned to expand into automobile manufacturing. He needed to make several business trips to Japan to consult with the automaker Isuzu. But his plan hit a snag. In the summer of 1993, the central government imposed an economic austerity program which tightened, among other things, restrictions on business travel abroad. A local official introduced Zhu to a travel agency operating under the provincial Public Security Department. After paying a fee and waiting for three weeks, Kang and his deputies obtained passports and visas for Japan.

In 1992, Rainbow Pipe purchased five trucks and ceased to use the services provided by a local transport company to ship coal and coke (its primary input) from the Kailuan Coal Mine and to deliver products to buyers in the province and beyond. Soon after that, the truck drivers reported to Director Zhu that, when they drove through different counties, they were frequently harassed by public security officers and forced to pay heavy road tolls. Zhu consulted an acquaintance in the county Public Security Department for advice. He was referred to a transportation service company under the Department, where he could rent military vehicle license plates for short-term use. The plates belonged to a missile base located in the county. Vehicles with such plates could deter harassment by local officials, pay no road tolls, and park freely in public parking lots. Also for a fee to that company, Rainbow Pipe was able to jump a long queue to pass the annual motor vehicle inspection quickly.

---

[27] As indicated in Chapter 3, the foreign partner in this case was a Southeast Asian company in which a large Chinese international trust investment company was the majority shareholder.

After being fined by the county Environmental Protection Office in 1990 (Chapter 3), Polyester Fiber hired an environmental engineering company under that office to make recommendations on how to clean up its two pollutant-producing chimneys. The company made some suggestions on cosmetic changes and offered a few "insider's tips" on how to pass the tests carried out by government inspectors. Three months later, the inspectors came again. After learning that the factory had been serviced by the backyard profit center, they gave it a clean bill based on the factory's report on what had been done subsequent to the last inspection. They also removed Polyester Fiber from the list of enterprises subject to random inspection, but suggested that it should commission the service of the backyard profit center at least once a year.

Coerced Sales and Purchases

There is, though, another type of transaction between industrial firms and backyard profit centers, known in Chinese as *qiangmai qiangmai* or coerced sales and purchases. Using the authority of their sponsoring agencies as a threat, many backyard profit centers have forced industrial firms to purchase their "services" or products that are not needed or priced at above-market levels; some of them have also imposed purchase orders for regular industrial firms' products or services priced at below-market levels. To the industrial firms concerned, whether or not to transact with the backyard profit centers is a matter of how much loss to incur as compared to the status quo.

Coerced transactions started in the early 1980s when increasing numbers of backyard profit centers forced industrial enterprises whose products were in short supply to sell part of their output at low prices and then used the products for arbitrage. With the decline of plan-allocated output since the mid-1980s, this practice has been overshadowed by coerced purchases of "services" and products from backyard profit centers. The following incidents illustrate some of the methods commonly used by backyard profit centers in involuntary transactions.[28]

As discussed in Chapter 2, in the mid-1980s Polyester Fiber moved out of the plan ahead of some state enterprises in the chemical fiber sector. It sourced its inputs and sold its output in the emergent markets. Its main product, polyester fiber, was widely used by weaving factories. The rise of large numbers of new industrial enterprises – especially township and village enterprises – in the textile sector drastically increased

---

[28] For examples and discussions of similar cases, see GPJYJ (1996), Liu Bing and Deng Yizhi 1999), and Liu Suinian (1991).

the demand for Polyester Fiber's output. During 1984–7, the market price for polyester fiber increased by more than 80%. But Polyester Fiber was not able to reap all the gains from the price change. In 1985, it received an order from a labor service company under the city's Textile Department, Polyester Fiber's supervising agency, requesting two tons of polyester fiber at plan-allocation price, which was below market price. That was followed by similar requests from an industrial materials company under the Economic Commission of the county where the factory was located and from a wholesale distribution center under the Industrial Material Allocation Bureau of the city government. Altogether, the amounts shipped to these backyard profit centers accounted for nearly 40% of Polyester Fiber's total output that year. In the next two years, a total of seven backyard profit centers made similar purchases from Polyester Fiber. It was not until 1988, when the market supply of polyester fiber greatly increased as a result of the relaxation of central control over imports and the growth of extra-plan sales by state enterprises, that Polyester Fiber was able to sell all its output at market prices.

But that was not the end of Polyester Fiber's involuntary transactional relationships with backyard profit centers. During 1986–90, the factory was forced to make frequent use of a hotel and a restaurant (which were torn down in 1990 to make room for the construction of a new office building) to accommodate its business guests and hold other functions. Owned by an "economic development" company under the Tax Collection Bureau of the county, those vendors charged Polyester Fiber "special" (higher) prices. Many other state agencies also introduced to the factory various "services" provided by their backyard profit centers at high prices. They included certification of professional titles for technical personnel, subscriptions to memberships of various associations, and various seminars (e.g., on safe use of electrical devices, the *Accounting Law*, land use regulations, food storage, tree planting and gardening, prenuptial education, and so on). There was an apparent threat of retaliation for noncompliance behind the "invitations" from the vendors or sponsors of these "services" that the factory otherwise would not have bought. Polyester Fiber's compliance protected it from incurring greater losses, but some other industrial firms became accommodating only after adverse actions were taken. Consider the experience of Superior Sound Electronic Products Co. (Superior Sound hereafter).

Superior Sound was one of the first and largest wholly foreign-owned enterprises in a southern special economic zone (SEZ). During the ten years after its formation in 1983, it steadily expanded its operation, and its work force grew from 160 to over 900. The overwhelming majority of the workers were migrants from inland provinces, such as Hunan and Sichuan. According to local government regulations, applicants for factory jobs in the SEZ need a permit for temporary abode from the local Public Security Office and a permit for temporary employment from the local Labor Department. Because of the fluidity of labor market conditions in the SEZ, turnover was high. In the early 1990s, Superior Sound on average hired 20 to 30 workers per month, most of whom were introduced by friends already working for the company. In the spring of 1993, the company was raided several times by the local police. The targets were potential job applicants who had not obtained the two permits but stayed temporarily with their friends in the factory quarters. Superior Sound was fined heavily for failing to exclude unauthorized personnel from its premises. During the raids, those who provided accommodation for their friends without the required permits were also detained. Since this involved quite a number of workers, the tightly scheduled production shifts were seriously affected.

In a meeting with the local police to resolve the crisis, Superior Sound's personnel manager was given a hint on how the problem could be avoided in the future. The police had formed a security service company in 1992, but its business was rather slack. A large company like Superior Sound could give it a boost. After weighing the options, Superior Sound decided to disband its own team of security guards and externalize their function to the security service company. The new team had twice as many security guards (totaling 40) as the company's own and cost nearly three times more. However, after this arrangement, no more raids were made by the police, though friends of Superior Sound's workers continued to come and stay in the factory quarters during their job searches. According to the personnel manager, the company was not alone. Four other factories in the area were also harassed and forced to contract the services of the security service company.

Coerced transactions with backyard profit centers constitute part of what is known in China as *san luan* or "three arbitrarily imposed levies" – (i) *tanpai* (cf. Chapter 3), (ii) extra or excessive fees, and (iii) irregular or excessive fines – arousing growing complaints among industrial enterprises and causing serious concern at the central government. A search of the *China Law and Regulation Data Bank* compiled by the State Council reveals that during 1982–93 the central authority issued a total of 26 directives and bans to curb the growth and spread of coerced transactions. But there is no sign that the problem has been effectively contained. In the 1993, 1994, and 1995 enterprise leader surveys mentioned above, for example, more than 80% of the enterprises indicated that they had difficulty resisting the obligations arbitrarily imposed by various state agencies. In the 1996 survey, 51.2% of the enterprise leaders claimed that such obligations had become heavier than before. The 1997 survey found a lower but still significant percentage (65%) of enterprises unable to resist exploitative demands from state agencies (CESS 1993: 6; 1994: 11; 1995: 17; 1996: 21; 1997: 12).

Collusion

A third type of interaction between backyard profit centers and industrial firms is collusion. It is often carried out through a deliberate effort by public enterprise leaders to transfer, sometimes with the tacit approval of their supervising officials, the profits and assets of their enterprises to backyard profit centers of state agencies. This appears to have become a rapidly growing phenomenon in the 1990s, especially since early 1992 when Deng Xiaoping called for a speedup of economic change. Three concurrent developments have followed.

First, in view of growing profit-making opportunities in the economy and a widening gap between their nominal pay and the income of many people (e.g., private owners, joint venture managers, and other professionals) in the nonstate sector,[29] large numbers of government officials have quit their jobs to pursue entrepreneurial activities full time.[30] Many have started their own businesses but maintained close ties with their former units, especially through various *guakao* arrangements (Lin and Zhang 1999; Wang Sibin and Wang Hansheng, 1998; Xu Weiguo 1993). Second, in the summer of 1992 the State Council enacted the *Ordinance on Restructuring the Management Mechanisms of State-owned Industrial Enterprises*. It greatly expanded the decision-making authority of state enterprise leaders over a wide range of issues, as indicated by the figures reported in Table 1.3. Third, although gaining significantly increased autonomy in decision making, state enterprise leaders continued to

---

[29] This income gap has fostered a sense of relative deprivation among many officials. In a survey of government officials conducted by the Sociology Department of Beijing University and the *Zhongguo Qingnian Bao* (China Youth Daily) in 1993, for example, 90% of the respondents ($n = 233$) regarded their salaries and fringe benefits as inadequate to support an average standard of living, and 66% claimed that their income levels experienced slippage relative to other people's during the previous few years. See Appendix A for more information about the survey.

[30] Such a practice is often referred to as *xiahai* or plunging into the sea (of business). There are no statistics about its exact magnitude. But there are indications that it involved quite a number of state agents. From 1992 to 1993 when the phenomenon reached its height, for example, the total number of employees in "government departments, Party agencies, and social organizations" decreased from 11.48 million to 10.3 million, registering a downsizing of 10.3% (GJTJJa 1997: 99). Assuming the number of retirees to be equal to that of the new hires during that period, a total of 1.18 million former state employees could have left for nongovernment jobs.

receive financial rewards significantly lower than those received by non-state enterprise leaders.[31] This has created a perverse incentive for them to make opportunistic use of their increased autonomy for private gain, even at a cost to their enterprises. Such behavior may be an important contributing factor to the seemingly puzzling phenomenon that in the 1990s the performances of state enterprises markedly deteriorated while their decision-making authority significantly increased.

Since the early 1990s, financial losses incurred by state enterprises due to the self-seeking behavior of their leaders have become a major topic in media reports. From 1995 to 1997, for example, a total of 302 state enterprise leaders in the city of Chongqing were prosecuted for managerial corruption that led their enterprises to incur heavy losses (*SDC*, No. 1, 1998). A 1997 investigation into 110 loss-making state enterprises reveals that managerial corruption was the main cause of their problems (*CND-Global*, December 30, 1997). In the 44 enterprises where in each case the amount of funds abused exceeded RMB 1 million, 190 enterprise leaders were found to have engaged in diversion of funds. Another investigation into 392 loss-making state enterprises in Inner Mongolia led to the dismissal of 74 factory directors for managerial corruption (*RMRB*, February 19, 1998).

The problem is not confined to enterprises with poor performances. Enterprises with sound performances have also been affected. For example, from 1990 to 1995 five managerial corruption cases involving several million yuan were uncovered at the Capital Steel and Iron Company (one of China's largest steel makers and a model enterprise); the top offender, Guan Zhicheng (assistant general manager), was executed (*RMLT*, May 1995). During a business trip to the United States in 1996, the director of the Kunming Cigarette Factory (a top performer in the state sector) disappeared, along with a large amount of factory cash assets (*MP*, April 19, 1999). In the same year, the director of the Changjiang Power Company (one of the country's largest power suppliers) disappeared from China and was several months later found to have

---

[31] In the 1994 CESS survey cited above (CESS 1994: 15), only 2.4% of the state enterprise leaders ($n = 2,048$) claimed that they were fully rewarded for their talents and the responsibilities and risks they took; 32% claimed they were grossly underrewarded, and 65.4% indicated they were partially rewarded for their work. Only 24% of the respondents said they were satisfied with their financial rewards. The 1996 survey found that the average monthly salary income of enterprise directors in 1995 was 1,024 yuan or only 55% higher than the average wage income of employees in the urban state sector (based on figures in the *Statistical Yearbook of China 1996*), whereas only 23% of the state enterprise leaders surveyed claimed they were satisfied with their financial rewards (CESS 1996: 11). In contrast, a 1995 national survey of 2,564 private enterprise leaders revealed that the median monthly income reported by the respondents was 2,000 yuan in 1994 (Zhang Xuwu et al. 1996: 161).

set up a large power station in the Philippines with funds embezzled from the company (*LW*, No. 12 1996). In 1997, the director of the Yuxi Cigarette Factory (China's largest tobacco product manufacturer and another model enterprise) was arrested along with his deputies for diverting large amounts of enterprise funds to private accounts (*RMRB*, January 26, 1998).

A major way to advance the self-seeking behavior of public enterprise managers is to form collusive alliances with backyard profit centers of state agencies.[32] This often involves the transfer from state enterprises to backyard profit centers of two types of kickbacks: profits and assets.

Profit Transfer

The most commonly used strategy for profit transfer is to make deliberate cuts in the prices of products sold to backyard profit centers and/or make extra payments for goods and services purchased from backyard profit centers. In either case, the profit of the public enterprise concerned is reduced. Through various arrangements, part of the transferred profit then becomes the private gain of the enterprise leader(s). Consider the following.[33]

In 1994, Southwestern Machinery faced serious financial difficulties. A major contributing factor was "triangular debt" (*sanjiao zhai*) – a debt chain involving a number of enterprises that transact with one another on credit (Li 1993: 289). One of its largest clients – a state-owned tractor manufacturer in a province in Central China – was unable to make payment for the purchase of two sets of milling machines (worth nearly 3 million yuan) from Southwestern Machinery. This severely affected Southwest Machinery's cash flow and production. The factory sent two representatives to the province to investigate the situation. They were told that the main reason for the inability of the tractor manufacturer to pay back the money was that it could not collect payment for products sold to a farm supplies distribution center, a private enterprise that had just been closed down. As the representatives' investigation deepened, however, they made a startling discovery.

---

[32] Such collusion, of course, can also take place between public enterprise leaders and individuals or organizations that do not have close or stable ties with state agencies. My point is not that backyard profit centers necessarily caused managerial corruption in public enterprises. Rather, their existence and expansion have had an enhancing and reinforcing effect on the incentives for opportunistic behavior on the part of public enterprise managers under the existing formal reward structure.

[33] For examples of similar cases, see *RMRB*, January 16, 1995, December 16, 1996, March 21, 1997, April 4, 1998, and July 26, 1999.

The farm supplies distribution center was a backyard profit center of the provincial Department of Agriculture. Before its closure, it had already cleared its inventory and transferred much of its funds to another backyard profit center under the department. Moreover, the payment it owed to the tractor manufacturer was actually a "farewell gift," for the director of the tractor company had had full knowledge of the upcoming closure. His daughter-in-law was an employee in the center and, after its closure, started to work in its sister company. Through its own supervising authority, Southwestern Machinery filed a complaint with the supervising authority of the tractor manufacturer. Eighteen months later, it paid back 75% of the debt, the result of a compromise solution reached between the two supervising authorities. But that payment was heavy enough to drag the tractor manufacturer into deep losses, as only a small fraction of the revenue for sales to the backyard profit center was retrieved. Its director resigned in the following year. But he soon started a private enterprise of his own. The registration record in the local office of the State Industrial and Commercial Administration showed that the equity capital of that enterprise was 1.8 million yuan, more than ten times the sum of his previous salaried income for ten years.

Asset Transfer

In 1993, Northern Machinery needed to find additional space for the construction of a new building to house a precision instrument testing facility to be imported from the United States. It made an offer to buy the land use right for two abandoned basketball courts in an adjacent stationery factory (a small state enterprise of 300 employees). After three months of negotiations, the two sides reached a tentative agreement. Northern Machinery would compensate the stationery factory at the market price for the transfer of land use rights in that area. But before the deal was finalized, the stationery factory abruptly pulled out. The reason was that it was approached by a real estate development company under its supervising agency. A de facto private enterprise, the developer had just learned about the availability of that piece of land. Two weeks later, the land use right was sold to the developer at about 40% of the price offered by Northern Machinery. The director and Party secretary of the stationery factory were subsequently made (paid) members on the "advisory committee" of the backyard profit center. In the winter of that year, the land use right was resold by the developer to a Sino-U.S. joint venture (which later used the land for the construction of an express mail sorting center) at a price much higher than the price of purchase from the stationery factory.

In the mid-1990s, there was a widely reported debate among Chinese economic policy makers and academic researchers.[34] The focus of the debate was a so-called *"Zhongce* phenomenon." *Zhongce* (China Strategic Holdings) was an investment company based in Hong Kong. It was set up in 1991 by Oei Hong Leong (Huang Hongnian), an Indonesian-born Singaporean businessman who lived in China during the 1960s. Starting from 1992, Oei purchased the assets of large numbers of Chinese state enterprises at low prices. After certain organizational restructuring, he resold them at much higher prices to foreign investors. Some claimed that this was a good way to turn poorly performing enterprises around quickly. But others argued that the assets of the state enterprises taken over by Oei were grossly undervalued, and his huge profit represented a heavy loss of state assets.

Without more detailed information about the valuation and negotiation processes, it is difficult to determine whether *Zhongce* indeed shortchanged the Chinese government with the same strategy – offering private incentives to the gatekeepers – used by the developer to acquire the land use right from the stationery factory.[35] But the debate did highlight an issue that has received growing media attention, i.e., "leaking and draining of state assets" (*guoyou zichan liushi*). According to a top official of the Bureau of State Assets Management (*JJRB*, December 4, 1995), from 1982 to 1992 at least 500 billion yuan's worth of state assets was lost due to collusive transfers and reckless management; from 1993 to 1995 the situation further deteriorated.

A major area where opportunities for collusive transfers of state assets into private hands have grown is organizational restructuring of state enterprises since the early 1990s. Among the methods used in such restructuring are merger, corporatization (i.e., reorganization as shareholding companies), and liquidation of enterprises with poor performance, all of which involve an assessment and transfer of assets. The implementation of these measures was accelerated after Deng Xiaoping's southern tour in 1992. In 1996 alone, for example, over 6,000 small and unprofitable state enterprises were closed down and their assets were liquidated (*WWP*, July 16, 1997). But this has been accompanied by extensive attempts at collusive "bargain hunting," including those

---

[34] See, for example, *CND-Global*, October 11, 1996; *JJRB*, June 17, 1996; *JRSB*, May 18, 1997; *GG*, No. 3, 1993; *RMRB*, February 21, 1995.

[35] In an interview with Asian Business News (now CNBC Asia), broadcast on March 15, 1998, Oei said that personal connections with government officials were very important to his successful business in China. But he claimed that he did not spend a single penny for bribery.

pursued by backyard profit centers.[36] In 1997, the 15th CCP Congress formally endorsed shareholding as an organizational alternative to the existing state enterprise system. But at the same time, the leadership also expressed serious concerns about the growing loss of state assets. It emphatically stressed the imperative need to safeguard them during the process of organizational restructuring. The message was prominently stated in a series of editorial comments published in the *People's Daily* and *Economic Daily* prior to the Party congress (*JJRB*, August 7, 1997; *RMRB*, August 7, 1997).

Summary

What the "backyard phenomenon" indicates is a decay of the state's ability to maintain its neutrality and integrity in the use of public authority and the management of public assets. The above account of the interactions between industrial firms and the backyard profit centers of state agencies shows three noteworthy aspects of the marketization process in China's reform era.

First, there are important differences between the economic space outside the plan and "the market" depicted within the Smithian view. Participants in marketized economic activities include not only regular players but referees that enforce the rules of the game. This directly affects the incentives and constraints faced by regular industrial firms in competition, transaction, and management. A hypothesis that can be derived from this finding is that, other things being equal, those that can both minimize the menaces of backyard profit centers and take advantage of the opportunities posed by them tend to have a competitive advantage over those that cannot do so.

Second, the decline of the plan, the expansion of market-oriented economic activities, and the acceleration of the privatization of economic assets in the 1990s have all been closely related to the brokerage of state agents. The role played by the self-seeking behavior of state agents in economic institutional change is a missing link in the economic competition thesis about the causal mechanisms of China's marketization. The uneven process of "growing out of the plan" among traditional public enterprises of different sizes, sectors, and administrative statuses, the widening gaps in resource allocation under the plan, the ability of many new enterprises to overcome their initial regulatory and resource con-

---

[36] For discussions of various aspects of this issue, see Huang Weiding (1992); He Qinglian (1998); Gong Xikui and Jin Hongwei (1995); Li Hanlin (1994); Xia Xingguo (1994); Xu Weiguo (1993).

straints, and the stagnation and even deterioration in performance among state enterprises in the 1990s despite significantly increased decision-making autonomy, for example, are all developments that cannot be adequately explained within a view focused on the push-and-pull effects generated by interactions among economic actors.

Third, industrial firms situated under different historical and structural conditions have different exposures to the menaces and opportunities posed by backyard profit centers, which may have an important impact on variations in their performances – especially between state and non-state enterprises. Although enterprises under the state plan were hit hard by the diversion of resources through backyard profit centers in the early years of reform, many new forms of enterprises (e.g., rural collectives, private enterprises, and foreign capital enterprises) were beneficiaries (and demand creators) of such diversions. Also, it appears that the lack of synchronism between the increase of decision-making autonomy and managerial reward in state enterprises, coupled with their spatial proximity to backyard profit centers (which, like state enterprises, are mostly located in urban areas, as indicated above), makes these enterprises more susceptible to the perverse incentives proffered by the latter for managerial corruption.

The above observations point to two related questions that need to be further explored. Why has the state been increasingly unable to contain the self-seeking behavior of its agents despite the development of formal/legal institutions aimed at addressing, among other things, problems related to such behavior? And what are the implications of the weakening of the state's self-monitoring ability for industrial firms situated under different initial and structural conditions during the reform? These will be the focus of discussion in the next chapter.

5

Erosion of Authority Relations: A Tale of Two Localities

To gain a clearer view of the influence of particularistic state action on the uneven pace and outcome of marketization among different firms, it is necessary to examine how the institutional settings of state action have been transformed. As noted in Chapter 3, an important change in the rules governing the behavior of state agents during the reform was administrative decentralization. This restructuring of authority relations, however, is by no means an institutional invention of the post-Mao era. In the first three decades of the PRC's history (during 1958–60, 1964–6, and 1970–5), there were a few rounds of large-scale delegation of decision-making authority from the center to local governments (Riskin 1987; Zhu Rongji 1985). A major difference between the two eras is that since the early 1980s state agents have gained increasing individual discretion in defining both the content and the scope of the agenda implemented in local jurisdictions. This change signifies serious erosion of vertical and lateral monitoring of decision making in the political process, which has been the main underpinning for maintaining the state's organizational health.

This chapter explores how traditional constraints on the self-seeking behavior of state agents have been weakened. Two cases,[1] an urban district and a rural township, are examined. The former is indicative of the environment in which state firms operate, whereas the latter encompasses essential features of the locales where large numbers of nonstate firms, especially TVEs, have grown. I first discuss the common mechanisms that have broadened the ground for the expansion of exchange relations in the political process. I then highlight the differences between the path-dependent authority structures under the local state that the two cases represent. This sets the stage for the next chapter's further discussion on the implications of dual marketization for industrial firms situated under different structural conditions.

---

[1] See Appendix B for a discussion of the selection of these two localities as case study sites.

The Local State as a Corporate Entity

The account below builds on a view developed by Oi (1992a, 1995, 1999) and Walder (1992a, 1994, 1995a) about the restructuring of authority relations in the state apparatus. It argues that administrative decentralization has made local – subprovincial – governments act increasingly like industrial corporations that actively manage, coordinate, and monitor the activities undertaken by their composite economic units – local public enterprises.[2] Although local officials respond to the incentives introduced by this institutional change, the outcomes of their responses vary under different historical and structural conditions.[3] In urban jurisdictions bureaucratic tugs-of-war tend to persist during decentralization, perpetuating slow and incoherent policy processes. But decentralized authority relations in rural townships tend to be much more rationalized and cohere toward a course of concerted collective action to promote local economic growth. Such a difference has been a major contributing factor for the performance variation between urban public (mostly state) enterprises and TVEs.

I share the underlying assumption of this view – i.e., local officials' behavior is driven by their calculations of self-interest.[4] It is also important to pay close attention to historical and structural contingencies in examining the orientation and outcome of the strategies local officials develop to safeguard and advance their self-interest. But I propose to broaden the angle of analysis from authority relations to exchange rela-

---

[2] The notion of the local state as a corporate entity was first introduced by Oi (1988) in an analysis of village government. It was later extended to the study of township and county governments.

[3] According to Walder (1992a, 1994, 1995a), urban jurisdictions inherited from the central planning system a wide span of administrative functions, many pre-existing formal rules, and entrenched departmental interests. To local officials, decentralization means a redistribution of authority, responsibilities, and rewards. The attempts to safeguard and advance narrowly based bureaucratic interests – both pre-existing and newly formed – in this redistribution have led to the development of new strategies in vertical and lateral bargaining among state agencies and between state agencies and their subordinate enterprises. This tends to exacerbate rather than alleviate the difficulties in the coordination of decisions and actions. As the lowest and most recently created administrative center of the state bureaucracy, however, township governments are not so entangled in deeply entrenched and widely stretched authority relations as urban jurisdictions. As compared to officials in higher (urban) level jurisdictions, township officials (i) have more clearly defined and closely clustered decision and income rights over local public assets, (ii) carry much lighter nonwage obligations to employees of local public enterprises, and (iii) have a smaller number of such enterprises to control and monitor. The financial and career incentives fostered under these conditions tend to align the pursuit of self-interest by local officials with the goal of maximizing local government revenue.

[4] It seems that what has happened in the reform is not that state agents have become more self-interested, but rather that the incentives and constraints they face in the pursuit of self-interest, as well as the form and outcome of such pursuit, have changed.

tions, and from the incentives to the constraints faced by local officials in their decisions and actions. I submit that local officials not only respond to formal institutional incentives but also seek to bend and modify the rules governing their own behavior.

The impetus for the intensification of such efforts stems from three concurrent structural changes in the political process during the reform. They include: (i) adoption of various formal contractual arrangements between different administrative levels to tackle the financial difficulties faced by the state, (ii) shift of emphasis from individual behavioral traits to task outcomes in the evaluation of the performance of local officials, and (iii) increase of inconsistencies and hence the need for ad hoc mutual adjustments in policy making and implementation. These changes have increased interdependence and fostered greater interest convergence among local officials, thus enlarging the ground on which to promote collusive collective action. Among the opportunistic adaptations by local officials are attempts to smuggle private agenda into solutions to the problems faced by the state, to stretch the limits of the "gray area" of their decisions and actions, and to coopt potential spoilers of collusion by making them share in the spoils.

To see this development in perspective, it is necessary to take a look at the behavioral constraints faced by Party-state functionaries under the prereform system.

Mutual Monitoring under Central Planning

A little more than thirty years ago, Franz Schurmann (1968) identified two cornerstones of communist rule in China: ideology and organization. He illustrated that it was through social, political, and economic control based on indoctrination and closely knit administrative commands that the Chinese Communist Party structured a new society and led the nation in carrying out the extraordinary social engineering designed by its top leaders. Subsequent research further revealed that between ideology and organization lay another important underpinning of behavioral manipulation, that is, state-fostered interpersonal rivalry to demonstrate loyalty and commitment to the communist cause (Shirk 1982; Walder 1986). This formed a basis on which a "divide and rule" strategy was effected by various loci of state authority to induce and orchestrate mutual monitoring among organizational members, thereby containing deviant behavior.[5]

---

[5] A perverse outcome of such a strategy, however, was a broadening of the basis and scope of factional conflict, which contributed to political events like the Cultural Revolution (Lee 1978).

These behavioral control mechanisms were based on three important institutional arrangements: public ownership of economic resources, central planning, and dominance of the CCP in decision making. The elimination of private economic activities in the 1950s closed off the avenues for individuals to make an independent living and made them totally dependent on the state. The central planning system severely limited exchange relations in economic life and structured a rigid order of divisions of labor through administrative commands under a gigantic hierarchy of authority relations. This confined the choice sets of individuals to the narrow roles the state assigned them to play. The dominance of the CCP, instituted by installing a Party cell as the command center in each and every organization, gave ideological indoctrination a central place in organizational agenda and made "politically correct" behavioral traits an important element in the reward system.

As both citizens in the society and members of the state establishment to govern the society, Party-state functionaries were closely subject to the impact of these institutions. Specifically, their calculation and pursuit of self-interest were significantly conditioned by the following behavioral constraints.

First, open pursuit of self-interest was not legitimate and any trace of it had to be disguised. The root of this constraint lay in Mao's belief that the pursuit of self-interest, especially individual material gains, would jeopardize the efforts to build a socialist society (Lee 1990). The message was not only sent out and reinforced through the mass media and the educational system (Chu and Ju 1993), but built into the formal incentive system through an organizational rule that selectively rewarded "good" behavior and invariably penalized the opposite (Schurmann 1968; Walder 1986). Moreover, Mao's advocacy of an egalitarian ideology and his concern about the rise of a bureaucratic elite class led to policies that restricted income differentiation among state agents and limited the formal financial rewards associated with position advancement (Meisner 1984). During the Cultural Revolution, for example, the bonus was totally abolished and many officials were promoted to higher positions without any pay raise. This dampened the aspirations of state agents for significant improvement in their financial condition through the formal reward system.

Second, diversion of public resources for private gain was difficult because of the lack of a legitimate space for economic activities to be conducted outside the plan. Although petty privileges were derived by state agents through various forms of in-kind consumption at public expense, the magnitude was not quite significant because of their irregular nature and the limited amount of the resources involved. During the Cultural Revolution, such privileges became a major target of attack and steps were taken to close off some "loopholes" in the use of organizational resources (Lee 1978).

Third, the interdependence between subordinates and superiors was highly asymmetric, and that between peers was seriously foiled by politicized interpersonal rivalries, thus containing collusive tendencies among Party-state functionaries. The central planning system gave those at the lower rungs of authority relations little resource allocation power and hence a weak position from which to influence the decisions of higher levels. Although higher administrative levels were held responsible for the performance of their subordinate levels, long and complex decision chains made it difficult to ascertain individual responsibilities, limiting the degree of dependence of the former on the latter. Within each administrative unit, attempts to maintain positional security and to gain vertical mobility under the highly limited and politicized opportunity structure drove Party-state functionaries to compete with each other for favorable assessment of their *bianxian* (manifest behavior), which often resulted in the use of various tactics of personal attack and sabotage. Such tension and conflict were further intensified by the inconsistencies in the functions, qualifications, and evaluation criteria between political functionaries and nonpolitical functionaries (Harding 1981; Lee 1990).

Fourth, long command chains, complex decision processes, and routineness of tasks made it difficult for individual state agents to make discretionary moves and to use uncertainty to cover up hidden agenda and justify attempts to significantly redefine or reinterpret the rules of the game. The CCP and the government had two structurally separate but functionally intertwined command chains (Zheng 1997). Within the government, administrative units often were under two sets of commands, i.e., those from the local command center (known as *kuai* or horizontal piece) and those directly from a pertinent authority at a higher administrative level (known as *tiao* or vertical line) (Lieberthal 1995: 169–70; Zhu Rongji 1985). Such arrangements subjected the decisions and actions at any administrative level to the scrutiny, monitoring, and authorization of multiple authorities, limiting the span of autonomous decisions, especially those by individual decision makers.

In the face of these rigidities, the pursuit of self-interest by state agents tended to be oriented toward various strategies of self-protection, such as accumulating credit for "good" behavior, and finessing for organizational slack through bargaining or inaction. The temporal movement between administrative decentralization and recentralization might increase inconsistencies in the policy process and thus, to a certain extent, broaden the room for the use of such strategies. But it did not legitimize open pursuit of self-interest by state agents, nor did it bring about any significant change in the pattern of mutual monitoring between administrative levels, between agencies, and between decision makers within each administrative unit. Although clientelist ties of instrumental relations existed among state agents (Oi 1989a; Walder 1986), they were rendered fragile and unstable by interpersonal rivalry, especially during the Cultural Revolution. Abuse of authority and embezzlement also occurred from time to time (e.g., Liu 1983), but they were contained in scope and scale (Gong 1994; Kwong 1997; Lu 2000). It was not until the start of the reform that exchange relations began to grow on a significant scale in the political process, as illustrated by the two cases detailed below.

Basic Structures of Grassroots Governments

The two grassroots-level governments examined here are located in Lotus Pond, in the eastern part of the North China Plain, and Gate Tower, in the heart of a northeastern provincial capital. The former governs a sparsely populated rural township where the traditional dominance of agriculture in the local economy has given way to rapidly growing industry and commerce since the late 1970s. The latter administers a densely populated urban district in one of China's largest industrial centers. According to the *Organic Law of People's Congresses and Governments at Various Levels* (amended in 1982), both are the lowest level of formal government administration in China.[6] See Table 5.1.

Figures 5.1 and 5.2, based on information obtained during 1993–9, illustrate several structural similarities between the two governments. First, each governed a number of lower level jurisdictions, called villages in the case of Lotus Pond and subdistrict administrations (*jiequ* or street blocks) in the case of Gate Tower.[7] Unlike the township or district government, these lower level jurisdictions did not have an independent budget of public revenue and spending, nor did they have the authority to enact local laws and regulations.

Second, government departments were divided into two categories: those that took orders only from local government leaders (e.g., the Cultural Affairs Department), and those that took orders mainly from their corresponding supervising bodies situated at the next higher

---

[6] Because of the status of the city as a provincial capital, however, the district director had the administrative rank equivalent to that of a county magistrate instead of an ordinary township leader.
[7] Each subdistrict administration in turn governed a few hundred households placed under the purview of several neighborhood committees.

Table 5.1. *Basic indicators: Lotus Pond
township and Gate Tower district*

Indicator	Lotus Pond	Gate Tower
Population		
1985	28,780	519,993
1993	30,250	570,000
1998	30,082	592,560
Number of villages/subdistricts		
1985	28	16
1993	38	16
1998	38	16
Gross economic output (million yuan)		
1985	47	740
1993	132	1,129
1998	193	1,920
Government revenue (million yuan)		
1985	11	96
1993	28	157
1998	39	206
Number of Party-state agencies at township/district level		
1985	19	49
1993	27	59
1998	29	61
Number of Party-state functionaries at township/district level		
1985	68	742
1993	117	1,083
1998	121	998

Source: Gazetteer (1993) and annual statistical reports (various years)
of the county in which Lotus Pond is located; gazetteer (1988) and
annual statistical reports (various years) of Gate Tower district; author's
interviews (Informants no. 183/1993, no. 236/1993, no. 243/1993, no.
423/1996, no. 427/1996, no. 479/1999, no. 496/1999).

administrative level – i.e., city or county (e.g., the Tax Collection
Bureau). The personnel appointment authority over the "outpost departments" lay in their supervising bodies instead of the township or district
government, as did the appropriation of their budgetary funds, including salaries. Under this dual command structure, local officials (especially
the township or district director) had to strike a balance between decisions originating from different levels.

Third, a large and growing number of local government departments
were not fully financed with budgetary funds. A significant part of their
expenses for personnel and administrative functions came from
off-budget funds. In Lotus Pond only less than 40% of the staff in the

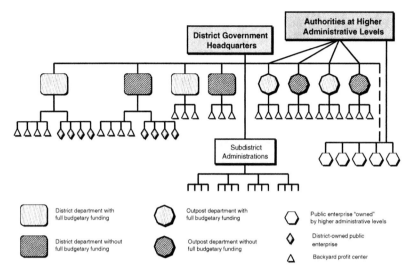

Figure 5.1: Organizational structure of district government in Gate Tower.

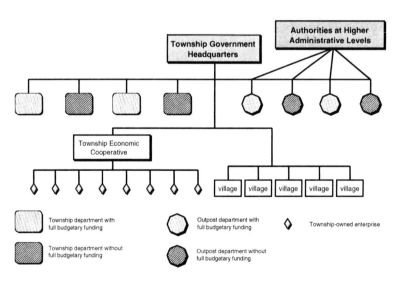

Figure 5.2: Organizational structure of township government in Lotus Pond.

township government were on budget-funded payroll. In Gate Tower, 11 (out of 61) government departments were totally financed with off-budget funds after 1987.

Fourth, those who commanded the headquarters of the two local governments – i.e., the Party secretary, the deputy Party secretary, the director, and the deputy directors – all had transient tenures. They were rotated every few years between different districts or townships. Some of them were transferred or even promoted to posts in city or county government departments, but few were promoted from within the local government. Their careers and financial rewards were closely tied to the fulfillment of the targets set by the city or county with regard to local social and economic development (e.g., tax revenue, employment, education, crime controls, etc.). The heads of the outpost departments in the district and township were also rotated regularly. Their performance, though, was evaluated mainly according to the narrower criteria used by their corresponding supervising agencies in the city or county government. Altogether, these most mobile officials accounted for 5–7% of the local government personnel. On the other hand, the overwhelming majority of the local Party-state functionaries had no career prospect beyond the district or township. Their mobility (if any) was confined to local departments, where promotion opportunities were limited by the several rounds of campaigns to downsize government establishment during the reform.

But there were some important differences between the two local governments. The district government of Gate Tower was much larger in size and involved a greater degree of divisions of labor among various functional departments than the township government of Lotus Pond. Also, public enterprises "owned" by the district government in Gate Tower were controlled by a number of local state agencies (e.g., the Industry Department, the Commerce Department, the Civil Administration Department, etc.), and there were a number of public enterprises that were located in the district but "owned" by higher level jurisdictions. In contrast, all township enterprises in Lotus Pond were controlled by a single authority called the Township Economic Cooperative.[8] Moreover, under each government agency in Gate Tower, there were several backyard profit centers, whose origins dated back to the mid-1980s. There were no such

---

[8] The Township Economic Cooperative was headed by a deputy township director. It ran all the township enterprises, managed a township cooperative fund, provided a wide range of economic services to villages and villagers (such as input supply, irrigation, technical support, equipment maintenance, information, sales of products, etc.), and coordinated and regulated collective economic activities at the village level, including record keeping, accounting, use of village funds, and enforcement of economic contracts (especially those concerning the farmland contracted to peasants).

entities in Lotus Pond. As will be shown below, these differences had a direct bearing on the varying ways in which the interests of local state agents were accommodated as well as on the varying effects of local state action on industrial firms.

Growth of Exchange Relations

Since the late 1970s the governments in Lotus Pond and Gate Tower have undergone changes similar to those in other locales – namely, depoliticization of decision-making agenda, decline of the plan amidst marketization, and decentralization. With these processes unfolding, many of the conditions that contained exchange relations among Party-state functionaries before the reform have been gradually weakened, opening up opportunities for local officials to redefine the scope and content of their agenda and decisions.

Enhanced Interdependence and Give-and-Take in Ad Hoc Contracting

A central institutional arrangement developed in the reform era is the adoption of a contract system (known as *chengbao zhi* in Chinese) governing the relationship between various parties in economic and (governmental) administrative activities. There are two types of contractual arrangements within the state apparatus: revenue contracts between different levels of government and spending contracts between the fiscal authority and other government agencies.

What a contract signifies is a relationship of exchange, centered around an agreement on the demarcation of rights and obligations between the parties involved. The common feature of these contracts is a negotiated formula for the calculation and determination of expenditure and revenue or public service objectives to which the contracting parties are bound, and a term regarding the distribution of funds, including the division and use of above-target surplus. This represents a major departure from the command hierarchy of the prereform system. A commonly binding term is now set between administrative superiors and subordinates, whose relationship increasingly gravitates from patronage toward partnership. Also, an incentive element is introduced to tie the outcome of economic and state actions to the rewards and latitude of the action takers. With the expansion of the scope of the contract system, *exclusive* areas of discretionary decisions and actions have also grown at subordinate administrative units. What this has led to is an increase of interdependence between different contracting parties, a reconfiguration of the interest structure of local officials, and an erosion of rigid authority relations in the allocation of resources and the coordination and regulation of economic activities. All this provides conditions conducive to the growth of exchange relations between the principals representing different contracting units.

Revenue Contract. Before the reform, the *tongshou tongzhi* (unified control of revenue and spending) system left little discretionary resources for lower level governments. In both Lotus Pond and Gate Tower, fiscal control lay entirely in the hands of the county or city government which extracted all the revenue from the commune or district, reviewed the spending needs of the commune or district, and appropriated annual expenditures. Because of the lack of a close link between revenue and spending and between the fulfillment of budgetary targets and the rewards to local officials, the fiscal control system provided little incentive for the local governments to maximize revenue. Creating and maintaining fiscal slack became a commonly used strategy (Informants no. 296/1994, no. 302/1995, no. 337/1996).

In 1980 and 1986, respectively, the local governments of Gate Tower and Lotus Pond were granted independent budgetary authority. This move was accompanied by the adoption of a revenue contract with the city or county government and the establishment of a local finance agency to draft budgets, review spending, and administer and supervise the daily use of government resources. What the local government was expected to do was to make sure that the revenue targets, mainly in the form of taxes, were met. Under the new system, there was a division between local taxes and taxes belonging to higher levels. But this distinction was less important than the total amount of the tax target for each year, since most taxes (except for the agricultural tax and some fees) were collected by the tax bureau, which was directly controlled by its supervising body at the city or county level. The role of the local governments was to facilitate this collection, and make sure that the tax base was well maintained.

The main spirit of the revenue contract between the grassroots level (township or district) of government and the higher level (county or city) was that a fixed amount of revenue estimated on the basis of the previous year's revenue figures was required of the latter. If a surplus was generated above the target, it would be shared by the two levels of government. Also, appropriation for spending at the lower level was tied to revenue – though not proportionally – and specified in the contract as well. Moreover, the local authority was given greater autonomy in making use of both annual budgetary appropriation and its share in surplus revenue which constituted a major source of bonus funds for local government employees.

Under the new system, the careers of local officials, especially top leaders, were closely tied to the fulfillment of the contract, which served as the main basis of performance evaluation and held the key to positional security and vertical mobility for top officials. In Gate Tower, of the five district directors appointed during 1985–93, three who fulfilled the revenue contract well were promoted to higher positions in the city government; in Lotus Pond, the number was four out of six (Informants no. 295/1994, no. 303/1995). Financially, local government leaders would be better off if the revenue contract were fulfilled or overfulfilled, which could bring to top township or district officials a year-end bonus, authorized by higher level authorities, on top of the regular bonus that they received with other local government employees. In Lotus Pond, for example, the year-end bonus for the three top leaders (the Party secretary, the township director, and the head of the Township Economic Cooperative) was more than half of their annual salary in 1993 (Informants no. 306/1995, no. 320/1995).

In response to these incentives, leading officials in Gate Tower and Lotus Pond adopted measures aimed at enlarging the tax revenue base of the local government during their tenures. A common strategy they pursued was to create or expand the production capacity of local public (mainly collective) enterprises and to promote their sales, as the bulk of the local budgetary revenue came from transaction taxes based on sales volume. From the mid-1980s to the mid-1990s, district and township leaders pressured local bank branches to extend loans to support such expansionary growth.[9]

But there was a twist here. Under the revenue-sharing arrangement, the more the township or district government overfulfilled the revenue target specified in the contract, the more was taken away by higher level authorities in absolute terms. To prevent "excessive contributions" to higher administrative levels, leaders of both localities sought to keep a limit on the degree of contract overfulfillment so they could retain as

---

[9] The strategy was rather effective in the mid to late 1980s, when market demand for many basic products remained strong and most state enterprises were still bound by the plan. Yet it encountered increasing difficulties in the 1990s, when competition intensified and the cost of borrowing increased. As a result, many local public enterprises accumulated large amounts of debt as well as excess production capacity. The two local governments had to rely increasingly on alternative sources of revenue, especially taxes and levies on private economic entities, to fulfil the revenue contract, bail out over-expanded enterprises, and finance daily operations of the local government. [Nationwide, the share of private enterprises in the total taxes paid by rural enterprises to the government increased from 21% in 1985 to 45% in 1998 (ZGXZQYNJBJWYH 1989: 569; 1999: 111).] In Chapter 7 I will discuss the moral hazard embodied in this short-term maximizing strategy, as well as its perverse effects, especially the intensification of predatory actions taken by local officials on less favored parties.

much surplus as possible at their own discretion. When it was clear that the revenue contract could be overfulfilled, they granted certain enterprises a temporary tax reduction known as *qianshui* or uncollected taxes owed to the government. The enterprises receiving the reduction could use the uncollected amount for their own operations, but it was subject to later collection or to partial extraction through nontax channels, such as various ad hoc fees (which belonged to the collecting authority) and covert payments. In both Gate Tower and Lotus Pond, for example, top local officials' trips abroad and local entertainment expenses were chiefly financed with such funds, and the providers of the "reimbursement service" were mostly enterprises whose leaders had a close personal relationship with (top) local officials (Informants no. 278/1994, no. 291/1994, no. 403/1996).

Along with the delegation of authority in revenue retention and spending under the revenue contract system the township or district government was granted greater authority over the organization and management of its revenue base, including the authority to approve or directly invest in new projects, to establish and regulate locally based enterprises, and to formulate local regulations. But this was not a process without strings attached. In Gate Tower, for example, what the city government was most willing to delegate were the burdens it did not want to bear. In the late 1970s, the city government took over the control and revenue rights of 141 industrial enterprises set up by the district government and subdistrict administrations. In 1992, 50 of these enterprises, most of which were in the red, were given back to the district. In other areas, in the mid-1980s the city government delegated those authorities that were too costly or too difficult to enforce (due to limited staff in the city government and a heavy workload), such as environmental protection, road services, and safety inspection.

But the district government did not simply take what it was given. It turned the burden shed from higher levels into an opportunity for expanding existing regulatory authority. In the case of the 50 industrial enterprises, for example, the district government bargained for and pushed through more flexible measures to manage them, including leasing and selling out some of them to generate off-budget revenue. The district government also gained the authority to modify rules adopted by the city as well as latitude in setting aside as bonus funds for the enforcement agencies part of the proceeds (e.g., fines) resulting from regulatory enforcement.

Spending Contract. A major legacy of the Mao era was a growing imbalance between limited budgetary resources and funding for large numbers of items and projects. This resulted in a large budget deficit in 1979. To maintain the operation of the state apparatus under increasing financial strain, in 1979 the Ministry of Finance introduced a provisional administrative expenditure contract system (*xingzheng kaizhi baogan zhi*) for Party and government agencies (Chen Rulong 1988, vol. 1: 300). It placed a cap on the spending of various agencies while granting them more leeway in the disposal of any budgetary surplus they could save, thus opening a gate for discretionary use of public resources. At the same time, all the nonprofit and nonregulatory units (namely, *shiye danwei*) were urged by the central authority to explore ways of self-financing, thereby reducing the burden on fiscal allocation.

Government agencies in Lotus Pond and Gate Tower adopted the administrative expenditure contract system in the mid-1980s. The main authority formulating and enforcing the contract was the local Finance Department. Despite the increase of budgetary funds authorized by higher level authorities in both localities under the revenue contract system, the growth in the number of government personnel and in administrative expenses outpaced that of budgetary funds. The need to reduce this gap provided a basis on which to justify an increase in off-budget revenue, which could be extensively used by local officials for self-defined purposes.

In Lotus Pond, the budgetary fund covered only the basic salaries of less than half of the township government personnel. All the units under the Economic Cooperative that provided services to rural economic activities (such as seeds, irrigation, agricultural machinery) were made self-financed profit centers. Their revenue, along with that from township enterprises and a cooperative fund (see discussion below), provided for the salaries of their staff and contributed to the pool of "self-raised" funds at the disposal of the township government. It was from that pool that the bonuses for the budget-funded personnel, including all top township leaders, were paid.

In 1992, the township government constructed a new office building. All the money needed was drawn from the self-raised funds in the Township Cooperative Fund, which also provided for the expenses for travel, socializing (*shejiao*), long-distance phone calls, entertainment, and accommodation for guests incurred by township officials. Monitoring by the fiscal authority at the county level mainly focused on budgetary expenditure under the spending contract. Given the legitimate purposes of some of the Fund's uses and given the fact that it was not allocated through budgetary channels but actually served as a primary supplementary source of budgetary allocation, the county government condoned the latitude of the township government in the management and utilization of the Fund so as not to weaken the incentive for township officials to maintain and expand this increasingly indispensable pillar of township finance (Informants no. 270/1994, no. 282/1994). Few people in the township government knew the actual size of the Fund, as some of the money was held in the accounts of the economic units and enterprises under the Economic Cooperative. According to a top township official, it was greater than the budgetary fund allocated to the township each year (Informant no. 275/1994).

The problem of a shortage in budgetary funds was more serious in Gate Tower, where the government was stretched out more extensively because of its size and the relatively more complex functions that it carried out. As the government grew in the reform, per capita distribution of funds in state agencies could not keep pace with the rate of inflation (Informant no. 409/1996). Increasingly, the *shiye danwei* (non-administrative units) under the district government became a burden. To address the problem, starting from the mid-1980s, the district government spun off large numbers of these agencies as self-financed units. In addition, while capping the spending by other government agencies, in 1987 the district government set aside eleven department-level agencies as completely self-financed units.[10] The budget funds requested through the Finance Department for these agencies were then turned into off-budget funds and transferred to other uses at the discretion of district leaders. To make sure that the allocation of funds for these agencies be continued in the annual spending budget authorized by the city government, the Finance Department first allocated the annual allotments to the accounts of these agencies and then transferred the fund back as "surplus" for redistribution.

The financial needs of the self-financed agencies were instead met by management fees from the enterprises that they supervised, including those that they set up entirely for this purpose, and by the fees generated from enforcing regulatory functions. The Economic Planning Commission, for example, was granted the authority to collect a management fee from enterprises run by subdistrict administrations, which were in return given greater authority in making use of the revenues they could generate. Also, the Commission was given the authority to approve the registration of new motor vehicles, which was a locally added regulatory requirement in the name of controlling pollution and traffic congestion. Part (30%) of the registration fee was kept by the Commission as revenue. In 1991, the budget fund nominally

---

[10] They included the Economic Planning Commission, the Labor Department, the Cultural Affairs Bureau, the Industrial Material Department, the Industry Department, the Commerce Department, the Price Control Department, the Fund Management Department, the Urban Construction Bureau, the Tertiary Sector Office, and the Foreign Economic Relations Committee.

allocated to the Commission (and then transferred back as "surplus") was 98,000 yuan, whereas the revenue that it generated from various fees under the self-financing scheme totaled 658,000 yuan. The disparity between the two figures explains why the Commission was willing to be fully self-financed.

As for the agencies and departments that were partially self-financed (i.e., only the fund for the basic salaries of those on budgetary payroll was allocated), the district government granted them permission to find other ways to supplement their spending. This resulted in the establishment of large numbers of profit-seeking entities under the auspices of various departments and agencies. By 1993, every department or agency in the district government had set up and run such entities. Their number was estimated to be in the order of 400 to 500 (Informants no. 272/1993, no. 296/1993).

The implementation of the revenue and spending contracts in Lotus Pond and Gate Tower suggests that the driving forces behind the behavior of local officials may be more diverse than the formal financial and career rewards associated with local governments' "public" agenda – fulfilling tax obligations to higher level authorities and providing public goods and services to the local community. The strategy to contain the level of above-target budgetary revenue (taxes) while maximizing off-budget revenue indicates that local officials were much more interested in generating funds that they could use in a discretionary fashion.[11] This limited the growth of the budgetary resources used under close fiscal monitoring, and signified a growth of informal incentives in the local fiscal process.

Whether or not the decisions and actions of local officials have led to optimal improvement in the provision of public goods and services is also in question. From 1987 to 1994, for example, the total spending by Lotus Pond's township government on local education, health care, and infrastructural facilities increased at an average annual rate of 3.4%. But during the same period, local government expenditure increased at an average annual rate of 7.6%; and the average annual growth rate of local government administrative and personnel expenses was 19% (Informants no. 297/1995, no. 304/1995). The disparity in fund allocation suggests that the priority of allocative decisions tilted toward items that brought more direct benefits to local officials. Note

---

[11] Nationwide, from 1986 to 1995 total revenue from all sources reported by township governments increased from 7.73 billion yuan to 102.1 billion yuan. In 1986 off-budget revenue was equivalent to about 20% of budgetary revenue; in 1995, the figure rose to 60%, registering a significant difference in the rate of growth between the two categories (ZGXZQYNJBJWYH 1994: 466; 1996: 544).

that these spending figures do not yet include the pockets of funds "deposited" in township enterprises and used by township officials for self-defined purposes.

Expanding the Gray Area of State Action

The reform in China is a trial-and-error process in which decisions become diffused, uncertainties grow, and new contingencies and problems arise. As various reform programs are introduced at different levels and modified in ways that vary across jurisdictions and over time, coordination and integration of actions become increasingly difficult. This not only creates new opportunities for state agents to bend and redefine the rules of the game and shape its outcomes to their own advantage, but also leaves open greater space where justification can be fabricated to legitimize the pursuit of such opportunities. The efforts to twist and eventually change the rules of the game are often referred to as *biantong* (bending the rules to get through). Here are some examples from the two local governments.

In Lotus Pond, the predecessor of the township government was the headquarters of a people's commune governing several production brigades, which in turn ran several production teams. When the people's commune was abolished in 1983, the collective assets of the production brigades and production teams under the commune were disposed of by rural cadres. Some embezzled collective assets as their own, others divided such assets and distributed or loaned them to peasants. To restore financial order, the county government required the newly formed township government to carry out a series of measures recommended by the Ministry of Agriculture. They were called *qingchan hezi, qingcai shouqian, yiqian zhuandai*, meaning "stocktaking collective assets," "verifying and collecting debts owed to the collective," and "turning such debts into loans."

In order for the collective assets to be restored and managed, an administrative instrument had to be instituted. This led to the creation of a cooperative fund in each village (the former site of the production brigade). But the need to reconstruct the books due to the loss of old records and the lack of sufficient and competent accounting personnel at the village level posed a problem to the management of these village funds. As a solution, the township government set up, under the Township Economic Cooperative, an umbrella organization called the Township Cooperative Fund, providing services in record keeping, accounting, and fund management. Under this arrangement, all villages became members of the township fund in which they were required to deposit all their cash assets. Items that entered the fund included the cash possessions inherited from the people's commune, the land-contracting fees paid by peasants to the village, the management fees of village enterprises, the land use fees paid to the village by nonfarm land users, and the various surcharges collected by villages.

Soon after the formation of the Township Cooperative Fund, it became evident to the township leaders that the pooled resources had the potential of being turned into financial capital. But in China rural credit was monopolized by the Agricultural Bank and its subsidiary the Rural Credit Cooperative.[12] Deposit taking and lending activities by any other organizations were banned. To tap the potential gains from lending, the township turned the fund into a "shareholding" pool and solicited, through village officials, subscriptions from individual peasants. Those who joined could get a year-end dividend at a rate of return 20% higher than the interest rate for savings in the Agricultural Bank. Labeling the fund a truly voluntary collective organization with participation by peasants and aimed at serving peasants through resource sharing, township leaders found a legitimate cover under which to absorb savings from peasants and lend out money for a profit.

In 1993, the size of the fund reached 10 million yuan, 80% of which was made up of subscriptions from peasants. Despite its claim to be an organization serving agriculture, nearly 90% of its lending actually went to nonagricultural activities. It was the largest pool of financial resources under the discretion of the township leaders, who determined who should get how much from the fund and on what terms. Like the Township Economic Cooperative, it assumed tax-exempt status, and contributed 5% of its revenue to the Cooperative as a management fee (which, as indicated above, was a major source of supplementary income of township officials). By law it was neither legal nor illegal,[13] but with

---

[12] In 1998 the Rural Credit Cooperative was delinked from the Agricultural Bank to become a separate financial institution directly regulated by the People's Bank.

[13] This undertaking would have been impossible, however, without the blessing of the county government. Lotus Pond was not the only township that set up such cooperative funds. Since the county government itself also wanted to find a way to tap the growing rural surplus and establish a locally controlled financial resource base outside the banking system, it backed the efforts of township leaders to develop the cooperative fund from an instrument to manage collective assets into a financial institution competing with the centrally controlled state banks. In 1987, the county was selected by the Ministry of Agriculture as a site for experiments in new institutional designs for the rural economy in the postdecollectivization era. Although rural finance was not on the initial agenda set by the Ministry, county leaders seized the opportunity to push for its inclusion on the grounds that development of a cooperative fund could be a way for the "collective" spirit of peasants to be restored and promoted (Informant no. 295/1994). In 1988, a county cooperative fund was set up to coordinate the operations of township funds. This gave instant recognition to the status of various township funds

shrewd maneuvering local officials nevertheless managed to make it survive and grow.[14]

In Gate Tower, as the size of the extra-budgetary revenue of different government agencies grew during the reform (it reached 25 million yuan in 1985, an equivalent of 54% of the budgetary revenue of the district government that year) (Informant no. 408/1996), the district government set up a Fund Management Bureau in 1987 to monitor the use of such revenue. Various government agencies were required to deposit their extra-budgetary revenues in a designated account of the bureau and seek its authorization for major spending items. Initially, the bureau was given a very lean budget to run its operation. But it soon discovered that the idle fund deposited in its account could be turned into loans for a profit. It pressed ahead in this direction and earned more than it received from budgetary allocation. Seeing this as a "one stone, two birds" solution, the district government withdrew its budgetary funding for the agency and made it a self-financed unit (*zishou zizhi danwei*) (Informant no. 411/1996).

Like those of the Cooperative Fund in Lotus Pond, its lending activities were not authorized by the banking regulations. But with the backing of the district government – in the name of "experimenting with new measures of administrative reform" – they were carried out. In fact, the Fund Management Bureau was not the only agency engaged in lending activities. The Auditing Bureau also made use of the fund temporarily frozen for its review for profit-oriented lending in order to "alleviate the inadequacy of budgetary funds"; and under the same cover many sub-district administrations issued internal bonds to raise funds from their subsidiary enterprises and staff and loaned out the money for a profit (Informant no. 409/1996).

The boldest move by the district government to bend the existing rules was a series of measures that it adopted in 1992 and 1993 that openly encouraged Party-state functionaries to leave their current posts and run profit-making entities, resulting in a proliferation of backyard profit centers. Streamlining government administration through downsizing was

---

and, because of the tie with the centrally sponsored experiment program, provided a shield against the challenge from state banks. Under the new arrangement, township governments continued to have full autonomy in raising and utilizing the funds under their auspices.

[14] In the spring of 1999 the central authority ordered a crackdown on these kinds of funds, demanding that they be merged into the Rural Credit Cooperative. The subsequent cleanup campaign that the county government was required to carry out revealed massive amounts of "bad loans" extended by township cooperative funds, including that in Lotus Pond (Informants no. 486/1999, no. 492/1999). For a discussion of the moral hazard problem leading to this, see Chapter 7.

cited as the main reason. By spinning off more government agencies as self-financed units and trimming the number of government personnel, the district leaders could spare more resources for alternative uses (including their pet projects) and vent the pressures from below for budgetary allocation (Informants no. 402/1996, no. 411/1996).

In the opening statements of the documents drafted for this purpose, Deng Xiaoping's 1992 speech (during his southern tour) calling for an acceleration of reform was prominently mentioned. Government agencies were also urged to provide support for the initial operation of the spin-off organizations. With the green light from the district authority, some government agencies went ahead to invent rules that facilitated their profit-making activities. The Labor Department, a self-financed unit, for example, demanded that newly hired, nonproduction staff in state and urban collective enterprises be trained at a vocational training course that it offered for a fee. Enterprises could not obtain permits for enlarging their workforce unless the new hires had certificates from the training course.

It is important to note that although part of the off-budget funds generated by the above agencies was used to finance their regular administrative functions, the bulk of the funds became discretionary resources used for other purposes defined by the leaders of the agencies (Informants no. 409/1996, no. 411/1996, no. 412/1996). Also, as the uses of such funds were not subject to close monitoring by the fiscal authority, what was meant by "regular administrative functions" became a fuzzy category.[15]

Sharing the Spoils: Co-Optation of Potential Spoilers

Before the reform, open pursuit of self-interest through collective action among Party-state functionaries was severely constrained by an institutional arrangement called the dual command chain between the Party and the government, as discussed above. Because of the emphasis on politically defined behavioral conformity in performance evaluation and the reward system, and because of the differences in professional qualifications and functional orientation between political and nonpolitical

---

[15] A division head that I interviewed in Gate Tower, for example, drove an Audi and carried a mobile phone. Both were provided by his agency for his unlimited use. A few days before my meeting with him, he had just driven back with his family from a vacation trip to the seaside city Dalian. The costs for the car, insurance, registration, inspection, driving lessons and license, maintenance and repair, parking, gasoline, tolls, and even traffic fines, plus those for the phone set and phone bill, were all paid for from the department's off-budget account for his "public" functions.

functionaries, there was a deep division of interests among state agents. The resultant interpersonal rivalries provided a major fulcrum with which to enforce a checks-and-balances mechanism of behavioral control through "divide and rule."

During the reform, the decline of the communist ideology and the shift of the focus of state action to economic development rendered redundant the political role of the Communist Party. In a report compiled by the central office of the city's CCP Committee in 1992, for example, the Gate Tower district was praised for making three major changes in its efforts to promote economic development: emphasizing the provision of service to the economy over the composition of the leadership team per se, emphasizing actual work results over the merits and shortcomings of individual officials, and emphasizing the actual contribution to the economy over the potentials and abilities of officials. Also, the main criteria used by the district in evaluating officials were recommended to other city districts. They included (i) coordination ability, (ii) expertise in administrative work, (iii) ability to support superiors, (iv) age, and (v) education. None of these has anything to do with political loyalty and ideological commitment.

But the Party has continued to function in the decision-making and implementation process of the state. In Lotus Pond, for example, a 1986 reform to separate the Party from the government resulted in a division of administrative work among the Party secretary, the township director, and one of the deputy Party secretaries. Although the interdependence between political and nonpolitical functionaries in the state apparatus has increased as the result of a shift in the basis of their financial and career rewards from individual behavioral traits toward the outcome of their collective administrative actions, this does not necessarily clear the way for self-seeking behavior. Interpersonal rivalries and factional divisions remain relevant factors in organizational relations despite the fading of the significance of political qualifications in the reward system, whereas whistle-blowing still offers an alternative for the advancement of self-interest. Both conditions pose a risk to attempts at trespassing. Moreover, taking unauthorized or illicit actions to realize or maximize the collective gains for interdependent actors often requires collusion from additional parties in the local state apparatus. Therefore, in order for exchange relations to thrive in the political process, active efforts must be made not only to cultivate and expand common ground among state agents but to co-opt potential spoilers.

In Lotus Pond, the annual bonus for top Party functionaries (the secretary and deputy secretary) was the same as that of the township director. Township leaders also paid special attention to the interests of outpost agencies like the Tax Collection Office and the Finance Office (until 1995, when it was changed from an "outpost" agency to an agency under the direct control of the township government). The measure taken by the township government to contain the degree of overfulfilling the revenue contract by not requiring some township enterprises to pay their taxes in full, described above, entailed at least tacit consent from both agencies. Although their budgets and personnel were not controlled by the township government, township leaders set up a special monthly allowance for their staff. It was paid out of the self-raised fund in the Township Economic Cooperative, and distributed to the staff of the agencies under various names during different seasons, such as an allowance for the Chinese New Year (*guonian fei*) in the spring, a subsidy for high temperature (*gaowen butie*) in the summer, a subsidy for busy work in the harvest season (*nongmang butie*) in the fall, and heating subsidies (*qunuan fei*) in the winter (Informant no. 295/1994).

In Gate Tower, similar strategies were used for co-optation. The staff quarters and the office building of the Tax Collection Bureau were both built by the district government using its off-budget resources, the cars of bureau leaders were provided by the district government, and the children of the bureau's staff attended the best schools in the district free of charge (Informant no. 202/1993). In 1990, the district set up a Foreign Economic Relations Committee to coordinate and promote externally oriented economic activities. In view of the fact that the district government was not authorized to engage in import and export directly, the Committee's import and export office teamed up with the Import and Export Company under the city's Commission on Foreign Economic Relations, becoming a subsidiary of that organization and paying it a management fee with part of the proceeds from direct foreign trade. To prevent this arrangement from being vetoed by the foreign trade authorities at higher levels, it set up an advisory board and invited 14 "leading officials" from the city and the province to become (paid) board members (Informant no. 222/1993).

In both Lotus Pond and Gate Tower, it was common practice that when a guest was treated to dinner by a leader of a government agency, large numbers of other, seemingly irrelevant people from that agency also showed up at the dinner table. One may interpret this simply as a way for those people to wine and dine free of charge. But there may be more to it. According to an accountant in the government of Lotus Pond who was a frequent banquet-goer (Informant no. 296/1994):

> It is not that we are so greedy as to attend each and every of these events. In fact, oftentimes it's physically very demanding, considering the fact that drinking contests have become a ritual. By making sure that many colleagues are present at the banquet,

the chief is not only justified in having the bill reimbursed but shows good will to us and clears himself of any future accusations of wrong-doing.

In Gate Tower, a large part of the revenue contributed by backyard profit centers to their sponsoring agencies was distributed among agency employees as communal benefits, such as housing, bonuses, and other subsidies,[16] despite the fact that not all the staff in those agencies were actively involved in running those entities (Informants no. 409/1996, no. 411/1996, no. 418/1996). Said a division head (Informant no. 430/1996):

> Well, we want to improve the welfare of our staff in the first place. . . . Besides, the fact that they know or know about such operations means that they are entitled to something from them. Otherwise, they may create trouble.

Mechanisms at Work

We can summarize what has been discussed above as follows. A high degree of shared interests among officials, broad grounds of justification for self-seeking behavior, and effective co-optation of potential spoilers are important conditions for the growth of exchange relations within the state apparatus. Before the reform, the lack of these conditions limited the scope and magnitude of exchange relations, sustaining authority relations as the modus operandi of state action. What set in motion the changes in the post-Mao era were the partial reforms to address certain imperative problems (e.g., budgetary shortfalls) faced by the state. But it is the self-interested, adaptive, and interactive behavior of local officials that has shaped the orientation of the process of change and carried it through.

This account brings additional light to the picture presented by the local development state perspective, which focuses on the institutional incentives engendered in the decentralization of authority relations. What I have sought to illustrate here are the opportunistic adaptations by local officials to overcome the institutional constraints on their discretionary power by enlarging the space for exchange relations to grow in the political process. The various contractual arrangements developed in the state apparatus were intended to rationalize control with incentives for administrative efficiency and revenue increase. Yet the resultant *exclusive* domains of decisions and actions have been expanded far

---

[16] The distribution of the benefits based on off-budget funds need not, however, be equal among all members of an agency (Informants no. 361/1996, no. 377/1996).

beyond the monitoring capacity of the system, and the self-seeking behavior of local officials in such domains has been fortified by strategies to fabricate justification and co-opt potential saboteurs.

Thus, decentralization in the reform is not simply a shift of the locus of authority, but a process in which monitoring has been seriously weakened between different administrative levels, between agencies, and between state agents. The motivating forces of the decisions and actions of local officials come not only from the financial and career rewards offered by the formal institutional incentives, but from the opportunities and gains from various forms of exchange among themselves. Despite the "public" image of the local state under which such interaction takes place, one should not lose sight of the private (individual or collective) agenda embedded in its drivers and outcomes. In fact, it is precisely because of the rise and deliberate promotion of the opportunities to blur the boundaries between "public" and "private" that local officials have strengthened their ability to justify their self-seeking behavior under legitimate covers.[17]

This being said, it should be noted that the growth of exchange relations in the political process has been a gradual and uneven process. In both Lotus Pond and Gate Tower, for example, officials interviewed in the mid-1990s indicated that in the mid-1980s they had been much more preoccupied with fulfillment of revenue contract objectives and implementation of other agenda from higher administrative levels, and more hesitant at open pursuit of self-defined agenda and involvement in entrepreneurial activities (Informants no. 337/1994, no. 351/1995, no. 396/1996, no. 398/1996). This earlier behavioral pattern can also be found in a study, based primarily on research in the 1980s, of a county government a few hundred kilometers away from Lotus Pond (Blecher and Shue 1996). It contrasts, however, with findings from studies based on data collected in the 1990s in economically more developed areas (e.g., Duckett 1998; Wank 1999), which indicate active and bold involvement of officials in profit making and favor exchange. It seems that several developments between the mid-1980s and the mid-1990s may have contributed to such a behavioral orientation. They include: worsening budgetary shortfalls (Wang 1995), growing uncertainties and inconsistencies in the policy process (Shirk 1993), intensification of a sense of relative deprivation among government officials in the face of faster growth of income and wealth for many economic actors – especially in economically prosperous

---

[17] This view also contrasts with Duckett's argument that entrepreneurial activities pursued by state agencies promote departmental interests by providing supplementary resources for personnel and administrative spending, thereby contributing to the provision of public goods and services (1998).

areas,[18] and massive replacement of old, ideologically more committed cadres by younger, pragmatic technocrats (Lee 1990). A hypothesis that can be tested to account for spatial and temporal variations is that the more these conditions are present, the more likely the mechanisms discerned above are brought into full play for the development of a political market under the local state.

Structural Variations

For industrial firms, the most immediate implication of the weakening of constraints on officials' self-seeking behavior is that the influence of particularistic state action on the distribution of advantages and disadvantages has become more fluid, increasingly individualized, and locally grounded. The mechanisms of political marketization in Lotus Pond and Gate Tower were similar, but there were important differences in the way local officials' interests were accommodated through exchange relations, and in the evolving milieu where exchange took place between local officials and outside favor seekers.

The first difference has to do with the locus of local officials' interests.[19] In Gate Tower, local public enterprises were not controlled by a single authority, but placed under the purview of a number of government departments, such as the Industry Department, the Commerce Department, and the Civil Administration Department. The revenues of these enterprises constituted the main base of the district government's tax obligation to higher level authorities. Under the revenue contract adopted in the reform, fulfillment of the tax target would help the district government secure approval for requested budget expenditures and bring financial and career benefits to district leaders as well as to the officials in the supervising agencies of local public enterprises. But the incentive for other government agencies was limited to providing a stable basis for fixed amounts of budgetary allocation. Officials in such agencies did

---

[18] See note 29 of Chapter 4.
[19] Two factors may have contributed to this difference: history and structure. Most township enterprises in Lotus Pond were formed in the reform era, but the majority of the public enterprises in Gate Tower and their administrative affiliations were inherited from the central planning system. Entrenchment of pre-existing regulations and departmental interests posed a major obstacle to the consolidation of control authority. Moreover, the size (hence the degree of division of labor) of the local government in Gate Tower was much larger than that in Lotus Pond. This not only affected the effectiveness of coordination of decisions and actions, especially those with regard to the accumulation and discretionary use of resources under different departments. It also added to the difficulty of balancing budgetary allocation among various administrative units, driving them to search for ways to expand their off-budget resource pools.

not get an extra bonus or nonpecuniary credit for the fulfillment of the revenue contract.

On the other hand, backyard profit centers were widely formed *outside* the formal organizational structure of the local state and extensively used to make collective and individual financial gains for the officials in their sponsoring agencies. Many of them used their authority and diverted resources to promote the growth of backyard profit centers.[20] This not only posed competitive pressures to local public enterprises in input supplies and output sales, as discussed in the preceding chapter. It also intensified the tendency of local officials, especially those not in charge of local public enterprises, to prey on the latter through various ad hoc levies or coerced transactions with their backyard profit centers.[21] Dispersion of the loci of authority in the district, divergence of interests, and difficulty in interagency coordination all made it difficult to curb the adverse effect of such predatory actions on local enterprises.

In contrast, the main avenue for officials in Lotus Pond to accommodate their interests lay *within* the formal organizational structure of the local government. As noted above, all the township enterprises were placed under the control of a single agency – the Township Economic Cooperative. Taxes paid by these enterprises constituted a major revenue target in the revenue contract between the township and the county government.[22] There were no separate profit-seeking entities under other township government departments. According to a top township official (Informant no. 297/1994), this consolidation of control was intended to concentrate resources where they could be best used.[23] Headed by a deputy township director, the Township Economic Cooperative managed township enterprises through various managerial contracts, ran a township cooperative fund, and provided various agricultural services to

[20] In the early 1990s, for example, even those in charge of local public enterprises diverted large sums of budgetary funds to real estate development projects undertaken by their backyard profit centers (Informants no. 328/1993, no. 366/1996).

[21] See, for example, the case of Elegance Furniture discussed in the preceding chapter.

[22] It is important to note that this course of more concerted collective action among local officials in Lotus Pond followed the same logic as the divergent strategies pursued by local officials in Gate Tower. That is, while performing the "public" functions of the state, local state agents sought to use their authority to accommodate their self-interest in a changing political process where traditional constraints on such a pursuit were increasingly weakened by the growth of exchange relations. What led to the different manifestations of this logic in the two locales were the varying degrees of difficulty in aligning the interest of local officials and confining the accommodation of self-interest to a common source. In Lotus Pond, overcoming this difficulty was facilitated by the small size of the local government and, relatedly, by effective use of administrative power to contain alternative self-seeking strategies.

[23] Physically, all the departments of the township government were housed in a three-story building.

villages. The management fees from township enterprises entered the cooperative fund, which was categorized as an off-budget fund and not subject to close monitoring by the fiscal authority. The fund provided for the salaries of over half the staff in the township government as well as the bonuses for all township government employees. It was also the main source for the expense accounts of top township officials and for the reimbursement of the entertainment expenses of various township government departments.

Another difference between the two locales concerns the spatial character of the public enterprises under the purview of the local government. In Gate Tower, a large number of the public enterprises located in the district were "owned" not by the district authority, but by the city, provincial, or central government.[24] Under China's fiscal regulation (Xiang Huaicheng and Jiang Weizhuang 1992), the main stream of revenue (i.e., income tax, management fees, and since 1994 part of the value-added tax) of a public enterprise goes to the level of its principal supervising authority. This seriously limits the financial contribution of "enclave enterprises" to the government in the locale in which they are situated. But these enterprises have to deal with or rely on the local government for a variety of matters, including employment of labor, land use, supply of utilities and other infrastructural facilities, licensing, and provision of social services such as health care and education of employees' children. Such an asymmetric interdependence between the local government and the economic enclaves within its territory tends to dilute the interests of local officials in the well-being of enclave enterprises. This, coupled with the fact that enclave enterprises do not have local state agencies as administrative patrons to provide protection through interagency ties,[25] makes them vulnerable targets for predatory local state action.[26]

---

[24] This division of jurisdiction among various levels of government was mainly a result of the prereform central planning system, which prioritized the allocation of limited resources according to criteria based on various ideological, political, economic, and strategic concerns. Those that were directly administered by higher levels of authority enjoyed better treatment in resource allocation than the others, as shown in Chapter 2. Under such a multitier control hierarchy, large numbers of firms administered by authorities above the level of township are located in places where the loci of their immediate supervising authorities are not situated.

[25] Fiscal decentralization in the reform has had the effect of significantly reducing the resource dependence of local governments on higher level authorities (Wong et al. 1995), which used to constitute a major lever for the latter to shape local state action. As a result, the ability of higher level supervising bodies to act on behalf of the enterprises under their control to pressure local governments for favorable treatment has been seriously weakened.

[26] In 1993 there were 47 "enclave" enterprises in Gate Tower. According to an official in the city government in charge of some of these enterprises (Informant no. 247/1993),

In Lotus Pond, there were no enclave enterprises. All the public enterprises were placed under the Township Economic Cooperative, which also coordinated the actions of the village economic cooperatives that oversaw the operations of village enterprises. This facilitated a "rational" prioritization of preferential treatment to TVEs,[27] and placed a constraint on predatory actions undertaken by renegade officials on local enterprises.

A third difference is that in Gate Tower those approaching local officials for special favors included not only locals but many outsiders. Local officials routinely received visitors from outside the district during and after work hours (Informants no. 352/1996, no. 357/1996). Many local hotels had long-term rental arrangements with nonlocal enterprises and governments for the use of some of their rooms as representative offices. In the words of a person stationed in one of these offices, a central part of their mission was to "deal with local government agencies here" (Informant no. 381/1996). The main reason for the large presence of outsiders is that Gate Tower, as a central urban district, is a major marketplace for input supplies, finished products, services, contracted work (e.g., construction), and employment. It is also a center of state administration, with a wide range of allocative and regulatory authorities, including the regional offices of major banks and other financial institutions. Furthermore, the dispersion of the loci of local state authority and the divergence of interests among local government agencies left open avenues for favor seekers, both local and nonlocal, to approach local officials for resources, regulatory flexibilities, and market access. As the head of the representative office of a suburban township government put it, "there are more inconsistencies in the policy process here than back home; this means opportunities for otherwise insignificant parties like us" (Informant no. 374/1996).

Lotus Pond was different, however. The nonfarm products produced by township and village enterprises were virtually all sold elsewhere. Except for occasional visits by some transaction partners of local enterprises, there was little presence of outsiders in the township. The overwhelming majority of township officials were locals, with extensive family and kinship ties based in various villages. They and the leaders of

---

after the late 1980s their performance deteriorated at a rate much faster than that of other public enterprises in the district. A major contributing factor was the intensification of unfavorable treatment by district state agencies (ibid.). When asked about this problem, some district officials openly admitted it (Informants no. 352/1996, no. 357/1996), citing an increasing shortage of budgetary funds as the main reason.

[27] This, again, was motivated not only by the incentives associated with fulfilling "public" functions of the local government, but by the private incentives embedded in the growing space of discretionary power.

local enterprises knew each other well, and there existed a stable pattern of interaction among them: Those contributing significantly to the budgetary and off-budget revenues of the local government were clearly most favored in resource allocation and regulation.[28] Although this did not prevent other economic actors from seeking preferential treatment from township officials, the efforts required were often rather formidable, especially if what they sought to do posed a challenge to the leading enterprises.

In sum, the political market in Gate Tower involved greater competing interests, more diverse and active participants, and more crowded avenues of favor seeking than those in Lotus Pond. This difference is closely related to the structural conditions that these locales share with their counterparts elsewhere in China. Since urban jurisdictions are where state enterprises are located and rural jurisdictions are the bases of the majority of nonstate enterprises, the case study findings from Gate Tower and Lotus Pond offer some clues to understanding the varying paces and outcomes of economic institutional change between the state sector and the nonstate sector. In particular, they provide a useful backdrop against which to explore what shapes the effectiveness of the efforts of firm leaders to manipulate state action in their favor.

---

[28] For example, Rainbow Pipe, the private enterprise introduced in Chapter 2, was the largest local government revenue provider in Lotus Pond. In 1993, about 30% of the economic output (an important indicator used in the evaluation of township leaders' performance) of the township came from this factory. But it was also a major beneficiary of various tax breaks and accumulated large sums of "uncollected" taxes that could be activated by township officials for various self-defined spending purposes. In 1994, the township government made a 2-million-yuan investment in one of its workshops and turned it into a joint-ownership enterprise. Also, Director Zhu (the private owner) was appointed a deputy township director and, at his request, was given the most flexible managerial contract among all the township enterprises in Lotus Pond.

6

Favor Seeking and Relational Constraints

With the persistence of particularism in state action and the expansion of exchange relations in the political arena, how firms fare in favor seeking has a direct impact on their competitiveness and profitability, as shown in Chapters 3 and 4. What, then, affects the ability of firm leaders to manipulate state action? In particular, what shapes the differences between state and nonstate enterprises in the effectiveness of their efforts to have the rules of the new economic game bent to their advantage and to profit from market-oriented economic activities?

To address this issue, it is important to examine both the means and the contexts of favor seeking. A widely noted phenomenon in studies of China's post-Mao transformation is that economic actors have made extensive use of *guanxi* – personal networks – as the main avenue of favor seeking. The focus of attention centers on the role of *guanxi* as a mediating mechanism, and the predominant approach to the analysis of this role is to examine it in terms of dyadic interactions between the parties involved in favor exchange. Much has yet to be said, however, about what shapes the outcomes of *guanxi*-mediated favor exchange, especially in the context of multiple-party interaction where decisions are interdependent between different dyads.

Following the clues developed in the preceding chapter, this chapter takes a close look at the relationship between favor seeking and the characteristics of the political markets faced by different firms. The focus of analysis is what may be called the "third party effect" on the use of *guanxi*. It concerns how the outcome of a dyadic exchange is affected by the interaction(s) of one or both of the participants with other parties. I argue that the competitive disadvantage of many state enterprises during the reform (especially the 1980s and early 1990s) has been partly due to their greater exposure to the downside of such an effect, which constrains the ability of their leaders to make effective use of personal networks to manipulate state action. This exposure is rooted in the path-dependent external and internal environments of these enterprises, where an adverse "third party effect" is enhanced by three major factors. They include: divergent interests among local officials, a crowded local political market, and handicapping organizational politics. To see the relevance of these factors, it is necessary to look at how *guanxi* is used as a means of favor seeking.

Personal Networks and "Third Party Effect"

From 1988 to 1996, I interviewed 168 enterprise leaders in China.[1] When asked about what they regarded as the most important factor for succeeding in business (see Table 6.1),[2] 143 of them said that ultimately *guanxi* with both officials and business partners mattered more than anything else.[3] Almost all the managers thought that the performance of their enterprises would be seriously affected if they could not cultivate and maintain good personal relationships with the officials who had various forms of authority over their activities. An essential aspect of such relationships is the exchange of favors. In Chapters 3 and 4 I have focused on the particularistic nature of state action in the reform. But there is a related issue that needs to be brought up: The orientation of particularistic state action has been greatly influenced by personalized interactions between officials and economic actors.[4] It was mainly through their personal connections with officials that the managers I interviewed sought special treatment in resource allocation, regulation of opportunities, and exemptions from state-engendered liabilities.

Moreover, the use of such connections was closely coupled with a provision of concrete benefits to the officials concerned. Such benefits were

---

[1] See Appendix B for details on the interviews.

[2] Table 6.1 is based on records of interviews with enterprise managers during 1988–96. Not all the managers addressed all the issues listed in the table. Since the interviews were conducted over a period of nine years, the changes within this time frame cannot be discerned from the summary information presented here. Despite such limitation, the managers' views do converge to a clear and consistent pattern that is both empirically and analytically meaningful.

[3] This finding was derived by asking the interviewees, first, to identify factors they deemed as important to their competitiveness and, then, to weigh the relative importance of the factors identified. A sharply different finding is reported in Guthrie (1999), which shows that *guanxi* with officials was perceived by firm leaders as having declining importance while no such change was found for *guanxi* among economic actors.

[4] In a 1992 survey of 1,440 private enterprise owners conducted by a group of Chinese sociologists (Zhang Xuwu et al. 1994: 120), 42.4% of the urban respondents and 39.4% of the rural respondents (the size of each group is not reported) indicated that their closest friends were cadres of various ranks. These percentages were the highest among the categories of social contacts from which the respondents were asked to choose their answers.

Table 6.1. *Enterprise leaders' views on guanxi (personal networks) and economic activities*

Opinion	Percentage of those sharing the opinion	
	State enterprise leaders	Nonstate enterprise leaders
(1) *Guanxi* with *both* officials *and* business partners is the most essential factor for success in business.	86 (*n* = 37)	94 (*n* = 131)
(2) Failing to cultivate close *guanxi* with officials has a significant effect on enterprise performance.	94 (*n* = 35)	96 (*n* = 129)
(3) Direct or indirect personal benefits are needed for gaining favorable treatment through *guanxi* with officials.	77 (*n* = 35)	91 (*n* = 126)
(4) Compared to the beginning of the reform era, it is now more difficult to gain favorable treatment through *guanxi* with officials without offering direct or indirect personal benefits in return.	93 (*n* = 29)	89 (*n* = 118)
(5) Compared to those of nonstate enterprises, leaders of state enterprises have a less free hand in offering personal benefits to officials in *guanxi*-mediated favor seeking.	100 (*n* = 32)	96 (*n* = 124)

Source: Interviews, 1988–96.

153

offered in various forms, including cash paid directly or in slightly disguised forms (e.g., deliberate losses to the officials in mah-jong – a game that can be played for gambling), "gifts" (cigarettes, liquor, jewelry, clothing, electronic and home appliances, etc.), "services" (e.g., free refurbishing of the officials' apartments, long-term use of cars, mobile phones, and pagers charged to the enterprises' accounts), in-kind consumption (e.g., banquets, junkets, and even prostitutes), "discounts" (e.g., for purchase of products sold or "resold" by the enterprises to the officials), benefits to parties designated by the officials (e.g., hiring the officials' relatives or friends, contributions to the construction of staff quarters for the officials' agencies), among others. It is also worth noting that such benefits appear to have become increasingly important in *guanxi*-mediated favor exchange, as Table 6.1 indicates.

Similar findings are legion in studies of contemporary Chinese society.[5] What they commonly indicate is that, despite the existence of many universalistic rules established in postrevolution China, people have relied extensively on particularistic, personal ties to get things done. Deeply rooted in folkways, widely cultivated, and constantly reinvented, such ties constitute an essential ingredient in the expectations and strategies of social interaction.

Much of the existing research on *guanxi* focuses on its ubiquity and importance in social and economic life, particularly its role in channeling influence from officials. Rigidities in the distribution of state-monopolized resources and opportunities under central planning are widely seen as a major reason why there were pervasive efforts to seek petty favors from officials for survival and personal advancement in the Mao era (1949–76) (e.g., Oi 1989a; Walder 1986). Some scholars further argue that such efforts have intensified in the reform because of the persistent influence of state power on the distribution of resources and opportunities (e.g., Bian 1994, 1997; Chu and Ju 1993; Yang 1994), and because of the need to sustain and expand market-oriented economic activities in the absence of well-functioning market institutions (Wank 1995, 1996; Xin and Pearce 1996).

A common theme that emerges from these views is that the political process has been porous and is now increasingly so. The preceding two chapters have shown how and why such porosity has increased in the reform. If the strong inclination of economic actors to rely on private

---

[5] See, for example, Bian (1994, 1997), Boisot and Child (1996), Chu and Ju (1993), Gold (1985), Hsing (1998), Oi (1989a), Pearson (1997), Tsui and Farh (1997), Vogel (1989), Walder (1986), Wank (1995, 1996), Xin and Pearce (1996), Yan (1996), Yang (1994), and Young (1995). The only study that produced evidence to the contrary is Guthrie (1998).

ties with officials to get things done is indeed in large part a reaction to the persistent potency and increasing manipulability of the state's allocative and regulatory power, what affects the outcomes of their favor seeking through *guanxi*? An important twist that needs to be explained in this regard, for example, is that state enterprise leaders appear to have faced greater constraints in tapping the full potential of their *guanxi* for manipulation of state action, as the findings on Opinion (5) in Table 6.1 suggest.[6]

Some scholars argue that the strength of the ties between the parties involved in social exchange has a direct impact on its outcome, especially when the exchange involves channeling influence from officials (e.g., Bian 1997). The rationale of this view is straightforward: The "return" on a personal tie is a function of the closeness of the social bond between the parties involved.[7] After all, blood is thicker than water, and it is a commonly observed fact that people with a strong sense of mutual trust and obligation tend to be more forthcoming than strangers in offering assistance to each other. Another view emphasizes what has been extensively discussed by Yang (1994) – i.e., the tactics of cultivating personal networks (see also Wank 1999). It suggests that whether one can well understand the intricacies and subtleties of complex interpersonal relations and master the skills and etiquette of communication and relationship building is likely to have a direct effect on one's ability to locate and "push the right button" to get things done.

Both views are useful, but neither extends far beyond dyadic interaction. The only "third party effect" noted in these studies is that the

---

[6] It should be noted that state enterprise leaders do use their *guanxi* to seek special treatment from officials. The top managers of Northern Machinery and Southwestern Machinery, for example, relied on their personal contacts in government agencies to gain most of the favors discussed in Chapter 3. Such interaction differed from traditional vertical bargaining in that it was motivated by the push-and-pull effects of markets rather than by attempts to maintain organizational slack, and extended far beyond the boundary of traditional superior-subordinate relationships between enterprises and their supervising authorities to involve officials who were not directly in charge of the operations of these enterprises. Moreover, bolder efforts were made to provide concrete personal benefits to the officials, such as hiring their children for easy jobs, sending workmen to refurbish their apartments free of charge, and inviting the officials to wining and dining. But these benefits paled in comparison to those offered by many nonstate enterprise leaders, who were able to use even bolder measures to get things done, such as more lavish spending on "gifts" and the use of cash as bribes.

[7] Although this is what Bian (1997) seems to focus on, his definition of "strong tie" includes "the time spent in interaction, emotional intensity, intimacy, or reciprocal services characterizing the tie." The last element in this definition bears no consistent correlation with the other elements. Its inclusion may not only decrease conceptual clarity (e.g., two persons without significant reciprocal services may have strong affection for each other, or vice versa), but run the risk of leading to a tautological explanation where the same factor (i.e., reciprocal service) constitutes both the cause and the effect of "strong tie."

exchange tie between two weakly connected parties may be significantly strengthened with the help or mediation of a third party (e.g., a mutual friend) to whom both are strongly connected (e.g., Bian 1997; Yang 1994). In the exchange relations between economic actors and officials, however, there exist three other types of "third party effect." They may significantly affect the outcome of favor exchange, hence meriting close examination.

First, a favor giver tends to be hesitant if the vested interests embedded in his or her existing relationships with other parties are at odds with what a favor seeker asks for. Second, a favor giver faces strong inducement to disregard expressive and normative concerns for instrumental gains if the same favor is sought by multiple favor seekers, whose offers of different levels of benefits in return combine to provide a clear frame of reference in which to gauge the opportunity cost for favor giving. Third, a favor seeker has to take extra precaution if knowledge about his or her act can easily be turned into a means to advance the interest of a third party (e.g., a personal rival) at the cost of the favor seeker.

In the following discussion, I elaborate on these possibilities and explain why the structural conditions faced by state enterprises make them more extensively exposed to the downside of these "third party effects."

Favor Seeking and State Agents' Vested Interests

The findings presented in Chapters 4 and 5 indicate two important features in urban areas: a clustering of backyard profit centers and a presence of multitier regulatory authorities in the same economic space. The interests of local officials are closely tied to the profits from backyard entities and to the various levies arbitrarily imposed on local enterprises, especially those "owned" by higher level authorities. At the same time, the formal structure of authority relations under the local state does not fully encompass the loci of the exchange relations that local officials are engaged in. This poses a major challenge to favor seekers whose enterprises bear the brunt of the predatory actions that sustain the vested interests of local officials.

As noted in the preceding chapter, each state agency in Gate Tower had established a number of backyard profit centers by 1993. There is evidence that this is by no means an isolated phenomenon (Lin and Zhang 1999; see also Duckett 1998). As illustrated in Chapter 4, the relationship between backyard profit centers and regular industrial enterprises is often a zero-sum one. The diversion of plan-allocated industrial materials, capital, and other resources by or through backyard profit centers, for example, means that the designated receivers are deprived of their necessary supplies and consequently have to pay extra to obtain them. State enterprises have been hardest hit in this regard, as they have been the main destination of plan-allocated resources. Furthermore, coerced transactions with backyard profit centers directly cut into the profits or assets of the affected enterprises, weakening their positions in competition.

Predatory state actions on enterprises not "owned" by the local government are also pervasive under China's multitier enterprise regulation system.[8] There are two types of "enclave enterprises" under this system. The first type consists of public enterprises that are "owned" by a particular level of government and operate in a locality where both its owner and a lower level government are located.[9] Gate Tower, for example, is where the headquarters of both the district government and the city government are located. City-owned enterprises are subject to the decisions and actions of district government agencies, especially the various ad hoc levies contrived by district agencies. The second type includes public enterprises that are located in a jurisdiction where the command center of its owner is not located.[10] A centrally controlled enterprise, for example, may be located in the city where Gate Tower District is located rather than in the capital city of Beijing.

The preceding chapter shows that the lack of contribution by enclave enterprises to the local government's budgetary revenue and their asymmetric dependence relationship with the local government make them vulnerable to predatory actions by local government agencies. It is therefore not surprising that extortionary demands from local officials have persistently been the focal complaint of large numbers of urban enterprises (e.g., CESS 1993–7; Luan Tao and Li Zhengzhi 1993). Again, state enterprises are most vulnerable to such adverse treatment, as all of them are enclave enterprises of one type or another, whereas most TVEs are spatially situated under the sole purview of the local governments that own them.

---

[8] See, for example, the survey results reported in Table 1.3. It should be noted that over 75% of the enterprises in the sample were state enterprises located in urban areas. This problem is also considered by a recent study (Steinfeld 1998) to be a major contributing factor to the difficulties faced by state enterprises, especially large ones that fall under the second type of enclave enterprise discussed below.

[9] My discussion of local government ownership of public enterprises draws on Granick's (1990) regional property rights perspective on state enterprises in China. For a similar view, see Walder (1995a).

[10] In 1992, 34.4% of state-owned industrial enterprises were in this category. The figure is estimated on the basis of an analysis of postal codes recorded in the 1992 national industrial firm data set.

For the leaders of adversely affected enterprises, the implication of these realities is twofold. On the one hand, asking local officials to contain or reverse their predatory actions directly affects the vested interests that they share with each other and with their backyard profit centers.[11] On the other hand, there are large numbers of predators to deal with. Neither condition makes it impossible to defuse (e.g., with the help of certain officials induced to override shared collective interests) the adverse effects of local officials' predation. But such an effort is likely to be very costly, particularly in comparison with favor-seeking efforts in contexts where the structural conditions for these forms of predation are minimal or absent. According to Director Wang of Everbright Heating:

> In this city, there are so many agencies at so many administrative levels that one has to deal with. I have three levels of immediate supervising authorities to deal with, and many more to look to and fend off. . . . It is hard to cultivate and maintain a good and close relationship with the key officials in each and every of the agencies that are relevant to our operation. . . . It's not because I don't have any friends out there, but oftentimes helping me means giving up what they could otherwise gain. It's not so difficult to have rules like fire control regulations bent, as the worst that can happen is the burn-down of our own buildings; but it's really not easy to dodge the various ad hoc levies, because they belong to the collecting agencies and constitute a major source of their discretionary funds and fringe benefits for their employees.

For Director Du of Red Star Heating, however, Wang's concern was not a big issue:

> I have been dealing with the officials in the township government since the days of the people's commune. Most of the old-timers are still here, though some have moved up. It is not so difficult to know the few new faces well. The whole government is located in one building, and *guanxi* grows naturally – both among insiders and between them and us. We are a key town-

---

[11] In 1989, for example, Northern Machinery faced a serious shortfall of steel bars because the city's Industrial Material Allocation Bureau diverted large amounts of plan-allocated supplies to several of its backyard profit centers for arbitrage. The head of Northern Machinery's sourcing department approached a key personal contact (a former middle school classmate) in the Bureau for help, but came back empty-handed. The reason was that the Bureau had just shifted 20 employees from its budget-funded payroll to the pool of personnel financed with off-budget funds, which mainly came from the profits of backyard profit centers.

ship enterprise, and we are in the same boat as the township authority. If the officials squeeze us too hard, they have little to count on tomorrow. In fact they try very hard to respond to our requests and protect us from unreasonable demands from the county authority – it's far away from us, anyway. . . . A small place like ours has advantages of its own.

This contrast should not be taken to imply that rural officials do not prey on local economic actors, however.[12] What it indicates is that they tend to refrain from doing so to their shared "cash cows." In urban areas, because of the divergence of interests among local officials under the dispersed and multitier authority relations in the local state apparatus, even a star enterprise like Northern Machinery could not keep itself from being affected by the self-seeking behavior of officials in renegade state agencies (note 11). Efforts to tackle this problem inevitably offset, in varying degrees, the special favors that many urban enterprises may be able to cultivate in other areas of interaction with local officials.

Crowded Political Market

In Chapter 5, I point out that, as the centers of economic and governmental administration activities, urban places tend to attract more outside favor seekers than townships in the countryside. There is also a historical reason for this, i.e., there have been broad and diverse avenues to the urban social space because of changes resulting from revolution, industrialization, and urbanization.

Unlike the Russian Bolshevik Revolution where urban proletarians played a central role, the Chinese communist revolution was based in the countryside. The millions of peasants who had joined the rank and file of the revolutionary army became the main source of cadres for the state bureaucracy after the victory of the revolution in 1949 (Song Defu 1994). They have worked, lived, and developed personal networks in urban administrative centers while maintaining social ties with their relatives in rural areas. Such ties provide a potential bridge for the latter to explore access to opportunities and resources outside their local social spaces.

The massive absorption of rural laborers into the urban work force in the 1950s further increased the social networks between urban and rural areas. A survey conducted by the Policy Research Office of the CCP's Secretariat in 1982 revealed that 70% of those who joined the urban work force before 1957 were recruited from the countryside (SJCYJS 1982:

---

[12] I will address this issue in the next chapter.

172–3). The local personal contacts that they have accumulated over time also provide a major stepping stone for their relatives in the countryside to explore access to the loci of state authority in urban areas.

In-depth case studies of rural industrialization during the reform clearly show that the social networks of rural entrepreneurs and officials have been a most important avenue through which to tap urban financial and human resources and input supplies, promote sales, acquire information and technology, develop business connections, and facilitate deal making (Byrd and Lin 1990; Ma Rong et al. 1994). Seventy-two of the 168 factory managers that I interviewed during 1988 and 1996 were based in rural areas. They all indicated that their primary contacts in urban areas were mostly people with family ties in their locales. It was through these contacts that they approached different levels of urban state authorities for various forms of help and assistance.[13] With the deepening of the reform process, such interaction has been further facilitated by the relaxation and eventual removal of stringent travel restrictions, and by the improvement in telecommunication facilities and services, such as telephone, pager, fax, and mobile phone.

The flocking of favor seekers to urban places adds a complicating factor to favor exchange with officials. The presence of large numbers of seekers for the same favor(s) forms a clear frame of reference for officials to evaluate the opportunity cost of favor giving. According to an official in charge of disciplinary affairs at the CCP Committee in Gate Tower (Informant no. 397/1996):

> Frankly speaking, the greater the number of people offering to trade favors with you, the more clearly you see the real worth of what you control. You then face two important decisions: whether to do it at all, and (should you decide to do it) whether to help your best friend first even if he does not give you the best deal.

What this suggests is that the clear contrast between different offers from competing favor seekers tends to intensify the temptation for the official(s) concerned to decrease the weight assigned to noninstrumental (i.e., expressive and normative) considerations in decision making.[14] This

---

[13] See, for example, the account of Flying Horse Motors' early development in Chapter 3.

[14] Hwang (1987) argues that *guanxi*-mediated social exchange is driven by diverse considerations. At one end of the spectrum, it is predominantly influenced by noninstrumental – expressive and normative – concerns among the persons involved (such as family members and close friends). At the other end, the primary driving force of social exchange stems from minimally ceremonialized reciprocity in accordance with cost-benefit calculations regarding narrowly defined self-interest. In between are exchange relations driven by mixed motives.

is particularly likely at a time when the moral vacuum left by the failure of Maoist ideological indoctrination is rapidly filled with various materialistic and utilitarian values that have surged during China's market-oriented reform and opening to the outside world (Madsen 1984, 1997).

A common trend noted by studies of social exchange in the reform era is that there is growing instrumentalism in the formation and use of *guanxi* (e.g., Bian 1994; Gold 1985; Chu and Ju 1993; Yang 1994). This is also indicated by the rather high percentage of those sharing the fourth opinion in Table 6.1. The situation is particularly acute in urban areas, which have political markets with large numbers of favor seekers, as well as a greater degree of commercialization and exposure to the cultural influence from abroad (Link, Madsen, and Pickowicz 1989; Schell 1989). As a result, narrowly focused cost-benefit calculations tend to rise as the deciding factor for the outcome of favor seeking, whereas the role of "strong ties" based on social bonding is reduced to facilitating access. In the words of Director Ma of Peak Equipment:

> True friendship is hard to find nowadays. Whether one has close *guanxi* with powerful cadres is one thing, and whether one can get things done through such *guanxi* is another. *Guanxi* is very important because it helps one open the door, which so many other people can open, too – through their own *guanxi*. But what one can walk away with from that door is a matter of business (*shengyi*) – I mean deal making (*jiaoyi*) – rather than a matter of the depth of one's cumulative relationship (*jiaoqing*) (with the cadres).

The essence of this observation is that, in the face of large numbers of favor seekers, a close personal relationship with officials is often not enough for securing special favors. Concrete material benefits not only are indispensable but need to be offered on terms that are more favorable than those of rival favor seekers, as the prize tends to go to the highest bidder first and foremost, especially when the favors sought are in limited supply.[15] Since multilateral interaction in favor exchange with officials frequently shifts the balance of benefits and costs with regard to each of the dyadic relationships centered around a particular favor giver,

[15] Director Ma, for example, was able to outmaneuver two other enterprises for the use right to a piece of land that Peak Equipment needed for its expansion in 1989. The main reason, according to Ma, was not that he had a closer personal relationship with the officials concerned (some of whom he barely knew), but the more substantial "benefits" (which he declined to specify) that he offered them.

stable commitment is difficult to sustain and opportunism is likely to result and spread.[16]

To be sure, doing business in a crowded political market is likely to be as costly for outside favor seekers as for their local counterparts. The difference, however, is that the former only partially and selectively count on the outcome from an exchange in such a market, but the competitive positions of the latter are overwhelmingly dependent on it, as most basic aspects of their operations are under the influence of local state actions. As Director Kang of Flying Horse Motors put it:

> We are like a guerrilla force. Our home base is away from where we fight the battles. We don't have to tie ourselves to a particular tree, waiting for it to blossom and bear fruit. If things don't work out in one place, we move on to another.

On the home front of enterprises operating under rural administration, the degree of crowding in favor seeking tends to be lower. Outside favor seekers are few and far between. More important, the clustering of the interests of local officials under an integrated authority structure leads to the formation of a pecking order for prioritizing the allocation of special favors. It also deters opportunistic behavior in favor granting, especially on a large scale.[17]

This does not mean that those at the lower end of the pecking order are deterred from seeking favors from local officials. The distribution of some favors, such as bending rules on environmental protection and labor right protection, may not result in a "winner-takes-all" outcome. These types of favors tend to be more actively sought than favors that are in limited supply, such as low-interest loans. But those that do not see the prospect of forming a close tie between their enterprises and the shared interests of local officials tend to refrain from competing directly with those that have established such a tie.[18] Another important trend in

---

[16] In the summer of 1992, Northern Machinery won (after several months of lobbying) a special foreign currency loan from the Economic Commission for importing equipment from abroad. But in the end it was only able to make use of 45% of the authorized amount. The remaining balance was "stolen" by two construction companies, which somehow learned about the loan and then made in-kind contributions (building materials) to the construction of new staff quarters for the Commission (Informant no. 274/1994).

[17] Some township officials in Lotus Pond claimed that they sometimes had to turn down requests for capital from relatives residing in their ancestral villages, as they might have affected the well-being of existing "key" township enterprises (Informants no. 282/1994, no. 290/1994).

[18] Director Zhu of Rainbow Pipe, for example, said that before it became clear that the products he developed had real market potential he did not approach local officials for help, because such an attempt "would be futile if I had no concrete benefits to show them."

rural social change during the reform is the revival of kinship networks. In some locales, the authority relations embedded in such networks have interlocked with those of the local state, turning the local state into a de facto clan organization (e.g., Lin 1995; Lin and Chen 1999). This poses a further constraint on the attempts of those on the edge to compete with those in the "inner circle" for the same kinds of special favors.

Collusion and Whistle-Blowing

Favor seekers often need to make unauthorized use of organizational resources to pave the way for obtaining favors, and the officials granting special favors in exchange for private gain can hardly do so without making inappropriate or illicit diversion of state-controlled resources and opportunities. Hence, *guanxi*-mediated favor exchange with officials is in large part a collusive act that breaks existing rules and thus involves a risk. Violation of the code of conduct for enterprise leaders and public office holders can lead to adverse consequences, ranging from disciplinary action to legal punishment.[19] To reduce risk and protect their mutual interests, colluding parties need to restrict the access of outside parties to the information concerning their private dealings. In the process of doing so, they must confront the constraints posed by the organizational environments in which they operate.

Neither state agencies nor economic organizations are devoid of internal politics, which spawns power struggles and interpersonal rivalry among key decision makers. Organizational politics is especially likely to be complex when the degree of relational stability and congeniality among key decision makers is low, making it difficult for them to trust each other and form a solid informal basis of common interests. In such a situation, any information on the trespass of existing rules by a decision maker can jeopardize his or her career if it falls into the hands of a personal rival. It follows that a decision-making group of small size and stable and self-selected membership may be more effective for containing the risk in collusion than a group of large size and unstable and externally appointed membership. The former may be more conducive to

---

[19] This is particularly likely to be the case in a political process where the policy orientation zigzags between different ideological and factional agenda and thereby creates opportunities for some decision makers to use evidence of "inappropriate" conduct to launch attacks on their personal rivals at the height of a change in the political climate. Lei Yu and Liang Xiang, for example, were both former governors of Hainan province who attempted bold reform measures. They were forced out of office by their political opponents on charges of inappropriate use of authority for personal gain (Informants no. 279/1994, no. 283/1994; *RMRB*, August 1, 1985, September 15, 1989).

fostering group cohesion, developing consensus, and sustaining cooperation. Assuming individuals are risk averse, therefore, collusive behavior is likely to be most active and fruitful between officials and "clients" who both face weak constraints from their respective organizational processes.[20]

In the reform era, this condition is most widely available in the interface between rural grassroots (i.e., township) level governments and the enterprises under their jurisdiction.[21] Small in size, township governments are mostly run by a circle of closely linked officials. Unlike that in governments at higher levels, decision-making power here is less diffused and more concentrated in the hands of a few key figures in charge of limited numbers of administrative units overseeing a rather wide range of combined and integrated functions. Although the township director and Party secretary are rotated periodically between different localities, their deputies and subordinates are all locals who know each other well and expect to stay where their roots are.

Other than rural collectives, many private enterprises, foreign capital enterprises, and joint-ownership enterprises also operate under the purview of township governments.[22] Most township enterprises and all the other nonstate enterprises operating under the purview of grassroots governments were established in the reform era. Their leaders, especially private owners, have the authority to fill their management teams with loyalists and conduct their business in an autocratic fashion. Major decisions are often made and monopolized by the number one person who is also able to keep virtually all the information on any external transactions to himself.[23]

Authority relations in state enterprises, especially large and medium ones, tend to be more complicated. Few of them are under the sole purview of grassroots government, as the county is the lowest level of

---

[20] Olson (1965, 1982) also emphasizes the importance of small group size to the success of collusive collective action. But his analysis is primarily focused on the "free rider" problem and incentives for commitment rather than on the risk factor.

[21] The size of the township government in Lotus Pond, for example, is only one-tenth that of the district government in Gate Tower (which is located in the heart of a provincial capital).

[22] In 1995, for example, there were 1.03 million rural collectives and 6.15 million rural private enterprises (including *getihu*) in the industrial sector (ZGXZQYNJBJWYH 1996: 99).

[23] Flying Horse Motors, for example, was in fact governed by a family despite its formal status as a village enterprise. Director Kang was in charge of general management and all external affairs. His son ran the production process, and his daughter controlled accounting and finance. Red Star Heating was run by the Du brothers, with the junior in charge of sales and finance and the senior looking after production and government relations. Peak Equipment, Modern Housewares, and Rainbow Pipe were each under the exclusive control of one person (i.e., Ma, Cheung, and Zhu).

supervising authority of state enterprises. They are monitored by a number of agencies (e.g., the industry specific departments, the fiscal authority, the planning authority, among others) whose actions do not follow a single command chain. Information concerning the interaction between a state enterprise and a supervising agency is likely to be known to other relevant agencies. The majority of state enterprises have been in existence for a long time,[24] and many still bear the scars of wounds in interpersonal relations from the highly politicized and divided work-place life (Walder 1986) under Maoist radicalism during the Cultural Revolution.[25] The top leaders are appointed by their supervising bodies and transferred periodically; few of them have full authority to handpick their deputies.[26] These institutional features may foster latent and manifest factional conflicts between political functionaries and nonpolitical managers, between "old-timers" and new appointees from outside, and between personal rivals, making it difficult for the top leader to engage in extensive informal transactions through private ties and to cut deals with outsiders and keep all the information to himself.[27]

[24] For example, only 28.2% of the state industrial enterprises that were in operation in 1992 were established after 1978 (1992 national industrial firm data set).

[25] At Southwestern Machinery, for example, decision-making authority was divided among four top leaders. The factory director mainly took care of government relations and sales. Personnel decisions were controlled by the Party secretary, whereas production and finance were controlled (separately) by two deputy directors. The director and the deputy director in charge of finance were longtime rivals. During the Cultural Revolution, they were both middle-level managers but belonged to opposing political factions. The reform brought their interests closer, but they still kept each other at arm's length. Although they lived only two blocks away from one another, they only paid visits, joined by other top factory leaders, to each other's apartments during the Chinese New Year. This relationship made the director extremely careful when he dealt with transaction partners and government officials. To him the use of any "flexible" means in such dealings was off-limits.

[26] According to the 1992 survey of 1,663 urban and rural industrial enterprises conducted by the World Bank and the Chinese Academy of Social Sciences (see Appendix A), the average tenure was four years for state enterprises and urban collectives ($n = 1,270$) and eight years for large township enterprises ($n = 281$); the percentages for enterprise directors who claimed to have the authority to pick their deputies are 20 ($n = 1,265$) and 40 ($n = 285$) for the two groups respectively (1992 World Bank-CASS survey data set).

[27] Interpersonal relations among top leaders at Northern Machinery did not feature such tension. In fact, from the early 1980s on, top enterprise leaders maintained a smooth working relationship among themselves. But there were subtle yet clear constraints on the latitude of the top decision maker. Collective decision making was the main mode of operation, partly because of its functional complexity and partly because of an institutionalized arrangement of involving the enterprise's Party leaders in decisions on important issues. Although in the reform the Party apparatus largely refrained from active involvement in day-to-day economic decision making, it maintained unrestricted access to all the information on decisions and continued to play a key role in monitoring. This, according to the Party secretary, was called "supervision and guarantee." The Party secretary was assisted by two deputy Party secretaries, who were also well

The consequence of such variations across different organizational settings is obvious. Enterprise leaders who are less constrained by internal politics can be more aggressive in using concrete benefits to enhance the effectiveness of their personal connections with officials in exchange for special treatment, especially where officials also face weaker relational constraints. In addition, officials tend to be more forthcoming in favor exchange when they can proceed in a clandestine fashion, through informal channels, with parties that have the same capability in information control. The tendency to collude between firm leaders and officials is likely to be weakened if one of the two conditions (weak constraints on both parties involved) is not present, and seriously contained if both conditions are absent.[28] Since this situation is what most state enterprises have faced in the reform, it imposes a major constraint on their effective use of personal networks for favor seeking.

Summary

History matters, partly because it shapes the contexts of social interaction. The "third party effects" discussed above are all embedded in the institutional legacies of the prereform political and economic system. The greater such effects, the weaker the competitive position of an enterprise in the new economic game. Since state enterprises, which are concentrated in urban jurisdictions, are more exposed than nonstate enterprises to these effects, such a structural difference constitutes a contributing factor to the uneven pace and outcome of marketization between the state sector and the nonstate sector, as noted in Chapter 1.

This account casts further light on the mechanisms whereby political markets have been developed in the reform era. It shows that the expansion of exchange relations in the political process in urban areas has been subject to the influence of interactions of competing interests, whereas such expansion in rural jurisdictions has been anchored in relatively

---

informed about many important decisions. The presence of these full-time political functionaries in the top echelon created a disincentive for the Party secretary to collude with the director for covert deals with outside parties. Any sign of such behavior might play into the hands of the Party secretary's immediate subordinates whose careers could be greatly advanced by any floundering on the part of the Party secretary. Such complexities in interpersonal relations did not necessarily make it impossible for factory leaders to seek favors from officials. But they did place a constraint on the latitude with which favor seeking was carried out.

[28] A precondition for such a pattern of effects has to be that there remains a certain degree of potency in the state's legal and regulatory power to enforce, at least superficially, its formal claim of neutrality, despite the compromise of state action by informal and particularistic agenda.

stable collusive alliances involving local officials and economic actors. Both processes have made the central planning system increasingly unsustainable. The growth of opportunism in social exchange as a result of intense competitive favor seeking in urban political markets has seriously drained the commitment and resources available to the implementation of the state plan. On the other hand, favor seekers based in rural areas have accelerated the decline of the plan by co-opting its guardians, weakening its main carriers (i.e., state enterprises based in urban areas), and enlarging the space outside the command economy through expansion of their own activities.

This being said, it is important to note that, aside from state enterprises, there are other enterprises in urban areas as well, such as urban collectives, foreign capital enterprises, and private enterprises.[29] Compared to state enterprises, relatively more of these enterprises operate under grassroots urban jurisdictions,[30] and they face fewer constraints from internal politics because of the much fuller authority of their leaders to select their deputies. But they do have direct exposure to backyard profit centers and face large numbers of rivals in favor seeking. This may have placed a certain limit on the overall advantage of nonstate enterprises over state enterprises in the use of personal networks for favor seeking.

Also, although state enterprises face strong constraints on the use of personal networks for favor seeking, they are by no means a homogeneous group. Some enterprises are better able to cope under such constraints than others. Large enterprises like Northern Machinery are generally better positioned than small ones to sustain ad hoc favorable treatment from officials, as there remains ground on which to link their operations to the interests of top supervising officials, who still need some showcase enterprises as their political capital.

Finally, since the enactment of the *Ordinance on Restructuring the Management Mechanisms of State-Owned Industrial Enterprises* in 1992 growing numbers of state enterprise leaders have gained greater autonomy in decision making over a wide range of issues, including the appointment of top managers. Where relational cohesion among enterprise leaders has increased as a result of such change, favor seeking and

---

[29] Everbright Heating and Peak Equipment, for example, are among these enterprises. According to the 1995 industrial census, in 1995 84% of the collective enterprises and 92% of those classified as "other" (vs. state and collective) enterprises operated in rural jurisdictions (GYPCBGS 1996: 4).

[30] In 1992, for example, 3% of the state enterprises ($n = 73,781$), 36% of the urban collectives ($n = 122,512$), and 29% of the joint-ownership and foreign capital enterprises ($n = 9,573$) in the urban industrial sector were placed under the purview of district governments (1992 industrial enterprise data set).

collusion with officials tend to be more effective. But this does not necessarily lead to a corresponding improvement in enterprise performance, which in fact has further deteriorated in the state sector as a whole. A major reason, mentioned in Chapter 4 and to be further addressed in the following chapter, is that cost-benefit calculations in the face of the competitive environments in the mid- to late 1990s have led many state enterprise leaders, especially those in small state enterprises, to re-orient the focus of their strategies to accommodate self-interest from increasing value-added in their enterprises to stripping enterprise assets.

7

Competition, Economic Growth, and Latent Problems

From 1978 to 1998 China's gross domestic product grew at an average annual rate of 9.7% (GJTJJa 1999: 58).[1] During the same period of time, exchange relations significantly expanded in both economic activities and the political process. These concurrent developments contrast sharply with images of economic stagnation and decline in countries with widespread corruption and rent seeking (e.g., Bates 1981; Mauro 1995; Myrdal 1968; Olson 1982; Rose-Ackerman 1999). In the preceding chapters, I have discussed how the growing political market has played an important role in bringing down the plan while shaping the competitive advantage of industrial firms in profit-oriented economic activities. In this chapter, I explore the seemingly puzzling concurrence of sustained economic growth and marketization of the political process.

I propose a two-step approach to this issue. First, it is important to explain why in the short run the rise of the political market has not resulted in the kinds of retarding effects on economic growth that figure so prominently in the literature on corruption and rent seeking. Second, it is equally important to examine latent problems that have developed during the past two decades and may fully manifest themselves down the road.

I argue that competition holds a key to understanding the short-term outcome of economic institutional change. The initial impetus came from the profit-making opportunities unleashed by sweeping rural decollectivization amidst huge pent-up demand in the late 1970s and early 1980s. Efforts to capture and expand such opportunities drove increasing numbers of economic actors and officials from the plan to markets. As a result, competitive forces quickly developed in both the economic and

---

[1] For a discussion of the inaccuracies of China's GDP data (especially those for 1998), see Rawski (2000).

the political process and reinforced each other. They brought down entrenched barriers to economic freedom and spread the effects of ad hoc changes in the rules governing economic activities. They also limited monopoly profits and contained the gains for uneven treatment of firms, forcing them to look beyond special favors for ways to compete on economic grounds while exploring additional areas for rule bending. All this created a major boost for output growth.

The gist of such an account is that during the 1980s and perhaps the better part of the 1990s efforts to manipulate state action gravitated toward gaining and broadening access to new opportunities of value creation outside the central planning system. In contrast, repartitioning of opportunities, resources, and economic gains within the existing institutional framework is a central feature of conventional "rent-seeking societies," where competitive forces are stifled in both the political and the economic process. Factors contributing to this difference, to be discussed below, include massive defection of grassroots officials from commitment to the plan, pervasive networks of social exchange, lack of institutionalized barriers to social exchange, and absence of strong organized interest groups in China.

There are, however, forces at work in other directions. An important trend of economic change in the reform is that the growth of value added has lagged behind that of assets among both state and nonstate enterprises in the industrial sector, which has been the leading contributor to China's GDP. What this suggests is that China's economic growth may have been increasingly driven by expansive investment rather than by a persistent improvement of productivity in the use of resources. The growth of investment has been fueled by foreign direct investment, budgetary overspending, public debt, and channeling by state banks of urban and rural residents' deposits. It is questionable whether these sources can continue to sustain growth over the long haul.

An important contributing factor to the lag between investment growth and value creation is excess capacity in many industrial sectors, which has been exacerbated by moral hazard problems under fiscal decentralization and by the deterioration of the organizational health of the state. Also, in view of the growing cost of favor seeking and the declining rate of return due to an intensification of competition in political and economic arenas, increasing numbers of public enterprise leaders have begun to shift the focus of their exchange relations with officials from production-based profit making to embezzlement of enterprise assets, creating further slack in production activities. Moreover, competitive favor seeking has stimulated state agents to enhance their efforts to divert public resources and abuse public authority. A result of this is an intensification of predation by state agents on less favored parties, which impedes innovation and productive activities and increases the tension between the state and the society.

The Rise and Decline of Monopoly Profits

When economic reform started in post-Mao China, it faced three important conditions developed under the old system: a differentiation of bureaucratic interests down the administrative hierarchy, a system of production and distribution featuring monopolies and monopsonies, and a serious shortage in the supply of many industrial products.

The central planning system established in the 1950s created an order of differentiated bureaucratic interests in the Chinese state. Administrative units at higher levels of the command chain had greater allocative and regulatory power than those at lower levels. A major determinant of such power distribution was the variation in the degree of importance attached by the leadership to the enterprises placed under the supervision of different loci of authority. As indicated in Chapters 1 and 2, enterprises controlled by central or provincial authorities were given more favorable treatment than those controlled by city or county authorities. Enterprises under the purview of urban subdistrict administrations and rural people's communes were at the bottom of the pecking order of resource allocation and faced enormous uncertainties and instabilities in input supplies, production, and sales. The disadvantage of these enterprises was reflected in the meager resource power of their supervising authorities. Thus officials in grassroots administrations had the least interest in maintaining the central planning system and were most receptive to alternative modes of economic activity that could make them more resourceful.

The central planning system also led to monopolies and monopsonies. In order to direct and keep track of the flow of resources and output effectively, the central planners fixed the pairing of transactions among economic organizations. Each enterprise was required to obtain inputs from state-designated suppliers at state-set prices and to sell its output to state-designated buyers at state-set prices. Self-arranged transactions between enterprises not paired by the central planners were generally not allowed. Although from time to time this rule was broken, especially by enterprises at the lower rungs of the resource allocation hierarchy, the scale and scope of self-arranged transactions were limited.[2] Because of such segmentation in the production and distribution of

---

[2] See Chapter 2.

industrial output, certain enterprises, especially those controlled by higher administrative levels of the state, were the sole input suppliers or output buyers of other enterprises despite the fact that in each subsector of industrial production there were usually quite a large number of enterprises producing the same or similar output.[3]

Still another legacy of the central planning system were imbalances between demand and supply. The leadership's hope that central planning could perfectly match demand and supply and eliminate the kind of wastage caused by free competition in capitalist economies never materialized in reality. Overemphasis on capital goods industries, coordination and communication problems under long and complex command chains, conflict between political and economic imperatives, and weak economic incentives to officials, managers, and workers were among the factors that contributed to a growing inability of the system to reduce slack in production and contain widening gaps in demand and supply among different lines of economic activities. The result was a serious shortage in the supply of many industrial products (including both capital and consumer goods) despite the existence of many pockets of underused capacity and redundant workforce.

The above three conditions set the stage for important changes to unfold in the reform. The demand for products in short supply created a potential opportunity for profit making through production of such output. Bureaucratic resistance to attempts at capitalizing on this opportunity tended to be easier to soften at the bottom of the state bureaucracy, where grassroots level officials were not firmly committed to maintaining the central planning system, especially the monopolies and monopsonies couched under higher level administrations. It is therefore not surprising that the growth of the nonstate sector economy started in areas of chronic shortage (e.g., consumer goods production) and took place under the auspices of grassroots level governments. What triggered such growth was the sweeping move to decollectivize the rural economy in the early 1980s (Riskin 1987: 284–315), which, coupled with fiscal decentralization, both opened opportunities and released and generated enormous resources for profit-making activities beyond agriculture.

The expansion process of the nonstate sector has been detailed elsewhere (see, e.g., Naughton 1995a). The economic competition thesis argues that it has contributed greatly to eroding the monopoly profits of

---

[3] It is important to note that the existence of monopolies and monopsonies before the reform did not lead to monopoly profits as defined in the context of a market economy. Under China's central planning system, prices did not reflect relative scarcity. Their levels were an indication of planners' preferences in allocating resources and distributing the gains from economic activities (Liu Guoguang and Zhou Guiying 1992; Zhu Rongji 1985).

traditional public enterprises (especially state enterprises) by offering an alternative source of supply and by demonstrating the gains of operating in the emergent markets. What the early comers acquired was actually a limitedly available right to operate outside the plan. This advantage formed a new source of (real) monopoly profits. But such profits were short-lived. Soon these enterprises faced stiff competition as they ran into each other during their expansion beyond their local economic spaces, as new enterprises were formed within their own neighborhoods, and as old public enterprises broke away from central planning (see, e.g., Jefferson and Singh 1999).

What needs to be more closely examined is how and why the above process has taken place. It is important to note that the space outside the plan was not a domain with open access. Entry by new players required permission from the gatekeepers, and resources were needed for operating in the new economic space. Without ad hoc regulatory treatment from local authorities and without the resources diverted (e.g., through back-yard profit centers) from the plan, nonstate enterprises could not have expanded so rapidly and generated growing competitive pressure on the traditional public sector and on each other. Also, the delayed but irreversible breakaway of traditional public sector enterprises from the plan has been a process involving extensive efforts led by certain enterprises to seek ad hoc favorable treatment from the state, such as exclusive rights in the form of various "one step ahead first" reform measures. But this has in turn triggered actions by other firms to follow suit, reducing the unevenness in regulatory treatment as well as the gains associated with it. The concurrent decline of monopoly profits, therefore, has been driven not only by competition among economic actors situated in different market niches and regulatory environments, but by their competition for ad hoc favors from state agents. The resultant exodus to the economic space outside the plan has both broadened avenues for economic growth and created a crowding effect, forcing enterprises to look beyond special favors for ways to improve profitability.

Entry and Expansion of New Enterprises in the Nonstate Sector

New enterprises in the nonstate sector fall into five categories: newly formed urban and rural collectives, private enterprises, foreign capital enterprises, and joint ownership enterprises. As discussed in Chapter 2, their entry and expansion in the industrial sector have been a major source of growing economic competition in the reform era. Although there have been central policies that opened the way for the development of these enterprises (e.g., laws and regulations on foreign capital enter-

prises), it is important to note that many such policies were formulated
to recognize and regularize changes that had already taken place beyond
the limits of the old system. It was primarily the gatekeepers of various
local economic spaces that initially opened the doors for the entry of these
new enterprises and bent local regulations to facilitate their growth.[4]

This fact has been extensively documented and discussed in studies
of rural collectives (e.g., Byrd and Lin 1990; Ma Rong et al. 1994; Oi
1998, 1999), private enterprises (e.g., Liu 1992; Shi Xianmin 1993; Wank
1996, 1999; Young 1995), and foreign capital enterprises (Hsing 1998;
Shirk 1994). Among the commonly reported favorable treatments
received by these new enterprises from local authorities are a lowering of
minimum equity capital requirements for TVEs, provision of guarantees
for borrowing from state banks, shortened processes of regulatory
approval for enterprise formation, expansion, and integration, permission
for private enterprises to fake themselves as collective enterprises, tacit or
explicit authorization of entry into areas not allowed by higher level
authorities, exaggeration of capital injected by foreign investors, flexible
accounting procedures, lowering of safety and environmental protection
standards, tolerance of poor treatment of labor, relaxation of restrictions
on import and export, tax reductions, and extended tax holidays.[5]

An equally important but sometimes overlooked fact is that favorable
treatment of new enterprises by local authorities is not extended in an
all-encompassing fashion, as noted in most of the studies cited above.
Rather, it must be sought and secured in an ad hoc fashion. With the
growth of the number of new enterprises in the nonstate sector, competition for ad hoc favorable treatment tends to intensify.[6]

This has two implications. First, to pre-existing public (especially state)
enterprises the newcomers in the nonstate sector posed a serious challenge, crowding their existing sales channels and eroding their traditional
revenue bases. Second, for the newcomers the increase of favor seekers
diminished the extraordinary gains accruing to any initially exclusive
rights to operate in various sectors outside the plan. This was due to the
difficulty of keeping other favor seekers from entering the same sector
in the same jurisdiction,[7] and to the inability of any of them to prevent

---

[4] In the 1980s, for example, regulations on TVEs were significantly modified several times
to address realities that had been created beyond existing rules (Ma Jiesan 1991; Zhang
Yi 1990). It was not until 1996 that the *Law on Enterprises under Township Authorities* was enacted.
[5] See also the discussion in Chapter 3.
[6] Table 3.1, for example, shows that during 1986–94 all but three of the 49 industrial
sectors experienced an increase in the number of newly formed enterprises, from both
the state and the nonstate sectors.
[7] In the 1980s, for example, the aluminum arbitrage operation of Modern Housewares
(Chapters 2 and 3) went quite well because it was the only major local source of supply.
But from the early 1990s when domestic producers of aluminum managed to increase

other favor seekers from entering the same sector in other jurisdictions (Montinola et al. 1995). The thinning of monopoly profits resulting from a multiplication of favor-seeking efforts under various local jurisdictions thus may have contributed to sustaining the economic competition among new enterprises themselves.

Furthermore, the expansion of new enterprises in the nonstate sector has been facilitated greatly by the resources that they have siphoned away, with the help of officials through their allocative decisions and/or through backyard profit centers, from the traditional public sector. Bank loans, industrial materials, energy and utility supplies, and technical personnel are among the resources that the state sector used to be guaranteed but has been increasingly unable to stop from flowing into the nonstate sector since the early 1980s. This has weakened the ability of state enterprises to sustain their traditional output levels, further reducing the means of many of them to make monopoly profits (if any).

In addition, as noted in Chapter 4, the nonstate sector has been the main demand creator for backyard profit centers. The multiplication of such entities since the mid-1980s has not only seriously hamstrung the plan but has also intensified the competition among themselves for favors from their sponsoring agencies. A result of this is the increase of supply of previously plan-allocated inputs, especially industrial materials (e.g., steel, timber, coal, cement), to outside parties. What has followed is a decrease to market levels of the initially high prices for industrial materials and hence a decline of the monopoly profits for arbitrage involving such items (Chapter 4). The greater availability of, and decrease of price discrepancies for, industrial materials have gradually narrowed the margin of profits accruing to certain nonstate enterprises because of their unique ability during the early years of reform to acquire through state agents industrial materials at "middle prices" between the plan and black or gray markets (Ma Kai 1992).

Breakaway of State Enterprises from the Plan

As indicated in Chapter 2, the entry and expansion of new enterprises in the nonstate sector not only have seriously undercut the performance of state enterprises but also illustrated the opportunity cost of continuing to operate under the plan. In response to such push-and-pull effects, many state enterprises have adapted their strategies, especially those for interacting with their supervising agencies. Such adaptations are

their sales outside of the state plan, local competition heated up. Mr. Cheung lobbied for a restriction on the registration of new local aluminum traders, but failed because the local *gongshang* office could not resist the intense efforts of newcomers to seek entry through their personal contacts with the gatekeepers (Informant no. 335/1995).

manifested in three strategies: to maneuver for organizational slack, to explore and capture market opportunities, and to turn state assets into private assets. The slack strategy has been widely seen as predominant and rooted in the governance structure of state enterprises.[8] But recent research findings have begun to broaden this once predominant view, especially its emphasis on the persistent insensitivity of state enterprises to new growth opportunities in their regulatory and market environments.[9] I discuss the market strategy here and leave the discussion of the asset-stripping strategy to the next section.

My case study findings are consistent with the view that the responses of state enterprises to marketization have gradually shifted from the slack strategy to the market strategy. Much of the evidence on the slack strategy concerns the early years of reform. But with the growth of the competitive pressures generated by new enterprises in the nonstate sector, increasing numbers of state enterprises have started to change course. Although bargaining has remained the main form of interaction with state agencies, its orientation has been shifted from finessing for slack to seeking growth opportunities for profit making outside the plan. What needs to be emphasized in this regard is that the pursuit of the market strategy and its success are both closely related to the efforts of state enterprises to manipulate state action.

A commonly used strategy to make up the losses due to an erosion of traditional monopoly profits is to generate new monopoly profits by bargaining for a leading position in exploring new frontiers of reform. The purpose of this approach is to create exclusive rights for moving out of the plan ahead of other state enterprises and thereby gain a competitive

---

[8] According to a principal-agent analysis informed by theories developed from past studies (e.g., Janos Kornai's works) on the state socialist economy, the governance structure of state enterprises drives enterprise leaders to rely on slack-oriented bargaining strategies despite the introduction of market-oriented reforms. This is due to two major factors. First, supervising authorities (the principal) depend on state enterprises (the agent) for nonfinancial functions (such as provision of employment) (Walder 1995b) and parochial financial gains (such as locally disposed fees in lieu of taxes) (Huang 1990). Such dependence makes it possible for state enterprises to bargain for soft financial discipline, protection, and subsidies, all of which add to organizational slack. Second, ambiguity and instability in the boundaries between different loci of state authority and between supervising agencies and state enterprises make it difficult to ascertain and individualize responsibility (Lee 1991; Naughton 1992b). Also, supervising agencies suffer from information deficiency due to large numbers of state enterprises placed under their regulation (Walder 1995b). These conditions weaken the incentive and capacity of officials to monitor state enterprises closely, adding further room for the latter to maneuver for slack.

[9] Weakening financial capacity of the state and increasing economic uncertainties faced by state enterprises, for example, are found to have led to a gradual hardening of financial disciplines by supervising authorities and even by enterprises themselves (Jefferson and Rawski 1994a, 1994b; Rawski 1994a, 1995; see also Naughton 1995a).

advantage based on institutional unevenness among peer enterprises. It follows the same logic of what was described by Vogel (1989) as "one step ahead first" measures (pursued in Guangdong's economic reform) and what Shirk (1993) termed as "particularistic contracting" between central and local authorities. What this represents is in essence a combination of rent seeking and profit seeking.[10]

It appears that large and "important" state enterprises tend to have an initial edge in gaining such ad hoc favorable treatment from their supervising agencies,[11] which have greater political and resource dependence on their performance than on that of other subordinate enterprises.[12] Northern Machinery, for example, has been a major beneficiary of ad hoc permissions for experimenting with reforms ahead of its peers in capital use, output contract, and labor practice during the reform (Chapter 3). According to factory leaders (Informants no. 255/1994, no. 267/1994), a key to this success was to maintain its traditionally high profile in the eyes of top city government leaders, who needed certain star enterprises (especially those that could showcase a politically correct point – i.e., it is possible to carry out reforms successfully in the ailing state sector) to boast about to higher level authorities and thereby secure and advance their own careers. To make the factory part of such indispensable political capital to local leaders, top managers of Northern Machinery not only sought to improve economic performance by marketizing its activities, but paid special attention to public relations and maintained very good ties with the official media and the propaganda agencies of the local Party-state apparatus. Arrangements were made periodically for top city leaders to tour the factory and "inspect work."

Ironically, the efforts that Northern Machinery made to gain an edge over other enterprises also set in motion forces that would eventually narrow the edge. If the "reform experiments" carried out by the factory proved to be successful, then it would be logical for such measures to be introduced in other firms, thereby making the gains from institutional

---

[10] See note 31 of the introductory chapter for a discussion of the distinction between profit seeking and rent seeking.

[11] The Chinese government uses a set of complex criteria, including production capacity, output, sales volume, number of employees, assets, etc., for the classification of enterprise scale (GJTJJb 1995: 314). The criteria were adjusted upward twice (in 1978 and 1992) in the reform era. Those classified as "large scale enterprises" are the leading enterprises in different industrial sectors. There remain, however, intersectoral variations in the criteria used. For example, the assets of a "large scale" enterprise in the textiles sector may be less than those of a "medium scale" enterprise in the petrochemical sector.

[12] It should be noted that officials providing special treatment to such enterprises may derive from this course of action both benefits in nonpecuniary forms (e.g., positional security and career advancement) and concrete material benefits, as discussed in the preceding chapter.

unevenness short-lived.[13] As one of Northern Machinery's deputy directors put it:

> We have been trying to keep one step ahead of other enterprises (in the same industrial sector). But they are quick to argue that they should follow the good examples we have set. It is hard for the supervising authorities to refute such an argument. Consequently, we have to keep looking for new areas of reform. It has become harder and harder to do so, but if we don't try harder others will – and surpass us.

Competitive Favor Seeking and Economic Growth

It is clear that the movement of both state and nonstate enterprises into the economic space outside the plan has been driven not only by competitive forces in the economic process, but by those in the political process. The multiplication of the latter has brought about three important effects. First, many pre-existing barriers to profit making through self-arranged exchanges have been lowered or overcome as a result of ad hoc rule bending by officials. This has enhanced the incentives and broadened the avenues for increasing numbers of economic actors to participate in market-oriented economic activities.

Second, with the brokerage of officials, large amounts of plan-allocated financial, physical, and human resources have been channeled from their designated users to those engaged in economic activities outside the plan. Neither group of enterprises is homogeneous, but the latter faces weaker constraints on profit-oriented economic activities and thus tends to be more productive in the use of resources than the former, as noted by most studies of economic change in China.

---

[13] The experience of Northern Machinery is similar to that of many other star enterprises in the state sector. The Capital Iron and Steel Company (known as *Shougang* in Chinese), for example, was a pioneer of reform in the state sector, largely because of its adoption of many "one step ahead first" measures based on the clout of Zhou Guanwu, its former director, in the central government (*Far Eastern Economic Review*, July 19, 1994, January 6, 1995). In the late 1980s and early 1990s, it was the most profitable steel mill in China. But then its performance declined, partly due to the political downfall of Zhou and partly due to the efforts of many other steel mills to follow suit. Yuxi Cigarette Factory, another star enterprise in the state sector, rose from a medium-sized tobacco product manufacturer to China's (and Asia's) largest and most profitable cigarette producer during 1980–90. Its success hinged greatly on an institutional unevenness between itself and other cigarette manufacturers in the heavily regulated tobacco sector, created by various forms of ad hoc favorable treatment from the provincial and subprovincial governments in Yunnan (Eng and Lin 1997). But what it did to bargain its way out of the plan was quickly imitated by other cigarette producers in Yunnan and those in other provinces, diminishing the initial regulatory unevenness and narrowing its profit margin in the 1990s (ibid.).

Third, although it is often *necessary* for enterprises to manipulate state action in order to excel, the difficulty of sustaining monopoly profit amidst intense competitive favor seeking has made it insufficient to rely on preferential allocative and regulatory treatment by officials as the primary source of profits. While exploring new ground for further rule bending, which may well amount to institutional innovation if the rules bent in an ad hoc fashion are legitimized and regularized,[14] enterprises can hardly prosper without innovation in economic activities. Among the case study enterprises that I have discussed in the preceding chapters, for example, the more successful ones are mostly those that have made extensive efforts in both areas.

Apparently, these effects work largely in the same direction as competitive forces in product and factor markets; they also draw on and reinforce the latter, which signal the opportunity costs of different modes of resource use and play an important role in shaping price fluctuations. This convergence of effects has driven large numbers of enterprises toward value-creation activities, contributing to the growth of economic output in the past two decades.

This view of the outcome of economic institutional change stands in contrast to the economic stagnation and decline prominently portrayed in the literature on corruption and rent seeking. Their retarding effects on economic development are traced to the following (Rose-Ackerman 1999; Tollison and Congleton 1995). First, currying favor involves wasteful allocation and use of resources (especially human resources), which otherwise could be developed (as in the case of human capital) and used for more productive purposes. Second, the beneficiaries of those gaining favors from officials are often not those making the most efficient use of resources. In fact, the monopolies created by them lead to underutilization of resources for value creation. Third, corruption and rent seeking provide perverse incentives for officials to contrive hurdles for favor seekers to overcome, breeding more unproductive activities. Fourth, pervasive corruption and rent seeking diminish the legitimacy of the government and foster disrespect for laws and regulations. This increases the governance costs in the economy and society, hinders innovation, and undermines the morale of the disadvantaged, who constitute the bulk of the workforce.

Noticeably insignificant during China's transition from central planning to markets are two important factors that contribute to the second

---

[14] Legitimation is important in this regard because it indicates an open acceptance by the pertinent public authority of a rule change. Unless they are legalized (which seems unlikely), therefore, violations of existing rules on environmental protection and labor rights protection do not qualify as institutional innovations even if they are widespread (and thus in a way regularized).

effect identified above: the repartitioning of economic opportunities, resources, and payoffs within the institutional confines of an existing system (especially one that is inefficient), and the relative stability of pricing power associated with monopolies. The origin of these lies in the initial conditions of the Chinese reform.

As noted above, because of their weak interest in the central planning system, large numbers of grassroots officials were both attracted to the enormous profit-making opportunities unleashed by rural decollectivization, and actively involved in favor exchanges with outsiders seeking to tap such opportunities under fiscal decentralization. This massive defection from the plan has not only made the old system unsustainable due to rule bending and resource diversion by the defectors, but also created a snowballing effect through their concurrent attempts to weaken the monitoring capacity of the system (Chapter 5), hence broadening avenues for more defectors and favor seekers to advance their interests at the expense of the old system. In the meanwhile, the actions of opportunistic officials have been decentralized and incohesive. This has resulted in a proliferation of competitive favor-seeking efforts both within and between different loci of state power, rendering the advantage of first movers significantly less effective as subsequent favor seekers gain the same rights. Consequently, it has become difficult to ration entry into the extra-plan space and to sustain broad pricing power for a few players.[15]

The outcome of competitive favor seeking in this context thus differs from that discussed in the conventional theory of rent seeking, which treats the competition for monopoly rights as a redistribution game that has little corrosive effect on the existing institutional framework. The initial focus of the theory (e.g., Krueger 1974) was the dissipation of monopoly profit (and the social waste) caused by competitive bidding among rent seekers, which can cause further wasteful uses of resources. Subsequent research has drawn attention to the institutional barriers to the efforts to challenge monopolies (Bardhan 1997). Olson (1982), for example, offers an elaborate account of the conditions that help sustain monopoly rights as well as the economic consequences of stable "collusive alliances." In particular, he identifies two factors conducive to the development of clublike political markets and the entrenchment of

---

[15] This contrasts with an argument made by Shleifer and Vishny (1993). They posit that the retarding effect of corruption on economic development is likely to be worse under a decentralized regime of state authorities than a centralized one, because the bribes that have to be paid for permits under the former tend to be greater and less effective. But they do not specify whether the acquirement of permits leads to greater incentives and opportunities for value creation or redistribution based on exclusive pricing power.

monopoly rights: institutionalized social segregation and organized interest groups – especially those that represent narrow interests but have broad influence in politics and economic life. Both tend to stifle efforts to challenge existing monopolies. It is interesting that both are conspicuously absent in China, making it difficult to sustain monopolies in both the old institutional framework and the formative economic space outside it.

Unlike India and many African countries that are well known for powerful special interests that retard economic growth (Bates 1981; Kohli 1990; Rudolph and Rudolph 1987), the bulk of the Chinese society has not been deeply divided along the lines of ethnicity, language, and religion. Han Chinese make up over 90% of the population, and most of the ethnic minorities live in remote, economically underdeveloped provinces. Although there are different local dialects, a standardized spoken language known as *Putonghua* has been adopted since 1955 and widely disseminated through the educational system and mass media. Confucianism, the traditional ideology, is not a religion, nor does it have any sectlike subdivisions. Although its core values were severely attacked in the Mao era,[16] some remnants, especially the emphasis on particularistic exchange through personal networks, have survived.[17] Under the central planning system, spatial mobility was restricted, especially between rural and urban areas. But there were various forms of migration that paved the way for the growth of social networks across the boundaries of different localities in the reform era.[18]

As to organized interest groups, they have not been extensively developed since the 1949 revolution. In fact, the communist state has restricted the formation and functioning of any formal organizations that aim to rep-

---

[16] Mao's ideal was to create a universalistic social order where all forms of social division would be eliminated and only "comradeship" would prevail (Vogel 1965). But in reality the politicization of social life did result in cleavages between people of different "class backgrounds" (Madsen 1984; Walder 1986). Although the resultant personal animosities may have persisted into the reform era, there is little sign that the official ideology has continued to function as an important separator in social interaction.

[17] It should be noted that this emphasis was intended to address instrumental and noninstrumental (expressive and normative) concerns and strike a balance between them (Yu Ying-shih 1984, 1987).

[18] Millions of former peasants who had joined the communist army became the main source of cadres after the revolution. They mostly settled and worked in urban administrative centers (Song Defu 1994). Large numbers of rural residents were recruited to work in urban enterprises during the industrialization drive from the 1950s to the 1970s (Xu Dixin 1988). Fourteen million urban youths were sent to the countryside during the Cultural Revolution, and most of them returned to their home cities afterward (He Guang 1990). Nationwide recruitment of college students and military soldiers and their assignment after school and service to units outside their places of origin also added important paths of social connections (Cui Naifu 1994). All these spatial movements have expanded the reaches of social networks.

resent the interests of certain segments of the society.[19] There have been various informal alliances of departmental interests in the state bureaucracy, but most of them have been unstable and unable to mobilize sufficient organizational power to sanction or ostracize opportunistic members (Harding 1981; Lampton 1987; Lieberthal and Oksenberg 1988; Shirk 1993).[20] The corporatist alliances formed under various grassroots governments in the reform do have a certain level of internal cohesion (Oi 1998, 1999; Whiting 1995).[21] But they lack the ability to influence what happens beyond their own jurisdictions; in fact they are fierce rivals.[22]

In short, because of the weak commitment of grassroots officials to the plan, the absence of entrenched institutional barriers to social exchange between people of different backgrounds, and a lack of cohesion among various loci of decentralized state authority, the political arena has become highly porous and accessible to large numbers of favor seekers from different quarters of the society. Since the most active favor seekers tend to be those without much vested interest in the central planning system, as shown in the preceding chapters, the multiplication of their efforts to use personal networks to manipulate state action to their advantage has rendered the old economic system increasingly unsustainable.

Undoubtedly, this course of action has likely involved considerable social waste, such as the time, resources, and talents devoted to securing special treatment, which otherwise could have been used more productively. But at the same time, competitive favor seeking has also contributed to drastic changes in economic institutions, unleashing enormous opportunities for value creation while containing the scale and scope of stable monopolies as well as their pricing power. As a result, the pie has grown much bigger, rather than simply being resliced within a given limit. Identifying and explaining the role of competitive favor seeking thus helps

[19] There have been various associations that operate under government auspices and claim to represent the interests of their members. Some have been better able than others to advance such interests within the boundaries set by the government (Unger 1996), though both the magnitude of their influence and the degree of their independence remain limited.

[20] The periodic swings between decentralization and re-centralization before the reform and the reshuffling of the Party-state bureaucracy during nationwide political campaigns (e.g., the Cultural Revolution), for example, added to the instability of organized bureaucratic interests.

[21] The revival of kinship organizations and their interlocking with local state authority in the countryside (Lin 1995; Lin and Chen 1999), however, do seem to pose certain constraints on competition within the local political market (especially at the village level). It should be noted that this development has been a gradual process and its impact was limited in the early years of reform. Also, the extent of its spread and the stability of the resultant authority relations remain to be ascertained.

[22] An example of this is the creation of various special policy enclaves under different local authorities to compete for investment and other resources. See, e.g., Shirk (1994).

reveal an important causal linkage in what has led to China's recent economic growth. This by no means negates the concomitant increase of social waste, which, however, may have been far outweighed by the growth of net output from economic activities in the short term. Nor should it be taken to gloss over the latent problems that have developed during dual marketization, which are the focus of the discussion below.

The Other Side of the Story

Although the record of China's recent economic growth has been impressive, it is important to look beyond output statistics for a fuller view of the more diverse outcomes of economic institutional change. A contrasting trend that has been in the making since the reform is that the profit rate has steadily declined in the industrial sector, as shown in Chapter 1. Concurrent with this is another trend among both state and nonstate industrial enterprises. The growth of value-added has lagged behind that of assets, particularly in the 1990s, as can be seen from the figures in the first two columns of Table 7.1. It is also worth noting that at the same time both fixed asset investment in the industrial sector and various sources of funds that can fuel the growth of such investment and working capital (i.e., foreign direct investment, bank deposits, budgetary overspending, and public debt of the government) have steadily increased.

A hypothesis that can be made about these concurrent trends is that the growth of economic output may have been increasingly driven by expansive investment rather than by a persistent improvement in the efficiency of resource use. To what extent this is true remains to be ascertained by economists. But what I discuss below – idle capacity, asset stripping, and intensification of predation by state agents on less favored parties – suggests a likely existence of the hypothesized causal link. All these problems have grown with the deepening of dual marketization.

Overbuilding and Underutilization of Capacity

As noted in Chapter 3, in the reform the authority to approve and regulate enterprise formation and licensing has been decentralized, thus broadening the avenues for entry into potentially profitable areas of business. This, however, has been accompanied by a growing problem, i.e., excess capacity, which has been particularly acute in the manufacturing of consumer goods that used to be in short supply. The main reason is that similar efforts have been made in many localities, leading to an oversupply of the same products and consequently underutilization

Table 7.1. *Return on assets in the industrial sector and various sources of asset formation*[a]

Year	Value-added/ assets (state industrial enterprises) (%)	Value-added/ assets (nonstate industrial enterprises) (%)	Capital construction investment in the industrial sector (100 million yuan)	Foreign direct investment (US$ 100 million)	Bank deposits from urban & rural residents (100 million yuan)	Budget deficit (100 million yuan)	Domestic & international debt (100 million yuan)
1978			273.2		210.6	10.17	35.31
1979			256.9			-135.41	43.01
1980	36	55	275.6		399.5	-68.90	73.08
1981			216.0			37.81	83.86
1982			260.6			-17.65	79.41
1983			282.3			-42.57	77.34
1984			341.6	12.58		-58.16	89.85
1985	36	52	446.5	16.61	1,622.6	.57	138.25
1986	34	48	531.6	18.74	2,237.6	-82.90	169.55
1987	34	47	682.8	23.14	3,073.3	-62.83	270.78
1988	36	49	812.6	31.94	3,801.5	-133.97	282.97
1989	34	45	822.5	33.92	5,146.9	-158.88	375.45
1990	30	40	952.6	34.87	7,034.2	-146.49	461.40
1991	29	40	1147.2	43.66	9,107.0	-237.14	669.68
1992	24	31	1458.3	110.07	11,545.4	-258.83	739.22
1993	29	44	2,004.5	275.15	14,762.4	-293.35	1,175.25
1994	27	36	2,761.7	337.67	21,518.8	-574.52	1,549.76
1995	23	29	3,236.3	375.21	29,662.3	-581.52	1,967.28
1996	21	30	3,726.7	417.26	38,520.8	-529.56	2,476.82
1997	20	29	4,119.5	452.57	46,279.8	-582.42	3,310.93
1998				454.63	53,407.5	-922.23	

[a] The data in columns 2–3 are for independent accounting industrial enterprises at and above the township level. Value-added refers to net material product for 1980–92 and industrial value-added for 1993–7. These indicators have slightly different definitions (Holz and Lin 2000). Assets refer to the sum of the net value of fixed assets and working capital, both of which were redefined in 1993 (ibid.). Because of these differences, comparisons of the ratios between the two periods may be inaccurate, though comparisons within each period are less affected by the changes in variable definitions.

Source: GJTJJa (1998: 269, 291, 444–7, 637; 1999: 265, 284); GJTJJb (1993: 103, 116); GJTJJc (1996: 115–17; 1997: 481; 1997: 501).

Table 7.2. *Selected statistics of industrial production (independent accounting enterprises at and above township level)*

Product	Number of manufacturers Before industrial reform	1985	1995	Use of capacity in 1995	Group profit rate 1985	1995
Bicycle	38 (1978)	672	1,081	55%	44.9%	0.2%
Motorcycle		194	1,535	55%	18.4%	8.6%
Sedan car		3	30	65%	41.6%	18.3%
Bus		53	135	30%	40.1%	−0.3%
Refrigerator	21 (1984)	110	186	57%	32.2%	8.1%
Washing machine	42 (1984)	132	89	43%	30.0%	2.9%
Air conditioner		44	408	34%	30.0%	6.4%
Beer		451	737	70%	24.1%	2.5%

Source: Fang Weizhong and Wu Jiajun (1989: 26–7, 161, 403); GYPCBGS (1987, volume 3: 90–121, 1180–95); GYPCBGS (1997a: 70, 166, 174, 182, 234–64).

of production capacities. The figures reported in Table 7.2 illustrate the situation.[23]

The intensification of economic competition apparently has had an effect on this. When output expands beyond effective demand, the less competitive producers are bound to falter or fail, consequently decreasing the utilization of their capacity. But the mismatch between demand and supply is not simply a result of miscalculations by economic actors. It is also related to problems that have developed in the political process, especially the perverse incentives and moral hazard under fiscal decentralization and the deterioration of the organizational health of the state.

In a recent study Gore (1999; see also Gore 1998) argues that, because the career advancement and financial rewards of provincial and municipal officials have been closely tied to the growth of output from the economic activities they oversee under fiscal decentralization, they have sought to mobilize resources for the construction of new projects or

[23] The capacity usage figures are computed as the percentages of the output levels of different products and their production capacities reported in the 1995 industrial census. They would look worse if the output that was produced but unsold in that year were also included in the computation. The situation remained serious three years after the census. According to a 1998 survey conducted by the State Statistical Bureau, half the manufacturers of the 900 major industrial products identified in the survey had a capacity utilization rate below 60% (*RMRB*, March 2, 1999). In another 1998 enterprise survey ($n = 3,180$), insufficient demand was rated by 33.8% of the respondents as the most serious obstacle to their operations (CESS 1998: 11).

expansion of existing projects under their purview. This type of investment often does not lead to efficient use of resources, but it boosts output growth (mainly reflected in the project builders' accounts rather than those of users) during the tenures of the leading officials concerned,[24] thus serving a political purpose. Since the growth of investment has outpaced the growth of slack resulting from overbuilding, the problem has not been fully exposed. When the tempo of investment slows down, as among many Southeast Asian economies during the Asian financial crisis in 1997–8, the bubble will burst and the economy will collapse to its true size.

A parallel can be found in rural industrialization, which has been driven by an expansionary strategy adopted by township and village authorities to promote the growth of collectives under their control (Byrd and Lin 1990; Ma Rong et al. 1994; Whiting 1996). As Kung and Lin (1999) note, since local officials are not true owners of public assets and thus do not bear the ultimate risk in asset use, they tend to focus on what is most closely related to their interests (especially short-term interests) rather than the economic fundamentals of local public enterprises. The expansionary strategy has therefore emphasized the growth of sales, which provide the base for the bulk of the tax revenue that local officials are obligated to generate,[25] thereby securing their financial and career rewards under the fiscal contract. But due to intense competition in product markets and the generally low level of technology among TVEs, stability in production is difficult to achieve, and frequent switches between different products have to be made for sales growth.[26] This involves building new capacities while reducing or abandoning the use of existing capacities.[27] Such a mode of operation, driven by short-term maximizing decisions of local political actors, has been facilitated by extensive uses of financial leverage (borrowing) (Lin Qingsong and Du

---

[24] An example of this is the expansion project imposed on Polyester Fiber by its supervising authority, discussed toward the end of Chapter 3.

[25] During 1985–98, transaction taxes on average made up 75% of the total taxes paid by TVEs, whereas the remaining 25% came from enterprise income tax (based on gross profit) (GJTJJa 1986: 217; 1987: 207; 1988: 289; 1989: 242; 1990: 396; 1991: 381; 1992: 393; 1993: 399; 1994: 364; 1995: 366; 1996: 391; 1997: 401; 1998: 422; 1999: 413).

[26] This is what happened among the rural collectives in Lotus Pond. According to the head of the township economic cooperative (Informant no. 349/1995), most of the township enterprises under it had to change their products almost every year to keep up sales. For more discussions on this issue, see Byrd and Lin (1990), Ma Jiesan (1991), Ma Rong et al. (1994).

[27] At Flying Horse Motors, for example, its expansion into the manufacturing of cars in 1994 turned out to be a big flop because of limited demand and oversupply. In 1996, only 30% of the capacity was used and the cars that had been assembled were sold at below-cost prices.

Ying 1997), exposing the enterprises to great risk.[28] With the increase of the cost for credit in the 1990s (Lardy 1998) and the narrowing of profit margin due to intense competition, however, expansionary growth has become increasingly difficult to sustain.

Moreover, the problem of overcapacity has been further exacerbated by widespread transgressions of the rules governing economic activities. In her best-seller *Xiandaihua de xianjing* (Pitfalls of Modernization),[29] author He Qinglian (1998) argues that ad hoc rule bending by state agents in exchange for private gain not only diminishes the effectiveness of the rules they enforce, but makes a mockery of the public authority such rules symbolize, resulting in growing disregard for law and regulation. A consequence of such a vicious cycle is a proliferation of substandard products and counterfeits, condoned by regulators (ibid.; *RMRB*, June 28, 1995, October 18, 1996, November 25, 1997, February 17, 1998, March 15, 1999, and July 6, 1999). There is also a concurrent weakening of entry barriers due to growing violations of regulatory requirements for environmental protection, labor rights, safety, and technical standards. As discussed in the preceding chapters, the intensity and effectiveness of the efforts by economic actors to manipulate state action have varied in different organizational and institutional settings. Those at a disadvantage (especially those in the state sector) thus tend to bear the brunt of unevenly regulated entry and competition in product markets, facing growing downward pressure on capacity utilization.[30] In the meanwhile, not all manufacturers of counterfeits and substandard products can sustain stable sales of their output, and some of those able to gain entry through regulatory violations may even be hit by unintended consequences of their own strategy, such as labor resistance and unrest, and destructive industrial accidents.[31] All this adds further slack to the economy.

From Production-Based Profit Making to Asset Stripping

Still another source of slack lies in a development manifested since the early 1990s: Increasing numbers of leaders of public enterprises that are

---

[28] According to the 1995 industrial census (GYPCBGS 1996: 519–20), the total debt incurred by township-owned enterprises was equivalent to 2.34 times their equity capital, which was even higher than the debt-equity ratio of state-owned industrial enterprises.

[29] For a review of the book, see Lin (2000).

[30] See Jin Bei (1997) and Zheng Haihang (1998) for discussions of these issues. For examples and discussions of similar cases, see GPJYJ (1996), Liu Bing and Deng Yizhi (1999), and Liu Suinian (1991).

[31] For a sample of reports on massive explosions in coal mines and fireworks producing facilities that did not meet regulatory requirements, see *RMRB*, March 3, 1995, December 15, 1996, November 19, 1997, October 31, 1998, and February 6, 1999.

less able to compete in both the political and economic markets have sought to promote their own interests at the cost of their enterprises. The main method is asset stripping, and a major result is a growing under-utilization of the physical and human resources of these enterprises.

The rise of this phenomenon is partly related to competition in the political market. Favor seeking is not a cost-free undertaking. To obtain preferential treatment, favor seekers incur various costs.[32] These include the time spent for interacting with officials in and outside of their offices,[33] various (in kind and pecuniary, direct and indirect, individual and collective) personal benefits extended to the officials, the use of resources to support certain formal functions or agenda as desired by the favor givers, or a combination of some or all of the above. The ability to influence the decisions of officials often has to be built up in a cumulative process to forge close ties, but there is no guarantee that the effort will subsequently pay off. In fact, administrative turnover in the state apparatus may result in transient tenures, turning the invest-ment in relationship building into a sunk cost. Moreover, given a limited supply of many favors (especially resources) within any given locus of state authority, the greater the number of favor seekers, the higher the cost of favor seeking relative to the net gains from the favors.

Also, industrial enterprises are situated in different structural condi-tions that influence the effectiveness of their favor seeking. Chapters 5 and 6 show that state enterprises tend to face greater constraints in the use of personal networks for special favors than nonstate enterprises. Within the state sector, large enterprises tend to have an edge over small enterprises in bargaining for preferential treatment, as noted above. It is therefore not surprising that small state enterprises have been the main loss-making segment in the state sector.[34] Among rural collectives, dif-ferential treatment by local officials in resource allocation and regulation tends to favor those making greater contributions to the formal and informal revenue bases of the local government (Ma Rong et al. 1994; Oi 1998, 1999; see also Chapter 5).

---

[32] In accounting, such costs are often included as production cost. An increase of produc-tion cost without a corresponding increase in output price is likely to lead to a nar-rowing of value added and profit margin.

[33] According to the director of Southwestern Machinery, for example, before the reform much of his time was spent on matters related to the internal operations of the factory. As the reform progressed, however, interactions with external parties took up the bulk of his time, which was divided between government officials and business partners. The same was true of the leaders of Northern Machinery (Informants no. 176/1992, no. 198/1992), where a special account was set up in the late 1980s to cover expenses incurred for various "socializing" functions undertaken by factory leaders.

[34] According to the 1995 industrial census, within the state sector large enterprises were the only group where total profits exceeded total losses (GYPCBGS 1996: 26). See also Lo (1997).

Withdrawing from the political market, however, may not be a viable option.[35] Maintaining even the barest level of production often requires the leader of an enterprise to enlist help from pertinent officials in securing recurrent loans from state banks, bending rules and regulations (e.g., those on accounting, environmental protection,[36] safety standards, employment practices, annual license review and renewal), reducing tax obligations, and containing various extra levies.[37] Although remaining in the favor-seeking game may not give an enterprise a great edge over its rivals, which are likely to pursue the same course of action, losing favor could increase its competitive disadvantage and, for the reasons just mentioned, even make its operation unsustainable. As Director Ma of Peak Equipment put it succinctly:

> Maintaining close contact with them [pertinent officials] is crucial to your ability to keep things going, though you won't necessarily be a lot better off. But if you stay away from them, you are most likely to be a lot worse off.

For leaders of public enterprises that can hardly afford to stay in the increasingly costly competition in the political arena and/or face great difficulty gaining the upper hand over their rivals, there is an alternative strategy. Instead of promoting their self-interest by improving the profitability of their enterprises to which their salaries and bonuses are tied,

---

[35] Substantial evidence of a combination of such withdrawal and high profitability would squarely contradict the hypothesis that effective manipulation of state action is a necessary condition for firms to succeed. One of the 46 factories where I conducted case studies during 1988–96 – Elegance Furniture (Chapter 4) – appears to have been in this category. The only preferential treatment it received from the local government was a one-year income tax exemption for 1983–4, which did not have much substantive effect in that the enterprise was still in the red during that year. Unlike many other factory leaders in the district, Director Liu did not spend much time socializing with local officials, some of whom called him a "talented oddball" (*guai cai*) (Informants no. 429/1996, no. 437/1996, no. 438/1996). Much of his spare time was spent for research on product development. Most of the capital was raised internally from retained profits, supplemented with limited amounts of bank loans borrowed at market rates. Despite a narrowing of profit margin in the early 1990s, it remained one of the more profitable enterprises in the district. But I have yet to find significant evidence of similar cases from secondary sources.

[36] This, of course, creates further hidden cost for economic growth. A World Bank report estimates that air and water pollution alone created costs equivalent to about 8% of China's GDP in 1995 (World Bank, 1997: 23). A study by the Chinese Academy of Sciences estimated that in 1995 the economic losses related to environmental pollution were equivalent to 3.27% of the GNP in that year (*JRSB*, May 7, 1999).

[37] Not all these favors (e.g., lax enforcement of regulations on labor practices, product quality, and accounting) are in strictly limited supply. But obtaining them is not a cost-free undertaking, not only because of the risk premium demanded by the officials for breaking the rules but because of their tendency to use rule bending as a way to bring themselves various additional benefits.

they can accommodate such interests by embezzling the assets of their enterprises, which neither they nor the supervising officials own. Among the commonly used methods are cooking the books for fund diversion, counting personal spending as production cost, getting kickbacks from colluding partners of transaction by underpricing output, overpricing input, and granting sales credit that could never be repaid (*RMRB*, January 16, 1995, July 26, 1995, March 21, 1997, February 20, 1998; see also Ding 2000; He Qinglian 1998).

These practices are, of course, illegal and require, at the least, collusion among managers and oversight from supervising officials. The magnitude of such embezzlement cannot be precisely ascertained, though it has become a major focus of attention among top policy makers and has been widely reported in the media since the mid-1990s.[38] The cases that have been exposed reveal massive amounts of funds embezzled and large numbers of enterprises involved.[39] Among the possible contributing factors are a significant increase in the number of enterprises (and hence a likely growth of competition in both the political and the economic processes),[40] an expansion of decision-making autonomy in state enterprises,[41] and a weakening of the state's monitoring capacity due to further growth of exchange relations in the political process, all of which reached unprecedented levels in the mid- to late 1990s.

A major consequence of this development is an accelerating increase of losses incurred by industrial enterprises (cf. Chapter 1). Moreover, it has also had an effect on further economic institutional change. In view of the growing number of loss-making enterprises in the public sector (including state enterprises, urban collectives, and rural collectives), in 1995 the central leadership adopted a new policy (*RMRB*, January 5, 1999), known as *zhua da fang xiao* (holding on to large enterprises and letting go small ones), to restructure large public enterprises into shareholding enterprises and allow small ones to have more flexible owner-

---

[38] In Chinese media this phenomenon has been characterized as "*qiong miao fu fangzhang*" or "impoverished monastery (the enterprise) under rich abbot (the manager)." For a sample of reports, see He Qinglian (1998); Jin Bei (1997); *RMRB*, July 19, 1997, August 17, 1997, October 20, 1999, January 11, 2000; and Zheng Haihang (1998).

[39] See, for example, *RMRB*, July 26, 1995, May 28, 1997, February 20, 1998, November 24, 1998, November 31, 1999, and December 14, 1999.

[40] The total number of industrial enterprises increased from 5.18 million in 1985 to 7.95 million in 1990, and further climbed to 10.01 million in 1994 before declining to 7.92 million in 1997 (GJTJJb 1998: 17).

[41] For a discussion of this, see section 4 (Collusion) in Chapter 4. Perhaps the most important effect of this change is that leaders of many small state enterprises have since gained the authority to choose their own deputies (CESS 1993–7). This has reduced the constraint on collusion among managers as discussed in the preceding chapter, thus opening the way for the pursuit of the asset-stripping strategy. Large enterprises, however, have not made much progress in this regard (ibid.). It is not surprising that most of the reports on asset stripping concern small state enterprises. See note 38.

ship arrangements, including outright privatization.[42] It remains to be seen whether this change will lead to a significant reduction in the slack created by large numbers of loss-making and underperforming enterprises. A serious problem that has to be tackled is the huge amount of debt that these enterprises owe to state banks,[43] which have absorbed the bulk of the savings of urban and rural residents and continued to grant loans to poorly performing enterprises (Lardy 1998). Since these debts have already been used to fuel existing output growth, massive default can pose a major threat to further economic growth.[44]

Predation on Less Favored Parties

In association with the increase of slack in economic activities there has grown another problem: the intensification of predatory state action. The increasing significance of this trend indicates a multiplication of the attempts at unproductive redistribution and a growth of constraint on innovation and productive activities.[45] The focus of favor exchanges in the political process has consequently begun to shift from seeking opportunities of value creation outside the plan to shaping the outcomes of redistribution among those pursuing market-oriented economic activities.

The problem was first exposed at the national level in 1982, when the State Council issued its first circular to curb excessive levies imposed by state agencies on enterprises (SJSFGS 1995: 30). Since then, the central

---

[42] This measure was implemented in both Lotus Pond and Gate Tower in 1998–9. Before its implementation, most public enterprises under both local governments, especially those in the "second and third tiers" (ranked in terms of importance), had already been deeply in the red. According to city and county officials (Informants no. 414/1996, no. 417/1996, no. 425/1996, no. 428/1996), the problem began in the early 1990s and worsened in the mid-1990s. Managerial corruption was singled out as the most important factor behind the trend. The fact that this could take place on a large scale suggests that condoning and perhaps even facilitating managerial corruption may have been pursued by some local officials as a way to get something for themselves from local public enterprises that were lackluster in performance and thus unable to make much of a contribution to the officials' formal or informal revenue bases.

[43] In 1997, the ratio of total debt to total equity was 1.89 for state enterprises, 2.4 for collective enterprises, and 1.45 for other enterprises in the nonstate sector (GJTJJa 1998: 444–6). What this means is that the total debt significantly exceeded the total capital owned by enterprises in all three groups, with collective enterprises being most exposed.

[44] In 1997, the liabilities of independent accounting industrial enterprises amounted to 6,614 billion yuan, equivalent to 143% of the bank deposits of urban and rural residents (4,628 billion yuan); state enterprises accounted for 58% of these liabilities (GJTJJa 1998: 325, 446). See Lin and Zhu (2001) for a discussion of the latest measures to "recycle" such debt.

[45] As noted above, these are among the retarding effects on economic growth identified by theories of rent seeking and corruption.

authority has issued various directives and restrictions on this issue every year, but to little avail. The magnitude of the phenomenon appears to have drastically increased since the late 1980s. In 1990 the CCP Central Committee and the State Council jointly launched a nationwide campaign to ban *san luan* or "three arbitrary levies" (*tanpai*, extra and unauthorized fees, and exorbitant fines). According to the directive issued by the central authority, the phenomenon "has persisted despite repeated bans (*lujin buzhi*), become increasingly serious, and posed an acute social problem, causing strong reactions from the masses" (ibid.).

A study conducted by the State Council in 1990 found that the taxes and regular fees imposed on enterprises increased from 4 in 1984 to 61 in 1989 (Luan Tao and Li Zhengzhi 1993: 4–11), of which 20 were taxes and 41 were various levies by state agencies; the various ad hoc charges were too many to count.[46] In 1987 there were 1,549 fee-charging state agencies in Beijing, which collected a total of 1.13 billion yuan. In the first ten months of 1992, the number of such agencies increased to 9,697, and the total amount of recorded levies rose to 3 billion yuan (BJSWYJS 1994: 266). A survey conducted by the Guangdong Price Control Bureau in 1996 found that only one-third of the nontax levies by government agencies in Guangdong province were authorized by the central and provincial governments (which were the only approving authorities for such levies), whereas the remaining items were contrived and imposed by lower level authorities (*ZGCJB*, April 2, 1996). Of the authorized charges, one-third exceeded the limits allowed by the pertinent regulations (ibid.). In a 1997 survey of 2,145 enterprises (CESS 1997: 20), 44.3% of the respondents reported an increase in ad hoc surcharges imposed on them while 49.5% claimed that they were required to pay more fees to government agencies than the preceding year.

The problem is not confined to the urban sector. It has also become widespread in the countryside, where TVEs have been the leading force of economic growth and, given the steady increase in their sales and tax payment (ZGXZQYNJBJWYH 1999: 8–9), should have made adequate contributions to meeting the basic financial needs of local governments. Peasants are the main bearers of the extra levies from local officials (Bernstein and Lu 2000; Li and O'Brien 1996). In 1990, the central authority issued an "urgent" directive to instruct local governments to reduce the financial burdens imposed by local officials on peasants. According to a subsequent directive issued by the State Council in July

---

[46] According to one report, for example, in 1992 nontax levies were imposed by state agencies on 1.16 million items and generated a revenue of 57 billion yuan (*JJRB*, September 17, 1993).

1992 (SJSFGS 1995: 83–4), during the two years after the 1990 directive, the problem was only

> contained in some areas. But it was not contained effectively in quite a significant number of areas. It has become a frequent practice [for local authorities] to impose arbitrary fees and surcharges on peasants. Recently, the complaints about excessive charges reported by peasants in person or through letters have significantly increased. In the nation as a whole, peasants' actual financial burdens have far exceeded the limit allowed by government policy, and there is a trend toward further increase of such burdens.

Nine years after the first "urgent" directive in 1990, still another "urgent" directive was issued by the Ministry of Finance to curb the various arbitrary levies imposed on peasants (*RMRB*, April 29, 1999).

Many such levies have been charged in the name of financing the provision of public goods and services. According to a report in the *China Financial and Economic News* published by the Ministry of Finance (*ZGCJB*, March 27, 1996), in the early 1990s more than 50% of the counties in China could not find sufficient budgetary funds to pay the basic salaries and medical bills of those on the government payroll, such as schoolteachers. The real problem, however, is not a lack of resources at the disposal of state agencies, but a dearth and depletion of resources slated for publicly announced agenda of the state. Large sums of government funds have been diverted from their intended uses to other purposes defined by officials (Luan Tao and Li Zhengzhi 1993: 4–5; *ZGCJB*, January 6, 1996, March 27, 1996, March 29, 1996), and from budgetary to off-budget categories (*JJRB*, September 17, 1993; *ZGCJB*, April 3, 1996, April 5, 1996). From 1980 to 1997 the government budget deficit increased from 6.9 to 58.2 billion yuan, whereas extra-budgetary revenue increased from 11.5 to 283 billion yuan (CZBZHJHS 1987: 139; GJTJJa 1999: 54, 56).[47] In 1993 one province was found to have a surplus extra-budgetary fund of nearly 2 billion yuan while its budget deficit totaled 1 billion yuan (*ZGCJB*, April 5, 1996). In 1994, the illicit funds in various little coffers uncovered by the fiscal authority in its annual fund use inspection increased by 300% over those uncovered in 1989. Most in the government agree that this only represents the tip of a huge iceberg (*ZGCJB*, March 27, 1996).

---

[47] These figures exclude the profits and depreciation funds controlled by the supervising agencies of state enterprises, which had been categorized as "extra-budgetary revenue" before 1993, as noted in Chapter 3.

A large part of the funds in off-budget categories (extra-budgetary funds and "little coffers") is not subject to effective monitoring of the fiscal authority. According to a 1996 report (*ZGCJB*, April 3, 1996), for example, only 45% of the extra-budgetary funds were deposited in fiscally designated accounts, whereas the fiscal authority had no clear and itemized record about the remaining amount reported. With a weakening of mutual monitoring between officials,[48] the guidelines on the use of extra-budgetary funds have lost their effectiveness (Deng Yingtao et al. 1990). As a result, such funds, along with those in little coffers, have been extensively used for various private purposes, such as the purchase of cars and mobile phones, banquets, bonuses, junkets, and sheer embezzlement (*JJRB*, September 17, 1993; SJSFGS 1995: 8; *ZGCJB*, March 27, 1996, March 29, 1996, April 2, 1996).

On the other hand, officials have been held responsible by their appointing authorities for the provision of public goods and services under their jurisdiction, which directly affects their mobility and positional security (Huang 1996; Whiting 1995). In view of the growing gap in public finance due to resource diversion, ad hoc exemptions granted to favored parties, underperformance among enterprises with excess capacity, and asset stripping by increasing numbers of public enterprise leaders, government officials need to find additional sources of revenue. Consequently, imposing contrived levies and erecting new regulatory barriers for extortion have been extensively used.[49] Moreover, since most of such levies are treated as off-budget funds at the discretion of pertinent officials, there is also an incentive for them to collect more than the amount needed to remedy the shortage of funds for public functions. In addition, this shortage provides a legitimate cover that officials can use to justify their self-seeking activities, as illustrated in Chapter 5.[50]

Those that bear the brunt of predation are most likely to be parties less favored by the officials, such as ordinary peasants and enterprises that cannot afford or fail to cultivate and maintain close ties with

---

[48] See Chapter 5.
[49] In Lotus Pond, for example, a large part of the "bad loans" owed to the Township Cooperative Fund (note 14 of Chapter 5) in the 1990s was invested in real estate speculation activities that turned out to be total failures. To cover the losses, the Township Economic Cooperative significantly increased the charges for its various services (e.g., seed improvement, repairing of agricultural machinery, and marketing assistance) to villagers and villages during the second half of the 1990s. The township government also imposed heavier ad hoc levies on villagers to maintain the basic funds for education, health care, and road improvement. At the same time, it continued to grant tax relief to its remaining "cash cows" – the large local enterprises (both public and private) that were still in business (Informants no. 488/1999, no. 493/1999).
[50] See also Lin and Zhang (1999).

them. With the intensification of predatory state action, the focus of efforts by many economic actors to manipulate state action tends to shift from making net gains to cutting the losses caused by the officials' predation, as illustrated by Polyester Fiber's experience discussed in Chapter 4. Such purely redistributive action does not change the marketized nature of the political process, but it undermines the performance of the enterprises affected and increases the tension between the state and the society.[51]

Summary and Reflections

The above discussion casts further light on the process and outcome of China's recent economic institutional change. It shows that the decline of the plan, the erosion of public ownership, and the growth of economic output have all been closely related to dual marketization. In particular, to a great extent it is through the intensification and interplay of competitive forces in both economic and political arenas that these changes have been brought about. On the other hand, the same forces have also created constraints and conditions that will affect further economic change.

Combining this analysis with those in Chapters 3 to 6, we can now put together some clues to addressing the three issues raised at the end of Chapter 1: the performance gap between state and nonstate enterprises, the presence of a significant number of enterprises from both groups in the same range of performance, and the decline of profit rate over time.

First, the first mover's advantage enjoyed by many nonstate firms in pursuing profit-making opportunities outside the plan, the dissipation of plan-allocated resources through diversion by state agents, and the uneven structural constraints on the use of personal networks for favor seeking, are among the factors that have contributed to the overall disparity in performance between state and nonstate enterprises, especially in the early years of reform. Second, many state enterprises have shifted from the slack strategy to the market strategy in response to the push-and-pull effects generated by growing competition in political and economic arenas. Some of them, such as Northern Machinery and its like, have been relatively successful. Their adaptations have limited the overall

---

[51] Sometimes such tension turns into open confrontation and conflict. For reports on large-scale demonstrations staged by peasants to protest excessive levies by local officials, see *JJRB*, April 24, 1989, January 25, 1990; *MP*, July 3, 1990, August 16, 1994, November 8, 1996. See also Bernstein and Lu (2000) and Li and O'Brien (1996).

advantage of first movers operating outside the plan. This, plus the fact that some nonstate enterprises situated in urban areas have also been exposed (albeit to a lesser degree) to adverse "third party effects" on the use of personal networks for favor seeking, has contained the disparity in performance between state and nonstate enterprises. Third, growing competition in political and economic arenas has made it difficult to sustain monopolies. It has also led to a growth of slack due to capacity overbuilding and an increase in the cost of favor seeking. These concurrent developments, coupled with the growing significance of asset stripping among both state and collective enterprises and the intensification of predatory state action since the late 1980s, may have shaped the trend of declining rate of return in both groups.

This account of the driving forces behind the behavioral changes and performance variations in the industrial sector indicates the importance of particularistic state action to the trajectory of China's economic transformation. The causal linkages it reveals need to be verified with more extensive and systematic empirical evidence in future research. It should also be noted that there are two pieces of evidence in the findings presented above that qualify the working hypothesis used to develop this account – that effective manipulation of state action is a necessary condition for firms to excel in the new economic game.[52]

First, the fact that intense competition has led many public enterprise leaders to refocus their efforts to manipulate state action from the market strategy to the asset stripping strategy since the early 1990s indicates that their interests are not always closely associated with those of their enterprises. Individually they may end up being "winners" for being able to manipulate state action to their own advantage, but their enterprises become "losers." A finer distinction between organizational and individual winners, therefore, is needed. Second, the narrowing of net gains for many favor seekers and the intensification of predatory state action during dual marketization raise questions about the relationship between the outcome of favor seeking and what is meant by "effectiveness" in the manipulation of state action. Given the growing importance of neutralizing state predation, the loss-cutting dimension of "favors," noted in the introductory chapter, merits close attention in the analysis of the exchange relations between economic actors and stage agents.

---

[52] See, also, note 35 for a discussion of evidence contradicting the hypothesis.

Conclusion

The main conclusion of this book is that the development of the political market is an important contributing factor to the demise of the central
planning system in China's reform era. To a great extent it is the restructuring and erosion of authority relations in the political process that have
reoriented particularistic state actions in the distribution of resources,
opportunities, and levies; and it is partly through or due to the brokerage of state agents in these areas that economic actors have moved away
from the plan and created outside it a new economic space as the center
of their profit-oriented activities. This analysis recognizes the view that
the growth of exchange relations and the concurrent intensification of
competition among economic actors have become a major driving force
of economic change. It also echoes the argument that promarket policies
of local governments have played an instrumental role in transforming
the Chinese economy. Yet it seeks to further these insights from the
economic competition thesis and the local developmental state thesis, out-
lined in the introductory chapter, with an account of what is underex-
plored in both of them – i.e., growing exchange and competition in the
political arena. In this chapter, I recount the mechanisms of dual marketization and discuss their relevance for understanding the process and
outcome of China's recent economic institutional change.

Dualism in Marketization

The rise and spread of markets for goods, services, and resources in the
reform era signify an expansion of exchange relations in the economy
and society, which has reshaped the means, rules, and outcomes of economic activities. Since this development evolves out of a centrally
planned economy governed by authority relations under the Party-state,
where and how the pre-existing barriers to exchange relations have been

197

brought down holds a key to understanding the dynamics and outcomes of marketization. The gist of my thesis is that exchange relations have grown not only in the economic process, but in the political process. It is through mutually reinforcing exchange ties in these two different markets that many of the observed changes in the economy have been brought about.

The process of economic marketization has been detailed elsewhere (e.g., Naughton 1995a; Perkins 1988, 1994). The focal issue that I investigate in this book is how such a process is related to a parallel in the political arena, which used to be overwhelmingly dominated by authority relations. The backdrop against which I cast my analysis is the formation of the competitive advantage of firms during the transition from the plan to markets. I have shown that the highly institutionalized differential treatment of firms by the state under the central planning system has given way to a regime of decentralized particularism in state action, where exchange ties between economic actors and local officials extend beyond traditional bargaining relationships between superiors and subordinates. Through such exchange ties, economic actors seek low-cost resources, ad hoc relaxation or removal of regulatory requirements, creation or protection of monopoly positions, and exemption from or reduction of government levies (including those created by state agents themselves). In return, local officials not only make collective gains from the contributions of economic actors to budgetary revenue and to extrabudgetary, discretionary resource pools, they also secure direct personal benefits, such as various "gifts," kickbacks, provision of in-kind consumption, accommodation of special needs, and reciprocal obligations that can be tapped in the future.

Concurrent with the growth of exchange ties between economic actors and officials is the growth of exchange relations within the state apparatus. This involves two types of exchange ties: those between different administrative levels and units, and those between officials – especially within the same administrative level or unit. The former are in large part embedded in various revenue and spending contracts adopted during the reform, which delineate the obligations and rights of various administrative levels and units. The latter are developed among officials with regard to the use of authority and resources under their collective control. Although the former represent an attempt to rationalize authority relations by creating incentives for revenue generation and reducing uncertainties in the demand and supply of resources, they have not only created a sheltered space for the latter to grow but also provided grounds on which to justify the expansion of the boundary of such growth, which eventually erodes the foundation of authority relations. Geared toward advancing the interests and self-defined agenda of the parties involved, expanding exchange ties between officials have gradually overtaken the exchange ties between administrative levels – centered around the formal functions and agenda of the state – as the main driving force of marketization in the political process.

To see how the expansion of the economic space outside the plan has been related to the growth of the political market in the reform era, attention needs to be drawn to three important issues: mutual inducement and accommodation between economic and political markets, collusion among officials, and competitive favor seeking among economic actors.

Mutual Inducement and Accommodation

The expanding exchange ties in economic and political arenas during China's transition from central planning to markets were closely related to and fed on each other. The efforts of economic actors to seek ad hoc favorable treatment from various loci of state authority were partly driven by the calculation that pre-existing barriers to economic freedom might be removed or bypassed through exchange ties with individual officials. There were also pockets of gray regulatory areas where economic actors were able to expand the boundaries of their freedom, but they needed to enlist the help of officials for a recognition and legitimation of the expanded economic space so as to perpetuate the changes that they initiated. Furthermore, the payoffs for newly acquired economic freedom might be amplified if the breaking away economic actors could gain access, with the help of officials, to the initially enormous resources commanded by the state and redirect them from the plan to markets. In addition, ad hoc relaxation of institutional and resource constraints on certain economic actors placed them in a more advantageous position to compete with peers who could not obtain such relaxation. In a nutshell, the political process held potential opportunities for overcoming bureaucratic constraints on economic decision making, ratifying unauthorized changes that were conducive to profit-oriented economic activities, channeling increasing amounts of resources from restricted use to potentially more gainful use outside the plan, and creating and maintaining allocative and regulatory unevenness among competing economic actors, as shown in Chapter 3.

The attempts of economic actors at capturing these opportunities were facilitated by the effects of market-oriented economic activities on the decisions and actions of officials. First, they provided opportunities for economic actors to make material gains that might be far greater than those made by officials through their formal remuneration system, thus contributing to a sense of relative deprivation among officials and creating or enhancing, in a perverse way, incentives for self-seeking behavior (cf. Chapter 4).

Second, as noted in Chapter 5, the expanding economic space outside the plan constituted a major source for the fulfillment by local officials of revenue obligations to which their formal financial and career rewards were tied, and for the discretionary resource pool (e.g., extra-budgetary funds and "little coffers") under their collective control. This drove local officials to take an active interest in the market-oriented economic activities under their jurisdiction and to bend existing rules to facilitate such activities, consequently inducing efforts to search for ways to weaken the organizational and institutional constraints on their collective use of decentralized authority and resources.

Third, the growing extra-plan space provided an institutionally ambiguous arena to which resources and authority could be diverted by officials for self-defined purposes, including making private gains. The diversions often took such forms as distributing state-owned capital and other resources at a substantial discount, collecting "admissions" for ad hoc entry, creating and maintaining exclusive rights, and providing exemptions from liabilities (such as taxes), especially those imposed by higher level authorities. Again, this increased the incentive for officials to cultivate ties among themselves so mutual monitoring on the diversion of authority and resources under their collective purview could be relaxed.

Fourth, variations in the prices for products and factors traded between economic actors provided a barometer of relative scarcity, indicating disparities between state-specified price and market price and signaling opportunities for officials to gain from arbitrage. Also, by illustrating variations in the prices and payoffs for alternative uses of resources and opportunities, the exchange relations among economic actors offered a frame of reference by which officials could clearly gauge the opportunity cost of their allocative and regulatory decisions. Although this did not change the particularistic nature of the actions of state agents, it reshaped the way the distribution of favors and liabilities among potential recipients was prioritized, consequently reshuffling the composition of winners and losers. As a result, firms that had a weak ability to bring individual or collective gains to officials were less favored than those that had a strong ability to do so. This is one of the reasons why many previously privileged firms (especially those in the state sector) have faced increasing resource constraints.

Collusion among State Agents

The political market thrives on collusion among officials in the use of public authority and assets for self-defined purposes. The state socialist economy is characterized by an absence of substantive owners of public property (which is taken care of by government officials), and by a lack of independent checks and balances on public accountability in the use of state authority (which is enforced by the officials themselves). How to motivate these caretakers of public assets and guardians of the state's neutrality to optimize the use of public property and authority according to announced public policy goals and to refrain from opportunism is a perennial concern in the structural design and change of the political and economic system.

Under China's preform system, long and complex command chains of central planning, total elimination of alternative forms of economic activities, and division of interests among officials combined to sustain an environment in which mutual monitoring played a key role in containing the tendency and efforts of officials to collude and divert public authority and assets for self-defined purposes. Although the system was economically inefficient, it provided a floor on which resource allocation could be carried out according to centrally defined political and ideological agenda.

In the account above (especially Chapter 5), I have shown that these conditions were changed in the reform, resulting in a weakening of mutual monitoring and a concurrent rise of collusive ties in the political process. The initial impetus for this development came from the pressing need to find quick fixes for problems (especially budgetary pressures) faced by the state at the end of the Mao era. To address those problems, some partial changes were made in the organizational and institutional parameters of state action. They included a shift from ideological indoctrination and political mobilization to economic growth, a modification of the rules regarding administrative financing, a shortening of command chains, a redefining and close pairing of delegated obligations and rights at various administrative loci, and a de-emphasis on behavioral traits in the performance evaluation of officials. These changes have homogenized the sources of financial and career rewards for officials, enhanced their interdependence in obtaining such rewards, and broadened the ground on which to increase the payoffs for collusion and to contain its costs.

Induced by the individual and collective gains from making alternative, unauthorized use of public authority and assets via exchange ties with economic actors, some opportunistic officials actively engaged in profit-seeking activities by accommodating requests from favor seekers (Chapter 3 and Chapter 6) and through backyard profit centers (Chapter 4). But officials are not a homogeneous group, and the self-seeking behavior of the more opportunistic ones faces constraints imposed by organizational politics in such forms as interpersonal rivalries and factional divisions. In order to use public office to advance self-defined agenda, opportunists need to consolidate their own rank and file, win over "middle-of-the-roaders," and neutralize committed communists (Nee and Lian 1994).

In the reform era, attempts to this end are manifested in two related strategies: fabrication of justification for self-seeking behavior and peer co-optation. Since officials are not the owners of the public assets under their collective control, and since they are the primary force to enforce public accountability, justification is needed for self-seeking behavior to be condoned by peers. The preceding chapters (especially Chapter 5) have shown three commonly used tactics for justifying private exchange ties in the political process: (i) increasing the dependence of the state's administrative functions on off-budget funds, (ii) twisting or redefining the restrictions on the self-seeking behavior of officials in the name of reform, and (iii) stretching the limits on discretionary decisions and actions in the gray area engendered by the uncertainties and inconsistencies in the reform process.

Although the decline of the communist ideology and the ascendance of the economic agenda in government decision making have broadened the ground on which to cultivate common interests among officials, not all of them are equally opportunistic and active in the effort to commodify public authority and assets under their collective control. The widespread practice of sharing a significant part of slush funds among members of the same state agency or decision-making circle indicates another mechanism that has facilitated the development of exchange relations in the political process, namely, provision of public goods to group members as a buffer against defection from collusive collective action.[1]

Competitive Favor Seeking and Institutional Change

Since the political market is not an open arena, securing access becomes important for competing economic actors in search of ways to excel. As noted above, the efforts by economic actors to seek favors from various loci of state authority are often aimed at creating and sustaining unevenness in input cost, regulation, and distribution of liabilities, which can

---

[1] In the literature on collective action, free riding has been commonly treated as a threat to sustaining cooperation (e.g., Hardin 1982; Olson 1965; Sandler 1992). This is true when the threshold of collective action hinges on certain levels of positive contribution from all group members. But when defection in the form of betrayal becomes the main obstacle to collective gains, when zero effort on the part of certain group members can be valued by other members as an asset relative to such defection, and when the gains to the key action takers from collective action without the active participation of certain members are sufficiently large, selective incentives may be needed – not to eliminate free riding, but to create limited free riding opportunities for potential spoilers.

significantly affect the balance of competitiveness among firms. The initial payoffs for such efforts are likely to be high when the number of favor seekers is limited. But the imbalances created by favor seeking among firms bring about a push-and-pull effect on other economic actors, which leads to a chain reaction driving more and more participants into the favor-seeking game. As the number of contenders increases and the unevenness between early comers and imitators decreases, however, the return on favors tends to decline, driving favor seekers to explore new grounds of rule bending. This has some important implications for the transformation of the economy.

First, competitive favor seeking has led to a gradual lowering or removal of many long-standing, institutionalized obstacles to economic freedom, including entry barriers, exclusive rights, restrictions on self-arranged production and transaction, and price control. The gains accruing to limited numbers of firms that were able to overcome these obstacles first gave them a competitive edge over those not able to do so. This change in the balance of competitiveness among firms not only exerted economic pressures on the latter but also demonstrated to them the opportunities in the political market. Efforts by latecomers to follow suit have increased the number of obstacles to be overcome. Although the successes have been achieved through ad hoc efforts, the cumulative effects are enormous, gradually blurring the line between "ad hoc" and "universal" changes.

Second, with the erosion of the institutional arrangements sustaining the central planning system, economic actors have gained increasing freedom to pursue profit-making opportunities outside the plan. At the same time, growing competitive forces in both the economic and the political process have increased the difficulty of sustaining monopoly positions and profits, making it insufficient to rely on special favors for economic success. The resultant efforts to innovate both in production and in rule bending have been important drivers for sustained economic growth during the transition from central planning to markets. Also, competitive favor seeking has shifted the locus of resource allocation from authority relations to exchange relations, as exemplified by the growth of backyard profit centers (Chapter 4). Increasingly, financial, physical, and human resources allocated by the state have been channeled from enterprises operating under the plan to those taking a more active part in market-oriented economic activities. This has increased the likelihood of resources being more productively used than under the plan.[2]

---

[2] See Bhagwati (1982) for a theoretical account of second-best situations where what he calls "directly unproductive, profit-seeking activities" may contribute to improving initially distorted resource allocation.

The diversion of resources from the plan has made it difficult for many state enterprises to sustain their operations, thereby increasing the pressure on them to break away from the plan. Their growing competitive efforts to move faster and closer to the economic space outside the plan and to catch up with first movers have accelerated the decline of the command economy. Also, in view of the intensification of economic competition, the weakening of the monitoring capacity of the state, and the increase in managerial autonomy, many public enterprise leaders, especially those of "laggard enterprises," have resorted to asset stripping for self-enrichment. The further deterioration of enterprise performance caused by this strategy has paved the way for the privatization of increasing numbers of small state enterprises, urban collective enterprises, and rural collectives since the mid-1990s. The resultant erosion of the dominance of strict state ownership in the economy represents an institutional change as important as the decline of the plan.

Third, the multiplication of exchange relations in the political process has sown the seeds for latent problems that may become full-blown down the road. Most notable among them are the growth of slack in the economy and the intensification of predatory state action. The surfacing and spread of these problems in the past decade indicate a deterioration of the state's self-monitoring capacity. They also suggest a possible increase in the retarding effects of the political market on economic growth. Such effects have thus far been contained in part because of the difficulty of sustaining monopolies amidst intense competition in both political and economic arenas, and in part because of the offsetting effect rendered by the drastic expansion of value creation activities outside the plan.

It is not clear whether the reconfigured interests in the political process will gradually develop into what Olson (1982) lamented in *The Rise and Decline of Nations*, i.e., stable alliances of collusion that hold broad power and stifle competitive forces. But as the central planning system fades into history, channeling resources from one mode of economic activity to another and bringing down the barriers embedded in the old system have become undertakings near completion. As a result, their stimulating effects on economic growth tend to diminish. At the same time, redistribution of resources and opportunities within the new economy has begun to assume increasing significance in exchange relations in the political process. If the problems identified above gain further momentum, then it is entirely possible that what has happened in China since 1978 only represents an extended detour from the normal trajectory of rent-seeking societies.

Markets and the State in China's Economic Transition

The foregoing summary leads us back to where the book began, i.e., the puzzles posed by the contrasts between Kornai's depiction of the limits and pitfalls of market reform under state socialism and the ascendance of markets in post-Mao China, and between the images of stagnation and decline in many rent-seeking societies and China's recent economic growth. It is now clear that a key factor that has made it possible for markets to prevail over the plan is an increasing dissociation of the interests of state agents from the old system. The initial push came from the least privileged segment of the economy – the nonstate sector, where decollectivization, coupled with fiscal decentralization, opened way for massive defection of grassroots officials from commitment to the plan while unleashing competitive forces in both the economic and political processes. These forces, driven by growing exchange relations involving economic actors and state agents, have kept monopolies at bay and oriented the pursuit of profits toward capturing value creation opportunities outside the plan, thereby sustaining robust economic growth for an extended period of time.[3]

The rise and spread of concrete markets for goods, services, and resources since the start of the post-Mao reform, however, have not been accompanied by a concurrent rise and institutionalization of what is known as "the market" – the three-pronged platform underlying a market economy, as discussed in the introductory chapter. Throughout the book I have shown that, although markets have become the center

---

[3] This explanation about the initial impetus and the mechanisms of economic institutional change also sheds some further light on a debate between the "gradualism" school and the "big bang" school about the nature of the Chinese reform (Jefferson and Rawski 1994a, 1994b; McMillan and Naughton 1992; Naughton 1995a; Rawski 1994a, 1994b, 1995, 1999; Sachs and Woo 1994a, 1994b; Woo 1994, 1999). The former focuses on the cumulative effects of piecemeal reforms that triggered growing economic competition. The latter emphasizes the effects of what in essence mimics an important outcome of political revolutions in the former Soviet Bloc, i.e., the rise of private economic activities, which are considered to have been ushered in swiftly but in disguised forms (e.g., reversion to family farms and influx of foreign capital) in China. If we bring the interests and actions of state agents to the center of the picture, it is clear that the impact of decollectivization and fiscal decentralization was indeed in a way revolutionary, as they led to the quick formation of a critical mass of bureaucratic interests strongly motivated to undermine the remaining central planning system based in the urban sector. On the other hand, the rise of private property rights has been an evolutionary process. The reversion to family farms changed the incentives for peasants but did not result in private ownership of land; and the growth of private economic activities in the rural non-farm sector and the urban sector did not gain momentum until the early 1990s (Kung and Lin 1999; Young 1995; Zhang Xuwu et al. 1994, 1996). The "bang" effect of rural and fiscal reforms of the early 1980s, therefore, may have been more pronounced in the political process than in ownership institutions.

of transactions and information, they often fall short of playing the key role in determining the relative payoffs to economic actors. The main reason is the lack of a relatively neutral state. As a result, participants in the new economic game can hardly excel without seeking ad hoc favorable treatment from state agents. The expansion of product and factor markets in economic transition, therefore, cannot be simply equated to an expansion of what mimics the Smithian image without taking account of the characteristics and impact of the coevolving political process.[4]

This view clarifies part of the confusion concerning the use of the notion "market" in the research on economic transition from state socialism. Nee (1989, 1991, 1996), for example, hypothesizes that the rise of market leads to a decline in the influence of redistributive political power on the distribution of economic opportunities and outcomes.[5] If "market" refers to concrete markets for products and factors, his argument faces the pitfalls identified above. If the notion refers to the ideal-typical image of full-fledged market mechanisms, then the hypothesis represents a tautological logic and cannot be empirically falsified (Walder 1996), as by definition "(the) market" in this context is free of the influence of redistributive political power and thus cannot "cause" it to decline.

A question that arises in this connection is whether the development of formal market institutions (i.e., pertinent laws and regulations) during the reform has created an increasingly effective constraint on the extent to which markets are handicapped by particularistic state actions. According to Guthrie (1999), the answer is affirmative, and such institution building represents the rise of a form of legal-rational authority enforced by the state. Findings presented in this book, though, call for caution. Compared to the Mao era, China today is indeed governed by a much more elaborate and broadly encompassing legal system. In the 20 years after the start of economic reform, the National People's Congress enacted 253 new laws and issued 106 directives on existing or new laws; the State Council enacted over 800 ordinances and regulations; and provincial legislatures enacted or approved over 7,000 local laws and regulations (*RMRB*, November 10, 1999). Many of these laws and regulations have been adopted to create an institutional environment com-

---

[4] It may not be appropriate to characterize the discrepancy between them as "market failure" either. The term invokes the assumption of an existence of institutional conditions that effectively limit the scope and scale of the pertinent anomalies. Also, it focuses attention on the resultant inefficiencies with reference to the ideal-typical market mechanism, rather than on any possible improvement of economic performance that the emergent "imperfect" markets may foster over a pre-existing system.

[5] For a collection of papers debating Nee's thesis, see *American Journal of Sociology* 101 (4, 1996): 908–1082.

patible with those of market economies and to reduce or eliminate irregularities and loopholes in economic governance,[6] hence redefining the institutional parameters and cost structures under which state agents and economic actors formulate their strategies.

The problem, however, is that the newly adopted formal rules have to be implemented by officials (especially those at lower levels) whose interests are often at stake. With the deterioration of the self-monitoring capacity of the state, it has become difficult to contain the gap between the rules on paper and the rules in action. Not surprisingly, despite repeated bans and restrictions, backyard profit centers, off-budget resource pools, predatory levies, and ad hoc rule bending for favor seekers have remained tenacious and pervasive, as shown in the preceding chapters. These forms of self-seeking behavior of public servants also make a mockery of the values they claim to uphold through the public authority they exercise. This tends to spawn widespread disrespect for laws and regulations, exacerbating the difficulty in enforcement and diminishing the legitimacy of the state (He Qinglian 1998; Shambaugh 1998). Under such conditions, a legalist state is a far cry from a legal-rational state, which in Weber's conception involves not only formalization of universalistic rules but, among other things, goal-action consistency and legitimacy based on people's identification with the core values embodied in the exercise of public authority (Weber 1978).

To explain what has driven and shaped the evolution of the formal and informal rules of the economic game, it is important to examine closely the changes that have taken place within the state apparatus (Walder 1995b, 1997). A major theme that emerges from the findings presented above is that the growth of exchange relations in the political process and competitive favor seeking have not only broken the old equilibrium of bureaucratic interests, thereby exerting a corrosive effect on the state-socialist economic institutions.[7] They have also posed to state agents private incentives that often times compete with the formal financial and career incentives centered on the implementation of newly adopted rules and public agenda of the state, creating problems that may threaten further economic growth.

---

[6] In 1994, for example, enterprise income tax rates were unified by the central authority in large part as a reaction to the serious erosion of tax revenue caused by extensive ad hoc tax breaks offered by officials to their favored parties under the previous multiple rate system (Wang 1996; Wong 1997). In 1997, the central authority introduced a new system of fee collection, known as *shouzhi liangtiao xian* (separating the accounts and administrative controls for fee collection from those for fee spending), which was aimed at curbing discretionary use of certain extra-budgetary funds.

[7] As noted in Chapter 7, this view contrasts with conventional theories on rent seeking and corruption, which focus on redistribution within the institutional boundaries of the existing political and economic system.

The pace and form of this development have nevertheless varied among different localities. Chapter 5 casts light on the conditions under which it may be contained or facilitated. Chapters 5 and 6 also discern a correlation between the varying orientations of particularistic local state action and the different historical and structural legacies that urban and rural jurisdictions carried over from the Mao era, whereas Chapter 7 highlights a growing link of redistribution between local officials' favor giving and predatory action. Where local officials' engagement in favor exchange with each other as well as outsiders is indeed aligned to the achievement of openly announced, broadly encompassing policy goals, a corporatist explanation is useful, and a parallel may be drawn to what some theories of East Asian developmental states characterize as "structural corruption" (Woo-Cumings 1999). Where the opposite situation is true or assumes increasing significance, however, the local developmental state theory needs to be complemented with an elaborate account of the evolving political market.

Among the factors that may obscure the nature of local state action is a perceived convergence between seemingly developmental policies and the formal incentives faced by local political actors. As noted in Chapter 5, only a very small number of (top) local officials are closely bound to the financial and career rewards and penalties under fiscal decentralization and political control of the CCP. How they respond to such incentives and constraints nevertheless holds a key to the orientation of local government policies, which may deviate from the expected path. During their normally transient tenures, for example, incumbent local leaders may pursue strategies (e.g., expansionary growth of local public enterprises) that aim mainly to fulfil short-term economic targets most relevant for the evaluation of their political performance.[8] The narrow focus of such action and the longer-term problems (e.g., overborrowing, underuse of capacity, and growing need to find additional revenue to finance the basic formal functions of the local state) resulting from the inherent moral hazard suggest that the primary beneficiaries of "developmental" policies may not be the main bearers of their costs (especially those that are hidden or deferred), raising questions about the extent to which such policies are truly encompassing. Moreover, as Chapter 5 and Chapter 7 indicate, the fulfillment of "developmental" targets need not hold in check the pursuit of self-defined agenda through collusive exchanges that local political actors – both top leaders and the rank and file – engage in with each other and with outsiders as long as the costs of such pursuit can be transferred to less favored parties. Revealing these divergent forces behind the encompassing facade of the local state helps

---

[8] See also Gore (1998, 1999) and Whiting (1996, 1999).

explain the seemingly inconsistent evidence about the "developmental" and predatory actions concurrently undertaken by local officials in the reform era (especially the 1990s) (cf. Chapter 7).[9]

It should be noted that what has been discussed in this book captures only a partial view of the growing exchange relations in the political process during China's post-Mao reforms. In *The Political Logic of Economic Reform in China*, Shirk (1993) offers a close examination of bargaining relations at the upper layers of the Chinese state. She argues that the formulation of central government policies on industrial reform has been greatly influenced by "particularistic contracting" involving Party, ministerial, and provincial leaders. The essence of such "enfranchisement" of authority is a give-and-take relationship, where in exchange for political support higher level leaders have made ad hoc allowance for subordinate parties to accommodate their parochial interests and increase discretionary power.[10]

At the other end of the state's political hierarchy Parish and Michelson (1996) identify another type of exchange relations: political patronage networks centered around locally elected officials and councillors in rural communities (villages), where direct elections have been gradually instituted since the late 1980s. The central feature of this clientelism, embedded in grassroots electoral politics, is local officials' dispensing favors in return for votes, though the scope and magnitude of such exchange have yet to be more clearly gauged.

What these vote-centered exchanges have in common with the exchanges surrounding the daily use of public office as portrayed in this book is that they both involve manipulation by special interests of state power for self-defined purposes. While it seems clear that together they have played an instrumental role in the destruction of the command economy, they have also brought about constraints on the construction of new economic and political institutions. In particular, they pose serious challenges to the re-building of the state.

A central issue facing modern states is how to institute effective mechanisms to address the encompassing interest that virtually all of them

---

[9] A question that arises in this connection is to what extent the stimulating effects on China's recent economic growth that have been attributed to the locally "developmental" policies pursued by grassroots governments actually stem from short-term maximizing behavior of local leaders and from the concurrent increase in ad hoc rule bending and resource diversion driven by competing but narrowly based special interests. Further research is needed to examine the circumstances under which this "identification problem" may occur and to provide empirical testing of the pertinent competing hypotheses on the causal mechanisms at work.

[10] Because of such particularistic rule bending, the old economic institutions have been rendered unsustainable. This conclusion provides a parallel explanation to the one offered in this book.

claim to take in the society.[11] This not only is important for maintaining the state's legitimacy and political stability, but, as recent scholarship suggests, holds a key to the facilitating role – characterized as "developmental" (Evans 1995), "market-augmenting" (Olson 2000), or "market-preserving" (Weingast 1995) – that the state may play in promoting economic growth. It entails an alignment of the interests of state functionaries – both top decision makers and the rank and file – to the publicly announced, encompassing agenda of the state, which in turn hinges on strong incentives for behavioral conformity and effective constraints on opportunism. In other words, a "Weberian bureaucracy" that is predictable, rule-bound, and authority-abiding holds a key to the success of modern state building (Evans 1995).

In the past two decades, the introduction of new laws and regulations governing the Chinese economy and society as noted above has been accompanied by various "rationalizing" measures to streamline government administration and reform the politically oriented nomenclatural system into a civil service system (Ma 1999; Tsao and Worthley 1995). While continuing to rely on traditional personnel appointment controls to influence the decisions and actions of local (especially provincial) political leaders (Huang 1996; Shirk 1993), the Party has also sought to strengthen the role of various internal watchdog agencies (e.g., the Ministry of Supervision, the Central Discipline Inspection Commission, the Anti-Corruption Bureau, among others) in monitoring the behavior of officials (Huang 1995), and periodically waged massive campaigns against corruption (Gong 1994; Kwong 1997; Lu 2000). But the outgrowth of exchange relations in the political process, especially at the lower rungs of the state apparatus, has created entrenched interests that are incongruent with, and oftentimes potent enough to undermine or defuse, vertically imposed constraints.[12] As discussed above, the widespread disregard for formal rules – both old and new – among those who enforce them, the fading divisions and rivalry between political and nonpolitical functionaries, the growing dependence of formal state functions on informal (off-budget) resources, the inducement of various offers from outside favor seekers, and the availability of avenues to prey on less-favored parties, among other things, all add to the difficulty of sustaining effective mutual monitoring among state agents and maintaining internal coherence in state action.

---

[11] For discussions of encompassing interest versus narrowly based special interests, see Olson (1982, 2000).

[12] A recent study (Zheng 1997) shows that the revolutionary logic of the Party poses another major obstacle to state building.

Are there any forces that may have been set in motion to curb the decay of the state's self-monitoring capacity? It is beyond the scope of this book to address this question.[13] One clue, though, can be discerned from the findings presented above. Chapters 4–6 show that opportunism tends to be most prevalent among state agents under dispersed loci of authority and overlapping administrative and regulatory structures, where divergent interests are likely to develop and impede the formulation and implementation of encompassing policies. Even at the level of the township, which has a greater degree of corporate coherence than higher level jurisdictions, local officials can still transfer the costs of politically motivated short-term maximizing decisions and of collusive private exchanges to or through villages. Unlike the township, however, villages are situated at the bottom of China's political structure and command no subordinate administrative units. As permanent local residents with virtually no exit from the local community, village cadres not only interact with fellow villagers on a daily basis but need the cooperation from the latter for the fulfillment of their political functions.[14] These structural conditions pose an extra constraint on officeholders' opportunistic pursuit of private agenda, which higher level officials normally do not have to confront directly.

Interestingly, after a decade of experiment, the National People's Congress enacted the *Organic Law of Village Committees* in 1998, making it mandatory for villagers to elect their governing bodies through open competition and secret ballot. Detailed and systematic evidence on the implementation of this law has yet to emerge.[15] Studies of the experiment under its prototype (the provisional version) during the preceding decade reveal considerable obstacles, including the continuing dominance of the CCP, bureaucratic resistance, and sabotage by incumbents; but they also find some containing effects on the abuses of power by village cadres, including manipulation of the process and outcome of village elections (Li and O'Brien 1996, 1999; O'Brien and Li 2000; Shi 1999). Should such effects be amplified and spread under the new law, the implications could be profound.

Totaling 739,980 in 1998 (GJTJJa 1999: 379), villages are the permanent homes of two-thirds of the Chinese population. The village economy accounts for about 40% of the GDP and up to two-thirds of

---

[13] See Lu (2000) for a perceptive discussion of the "organizational involution" of the state.

[14] See Yan (1996) for accounts of the relational constraints that everyday interactions with villagers pose on the power of village cadres. See Lin (1995) for a discussion of the communal norms that village leaders have to ponder in decision making. Eng and Lin (2000) provide an analysis of communal authority based outside the state system that village cadres have to reckon or align themselves with.

[15] For discussions on the evolution and initial impact of village elections in rural China, see a special issue (No. 162) of *The China Quarterly* published in June 2000.

the workforce of the country (GJTJJa 1999: 21, 55, 136–7; ZGXZQYN-JBJWYH 1997: 121, 1999: 111).[16] The development of truly encompassing public authority at the vast rural grassroots thus may provide a major cushion for political stability and a powerful engine to sustain economic growth, thereby demonstrating the value of democratization. Growing attention of village cadres to their electorates (Manion 1996a) may also make it more difficult for higher level officials to transfer the costs of their self-seeking behavior, hence setting off a ripple effect that disrupts the existing patterns of redistribution and intensifies the tension in the political system. History will tell whether this combination of potentially stabilizing and destabilizing effects will materialize and develop into a push-and-pull mechanism for further, more fundamental transformation of political and economic institutions.

[16] The size of the village economy is estimated by deducting the value-added and workforce of township-owned enterprises from the value-added and workforce of the rural sector.

Appendix A

Statistical Data Sources

Data Sets

1992–7 National Industrial Firm Data Sets

The data sets were compiled by a commercial subsidiary of a central government agency for the development of data bases for business enquiries. For confidentiality reasons, indicators related to the identity of the firms (such as firm name, address, and telephone number) were withheld. The data sets that I used in this book contain firm level information on firm code, zip code, ownership form, firm size, 4-digit industrial sector classification, starting year, total number of employees, sales revenue, net value of fixed assets, working capital, pretax profit, and administrative level of the firms' direct regulating authority. The data sets for the years through 1995 cover all the independent accounting industrial firms (see note 3 in Chapter 1 for definition) regulated by authorities at and above the level of township (*xiang zhen*) – the lowest administrative level of the government. The data sets for 1996–7 include only industrial enterprises of this category that had annual sales revenue exceeding 2 million yuan. Industrial activities carried out by firms at the village level and by self-employed persons (*getihu*) are not recorded in the data sets. Despite these limitions, the data sets offer a comprehensive coverage of essential information on economic activities in the most formalized industrial organizations. See Table A.1.

Industrial Firm Data Sets for Provinces A and B

These data sets were compiled by the statistical office of a coastal province (A) in southern China and that of an inland province (B). The providers of the data sets requested that the names of their provinces not be revealed. The data sets include all the indicators in the national

213

Table A.1. *Number of enterprises in different data sets*

	National		Province A		Province B		1992 CASS-World Bank survey		
Year	State enterprises	Nonstate enterprises	State enterprises	Nonstate enterprises	State enterprises	Nonstate enterprises	State enterprises	Urban collectives	TVEs
1984									176
1985									191
1986			1,485	3,919			933	334	191
1987			1,771	5,466			941	336	189
1988			1,858	4,341	2,971	7,652	953	347	290
1989			1,947	6,884	3,064	8,393	956	359	292
1990			1,997	6,958	3,125	8,770	946	356	290
1991			2,105	8,886	2,958	9,233			
1992	72,227	319,410	1,921	10,266	3,433	11,294			
1993	65,950	305,864	1,793	11,320	3,260	12,438			
1994	63,130	300,893	1,799	11,320	3,328	14,595			
1995	72,024	358,513	1,036	13,824	3,456	16,392			
1996	37,118	141,460	900	5,817	1,446	8,214			
1997	33,126	145,298		6,546	1,732	8,425			

industrial firm data sets and same types of enterprises. The data sets for province A cover the period 1987–92, and those for province B cover the period 1988–92. The data for the period of 1993–7 were derived from the national data sets described above.

1986 CASS-World Bank Survey

This questionnaire survey was conducted by a team of researchers from the Chinese Academy of Social Sciences and the World Bank in 1986 it covered 115 township and village enterprises in four counties: Wuxi (of Jiangsu province), Shangrao (of Jiangxi province), Jieshou (of Anhui province), and Nanhai (of Guangdong province). Details of the survey are described in Byrd and Lin (1990).

1992 CASS-World Bank Survey

This is a questionnaire survey conducted by a team of researchers from the Chinese Academy of Social Sciences and the World Bank in 1992. The sample ($n = 1,633$) includes 967 state enterprises, 366 urban collective enterprises, and 300 township and village enterprises. The survey consists of two sets of questionnaires: a questionnaire on managerial decision making, which is analyzed in Chapter 1; and a questionnaire aimed at collecting retrospectively a wide range of enterprise information (including, for example, statistics on input and output, finance, personnel, technology, etc.) for the period 1980–90. Details of the survey are described in Xu, Jefferson, and Rathja (1993) (see also Jefferson and Singh 1999).

1993 Beijing University and *Zhongguo Qingnian Bao* Survey

This survey was conducted jointly by the Sociology Department of Beijing University and the *Zhongguo Qingnian Bao* (China Youth Daily) in 1993. The respondents ($n = 611$) were state employees in *jiguan danwei* (agencies and departments with regulatory functions or administrative authority) ($n = 235$) and *shiye danwei* (nonregulatory entities – e.g., research institutes, hospitals, newspapers) ($n = 376$) in Beijing. Only the data on the former group were included in the data analysis in Chapter 4 (note 29). The sample distribution was determined on the basis of availability of access – the interviewees were the personal acquaintances of the interviewers – rather than random selection. Despite potential sampling bias and limited sample size, the information obtained on many sensitive issues (e.g., composition of personal income), which may be more reliable than that generated from random and larger samples, still offers some useful clues.

Further Note

All the data sets were cleaned after being obtained from the various sources. Where possible, missing values for asset data (i.e., net value of fixed assets and working capital) in the panel data sets were estimated by taking the average of the figures for the immediately preceding and ensuing years.

In the calculation of profit rate, net value of fixed assets was used without adjustment to a common price. This could pose a problem for temporal comparisons in that under the asset reporting procedure followed by industrial enterprises in China the total net value of fixed assets of a firm is the sum of each year's newly added capital stock minus annual depreciation at current price. As a result, the incremental effect of the price increases of capital goods is not excluded. There are two major reasons why I did not attempt to adjust this part of the input data. First, there is a lack of accurate information on the vintage of capital stock and on the changes in the prices for capital goods used by different enterprises. Second and perhaps more important, depreciation of fixed assets in the industrial sector has been carried out at very low rates (e.g., Liu Guoguang and Zhou Guiying 1992), resulting in an inflation of fixed asset value. It is therefore not implausible to assume that this inflation cancels out a great part of the price increase effect on newly added capital stock, especially before the mid-1990s (Holz and Lin 2000). This does not eliminate data inaccuracies, but it may be a simpler and safer alternative to using inaccurate deflators to adjust capital stock value.

Appendix B

Methodological Note on Case Studies

The Factories

The case study materials on the factories used in this study were mainly accumulated during 1988–96.[1] I started the field research when I was a doctoral student. My topic was the interaction between enterprise leaders and government officials. The selection of the factories was entirely based on access availability: My acquaintances or friends in China introduced me to their acquaintances or friends holding important positions in factories (director, deputy director, Party secretary, deputy Party secretary, owner, and chief accountant). In addition to meeting with me, some of those enterprise leaders also helped to expand the pool of my interviewees by arranging meetings with their colleagues.

The disadvantage of this approach is apparent – it did not produce a random and representative sample. But a random and representative sample may generate little useful information (Babbie 1992: Chapter 11), especially when providing accurate answers to the questions posed by the researcher is perceived by the informants as having the potential of affecting their interests. A tradeoff often has to be made. My use of the above method of information gathering was based on two related considerations. First, the usefulness of the information that I sought depended greatly on the willingness of the informants to reveal what they knew. Shorter social distance was conducive to increasing the

---

[1] In addition to the interviews described below, I have (since 1988) also accumulated notes on meetings with other informants, including academics, Party and government officials, middle-level managers, and ordinary workers. Some of the information from these sources is used in the book. Also, I have made extensive use of printed materials in Chinese, including newspapers, journal articles, books, and various government reports and documents. It is important to note that I used such materials mainly for factual information rather than for the interpretations they provided. Although I have tried to be careful in the selection and use of such materials, it is beyond my ability to ascertain their accuracy.

likelihood of their cooperation. Second, granting an interview involves an opportunity cost. With the increase of uncertainty and competition, time had become increasingly precious for enterprise leaders. Spending time with a stranger for discussions that contributed nothing to their business operations would bring them nothing but a net cost. But talking to someone introduced by a friend or acquaintance meant the addition of a favor (however small) in the equation of social exchange between the interviewee and my contact(s). Because of this, few enterprise leaders that I approached rejected my request for a meeting, though not all the ones that I talked to were equally willing to answer all the questions I raised.

I interviewed 168 enterprise leaders. They were affiliated with 46 enterprises located in 7 provinces and 2 centrally administered municipalities. These enterprises encompassed all the major ownership forms – state enterprise ($n = 37$), urban collective ($n = 26$), rural collective ($n = 39$), private enterprise ($n = 22$), foreign capital enterprise ($n = 28$), and joint ownership enterprise ($n = 16$). Their activities spanned a wide range of industrial production, including mining, material processing, manufacture of parts and components, and manufacture of end products. Thirty-two of the enterprises were established before 1980. The 12 cases discussed in this book were among those to which I paid several visits. See Table B.1.

Most of the interviews were conducted during work hours in the factories. The time of each meeting varied significantly, ranging from 30 minutes to 4 hours. My identity (first as a student studying overseas and later as an academic working in Hong Kong) was fully revealed to the interviewees. A tape recorder was not used. Instead I took notes during the conversations. At the end of the day I read through the notes and sometimes added a few more pieces of information that I had not written down but was able to recollect. None of the interviewees was paid or given a gift. Sometimes I treated them to a meal after a meeting, but more often than not, I was the one being treated.

The questions that I asked at each enterprise were centered around the issue of how it dealt with the opportunities and constraints it faced. Several key questions were raised at each meeting, though I did not use a uniformly structured questionnaire. They concerned the history of the enterprise, its main products and technology, its relationship with various government agencies, important events and government policies that affected its operation and performance, its internal organization, its input and output markets, and the competitive strategies adopted by its leaders. Whenever possible, I sought to verify important parts of the information provided by an interviewee through consistency checks

Table B.1. *Profile of case study firms (in order of first appearance)*

Name	Starting year	Ownership	Region	Main products	Performance[a] (1980–96)	Time of case study	First appearance
1. Northern Machinery	1949	State	North China	Milling machine	High→fair	1989, 1992–4, 1996	Chapter 2
2. Polyester Fibre	1973	Urban collective	North China	Polyester fibre	Low→fair →low	1988, 1989, 1992–4	Chapter 2
3. Red Star Weaving (Red Star Heating)	1972	Commune/ township	East China	Cotton weaving Water heater	Fair→low →fair	1993, 1995–6	Chapter 2
4. Flying Horse Motors	1979	Brigade/village	East China	Motorcycle Small diesel generator	Fair→high →fair	1995–6	Chapter 2
5. Peak Equipment	1983	Private→ Sino-foreign	North China	Water pump	Fair	1988–99, 1993, 1995	Chapter 2
6. Modern Housewares	1983	Sino-foreign	South China	Kitchenware Window frame	High→fair	1988–99, 1993, 1995	Chapter 2
7. Everbright Heating	1986	Urban collective→ Sino-foreign	North China	Heat converter Heating devices	High→fair →low	1988, 1992–4, 1996	Chapter 2
8. Rainbow Pipe	1989	Private→ shareholding	North China	Water pipe	Fair→high →fair	1994–5	Chapter 2
9. Southwestern Machinery	1959	State	Southwest China	Milling machine	Fair→low	1994, 1996	Chapter 3
10. Guardian Work-wear	1988	Sino-foreign	South China	Glove, face mask	High	1988, 1992, 1995	Chapter 4
11. Elegance Furniture	1979	Urban collective	Northeast China	Furniture Interior decoration	Fair	1996	Chapter 4
12. Superior Sound	1983	Wholly foreign-owned	South China	Audio products	Fair	1996	Chapter 4

[a] Performance is defined as a firm's profit rate relative to the average sectoral profit rate [calculated based on statistics reported in GJTJJa (various years) and GJTJJb (various years) during the same period of time].

219

during the conversation, through asking the same questions of other knowledgeable interviewees, and through a repeat of the same questions during subsequent visit(s).

In addition to meeting with enterprise leaders, I also requested and, in most cases, obtained printed materials and statistics on the enterprises that I visited. I normally toured the factories during the visits. In some cases, I was able to meet with middle level managers and workers as well.

The Two Local Governments

The information about the two local governments discussed in this book was also collected on the basis of access availability rather than random sampling. It is generally more difficult to study Chinese government agencies than enterprises because government officials consider their information to be of greater sensitivity. Thus gaining access is a crucial first step for any attempt to probe into the inner workings of the state bureaucracy.

My access to Lotus Pond Township was arranged with the help of several officials (acquaintances or friends) at the Ministry of Agriculture. In 1987, the county where Lotus Pond was located was selected by the Ministry as an experimental zone for the development of pilot programs of rural reform. The local officials thus had a direct working relationship with the Ministry. I made my first visit to the county in 1994 and met with top officials of the experimental zone office. During the visit, I asked if I could visit and study a township with an average level of economic development. It so happened that the son of an official in the office was then the township head of Lotus Pond. The official offered to help make the arrangements.

Between 1994 and 1999, I made five week-long visits to Lotus Pond. During my stay in the county and the township, I ate almost all my meals with the local officials, who insisted on paying the bill. As a token of appreciation for their help and hospitality, I brought with me each time a few cartons of cigarettes for the officials. I interviewed all the top decision makers and major department heads (totaling 19) in the township. My questions focused on the evolution of the township government from the days of the people's commune to the late 1990s. In particular, I raised questions about the organizational structure and change in the township government, important events in the township's recent history, its relationship with the villages under its jurisdiction, with local enterprises, and with the county government. Each meeting lasted for about two hours. Some of the top officials were interviewed more than once. As in the factories, I posed the same questions to different interviewees and at different times to check the accuracy and consistency of the information that they provided. Again, no tape recorder was used. In addition, I obtained printed materials (reports, regulations, documents, etc.) and statistics on the township. During the visits, I also met with officials in three villages, and conducted case studies at two local enterprises. One of them, Rainbow Pipe, is discussed in this book.

The local government of the Gate Tower District was first studied by a group of faculty members at a university in Beijing. In 1992 they took some of their students to conduct a household survey in the district, which was the home place of one of the faculty members. During their stay there, they were approached by officials from the district government for help in conducting a policy study for the local government's medium term social and economic development plan. Seeing this as a rare opportunity to take a close look at the operation of the local government, they asked to combine the policy study with a parallel academic study of the evolution of the district government from the early 1950s. The district officials agreed. Government agencies were instructed to cooperate with the university researchers during their subsequent trip to the district in 1993. In seven weeks they visited most of the agencies of the district government and the Communist Party (including two subdistrict administrations), conducted 137 in-depth interviews, and collected a large amount of archival information, including reports, documents, circulars, gazetteers, statistics, regulations, and various other local publications.

I knew some of the faculty members in the research team and had collaborated with them in other research projects. They were generous enough to grant me full access to the materials they collected from Gate Tower. After combing through more than 20,000 pages of interview notes and printed materials, in 1996 I made a fact-finding visit with the help of a scholar at the local social science academy. I also joined (in 1999) the university research team in one of its several follow-up study trips to the district. During the two visits, I interviewed 22 officials in 14 government agencies. Some of them had been interviewed by the university research team before. My questions were similar to those raised at Lotus Pond. Since I had already examined the pertinent background information before the trip, I focused my questions on issues I wanted to clarify or further explore. I also studied two local enterprises, one of which (Elegance Furniture) is discussed in Chapter 4.

Obviously, the fieldwork materials used in this book can only shed limited light on the complexities in the changing political and economic processes of China. It remains to be seen to what extent the enterprises and local governments wherein I did case studies are similar to those in other parts of the country. I see what I put into this book as an effort to identify important causal processes and develop falsifiable hypotheses about them. It is my hope that verifying such hypotheses with more substantial empirical evidence, contrasting my findings and those from other studies, and investigating the circumstances under which differences arise will lead to the discovery of more useful clues to understanding China's economic and political transformation.

Bibliography

Part I. Chinese Materials (cited by full name of author or abbreviation of author/publication)

BJRB (Beijing ribao) 北京日報 (*Beijing Daily*).

BJSRMZF (Beijing shi renmin zhengfu) 北京市人民政府. 1993. 關於北京市黨政機關與所辦經濟實體脫鉤工作情況的總結報告 (Report on the Work to Delink Agency-Sponsored Economic Entities from Their Sponsoring Party and Government Agencies in Beijing). 北京：北京市人民政府. (Internal document).
————. 1995. 關於檢查經濟實體工作的總結報告 (Report on the Investigation into Economic Entities Sponsored by Government Agencies). 北京：北京市人民政府. (Internal document).

BJSWYJS (Beijing shiwei yanjiu shi) 北京市委研究室. 1994. 北京市十個系統，各縣區調查報告選編 (A Collection of Selected Current Affairs Reports on Ten Administrative Systems, Counties, and Districts in Beijing). Internally circulated document.

BJWB (Beijing wanbao) 北京晚報 (*Beijing Evening News*).

BJWYH (Bianji weiyuan hui) 編輯委員會. 1984–98. 中國對外經濟貿易年鑒 (Almanac of China's Foreign Economic Relations and Trade). 香港：中國廣告有限公司.

BSBXZ (Benshu bianxie zu) 本書編寫組. 1995. 當前經濟發展與體制改革的主要任務 (The Main Tasks for the Current Economic Development and Structural Reform). 北京：中共中央黨校出版社.

BYT (Banyue tan) 半月談 (*Fortnightly Review*).

CZ (Caizheng) 財政 (*Finance Monthly*).

CESS (China's Entrepreneurs Survey System) 中國企業家調查系統. 1993–8. 企業經營者問卷調查報告 (Report on Annual Questionnaire Survey on Enterprise Leaders). 北京.

Chen Ruisheng, Pang Yuanzheng, and Zhu Manliang 陳瑞生，龐元正，朱滿良 (主編). 1992. 中國改革全書：政治體制改革卷 (An Encyclopedia of China's Reforms: Volume on Reform of the Political System). 大連：大連出版社.

Chen Rulong 陳如龍 (主編). 1988. 當代中國的財政 (Public Finance in Contemporary China). 北京：中國社會科學出版社.

Chen Yuan 陳元 (主編). 1994. 中國金融體制改革 (Reforming China's Financial System). 北京:中國財政經濟出版社.

Cui Naifu 崔乃夫 (主編). 1994. 當代中國的民政 (Civil Administration in Contemporary China). 北京:當代中國出版社.

CZBZHJHS (Caizhengbu zonghe jihua si) 財政部綜合計劃司. 1987. 中國財政統計 *1950–85* (Financial Statistics of China 1950–85). 北京:中國財政經濟出版社.

Deng Yingtao, Yao Gang, Xu Xiaobo, and Xue Yuwei 鄧英淘,姚剛,徐笑波,薛宇偉. 1990. 中國預算外資金分析 (An Analysis of China's Extra-budgetary Funds). 北京:中國人民大學出版社.

Fan Xiumin and Ma Qingqiang 范秀敏,馬清強 (主編). 1994. 鄉鎮企業發展論 (On the Development of Township Enterprises). 北京:中國統計出版社.

Fan Yongming 樊勇明. 1992. 中國的工業化與外國直接投資 (China's Industrialization and Foreign Direct Investment). 上海:上海社會科學出版社.

Fang Weizhong and Wu Jiajun 房維中,吳家駿. 1989. 工業企業虧損調查研究 (An Analysis of Losses Incurred by Industrial Enterprises). 北京:經濟出版社 (內部發行).

Fei Kailong and Zuo Ping 費開龍,左平 (主編). 1991. 當代中國的工商行政管理 (Industrial and Commercial Administration in Contemporary China). 北京:當代中國出版社.

Fei Xiaotong 費孝通. 1985. 鄉土中國 (Rural China). 香港:三聯書店.

Feng Tongqing and Xu Xiaojun 馮同慶,徐曉軍 (主編). 1993. 中國職工狀況 (Current Status of Chinese Urban Employees). 北京:中國社會科學出版社.

FZRB (Fazhi ribao) 法制日報 (*Legal Affairs Daily*).

GG (Gaige) 改革 (*Reform*) (monthly).

Gao Shangquan 高尚全 (主編). 1987. 中國:發展與改革 (China: Development and Reform). 北京:中國黨史資料出版社.

GJTGW & GJGSJ (Guojia tigai wei & guojia gongshang ju) 國家體改委,國家工商局. 1993. 中國個體私營經濟調查 (A Survey of Self-employed Individuals and Private Enterprises in China). 北京:中國軍事譯文出版社.

GJTJJa (Guojia tongji ju) 國家統計局. 1981–99. 中國統計年鑒 (Statistical Yearbook of China). 北京:中國統計出版社.

GJTJJb (Guojia tongji ju [gongye jiaotong tongji si]) 國家統計局 (工業交通統計司). 1988–98. 中國工業經濟統計年鑒 (Statistical Yearbook of China's Industrial Economy). 北京:中國統計出版社.

GJTJJc (Guojia tongji ju [guding zichan touzi tongji si]) 國家統計局 (固定資產投資統計司). 1996–8. 中國固定資產投資統計年鑒 (Statistical Yearbook of Fixed Asset Investment in China). 北京:中國統計出版社.

GJTJJd (Guojia tongji ju) 國家統計局. 1993–8. 中國勞動工資統計年鑒 (Statistical Yearbook of Labor and Wages in China). 北京:中國統計出版社.

GLSJ (Guanli shijie) 管理世界 (*Management World*) (monthly).

GMRB (Guangming ribao) 光明日報 (*Guangming Daily*).

Gong Xikui and Jin Hongwei 宮希魁,金紅煒. 1995. 中國隱形經濟問題研究 (A Study of the Stealth Economy in China). 大連:大連工學院出版社.

GPJYJ (Gongping jiaoyi ju) (國家工商行政管理局) 公平交易局. 1996. 不正當競爭案例精選 (A Selection of Unfair Competition Cases). 北京:工商出版社.

GRRB (Gongren ribao) 工人日報 (*Workers' Daily*).

Gui Shiyong 桂世鏞. 1994. 中國計劃體制改革 (Reforms in China's Planning System). 北京：中國財政經濟出版社.

Guowu yuan 國務院. 國務院公報 (Gazette of the State Council) (daily).

GWYYJSKTZ (Guowu yuan yanjiu shi keti zu) 國務院研究室課題組. 1992. 中國社會保險制度改革 (Reforms in China's Social Security System). 北京：中國社會科學出版社.

—— 1994. 我國所有制結構變革的趨勢和對策 (Changes in the Ownership Structure of Our Country: Trends and Policy Proposals). 北京：中國經濟出版社.

GYPCBGS (Gongye pucha bangong shi) 工業普查辦公室. 1987. 中國人民共和國1985年工業普查資料 (Statistics of the 1985 Industrial Census of the People's Republic of China). 北京：中國統計出版社.

—— 1996. 中國人民共和國1995年第三次工業普查摘要 (Statistics of the 1995 Third Industrial Census of the People's Republic of China). 北京：中國統計出版社.

—— 1997a. 中國人民共和國1995年第三次工業普查資料：行業卷 (Statistics of the 1995 Third Industrial Census of the PRC: Volume on Industrial Sectors). 北京：中國統計出版社.

—— 1997b. 中國人民共和國1995年第三次工業普查資料：國有，三資，鄉鎮卷 (Statistics of the 1995 Third Industrial Census of the PRC: Volume on State-owned, Foreign-funded, and Township Enterprises). 北京：中國統計出版社.

—— 1997c. 中國人民共和國1995年第三次工業普查資料：地區卷 (Statistics of the 1995 Third Industrial Census of the PRC: Volume on Regions). 北京：中國統計出版社.

He Guang 何光 (主編). 1990. 當代中國的勞動力管理 (Labor Force Management in Contemporary China). 北京：中國社會科學出版社.

He Qinglian 何清漣. 1998. 現代化的陷井：當代中國的經濟社會問題 (Pitfalls of Modernization: Economic and Social Problems in Contemporary China). 北京：今日中國出版社.

Huang Weiding 黃葦町. 1992. 中國的隱形經濟 (China's Stealth Economy). 北京：中國商業出版社.

IFTE & IPA (Institute of Finance and Trade Economics, CASS, and Institute of Public Administration, NY). 1994. 中國城市土地使用管理 (Urban Land Use and Management in China). 北京：經濟科學出版社.

Ji Long 季龍 (主編). 1991. 當代中國的集體工業 (Collective Industries in Contemporary China). 北京：當代中國出版社.

Jin Bei 金碚. 1997. 何去何從——當代中國的國有企業問題 (Where to Go? A Study of State-owned Enterprises in Contemporary China). 北京：今日中國出版社.

JJCKB (Jingji cankao bao) 經濟參考報 (*Economic Information*).

JJRB (Jingji ribao) 經濟日報 (*Economic Daily*).

JJXXB (Jingji xinxi bao) 經濟信息報 (*Economic Information Times*).

JJYF (Jingji yu fa) 經濟與法 (*Economy and Law*) (monthly).

JRSB (Jinrong shibao) 金融時報 (*Financial News*).

Kang Shizhao 康式昭 (主編). 1992. 中國改革全書：文化體制改革卷 (An Encyclopedia of China's Reforms: Volume on Reform of the Cultural System). 大連：大連出版社.

Li Hanlin 李含琳. 1994. 國有資產大流失 (Serious Losses and Disappearance of State-owned Assets). 蘭州：蘭州大學出版社.

Li Peilin and Wang Chunguang 李培林，王春光. 1993. 新社會結構的生長點 (A Pivotal Point for the Growth of a New Social Structure). 濟南：山東人民出版社.

Li Weizhi 勵維志. 1994. 中國共產黨制度建設史綱 (A Brief History of the Chinese Communist Party's Institution Building). 天津：天津社會科學出版社.

Li Yining 厲以寧. 1992. 中國經濟改革與股份制 (China's Economic Reform and the Shareholding System). 北京：北京大學出版社.

LW (Liaowang) 瞭望 (*Outlook Weekly*).

Lin Qingsong and Du Ying 林青松，杜鷹 (主編). 1997. 國有企業與非國有企業比較研究 (A Comparative Study of SOEs and Non-SOEs). 昆明：云南人民出版社.

Ling Hu'an and Sun Zhen 令狐安，孫楨 (主編). 1992. 中國改革全書：勞動工資卷 (An Encyclopedia of China's Reforms: Volume on Labor and Wages). 大連：大連出版社.

Liu Bing and Deng Yizhi 劉兵，鄧益志 1999. 反不正當競爭案例精選分析 (An Analysis of Selected Cases in the Implementation of the *Law against Unfair Competition*). 北京：法律出版社.

Liu Guoguang and Zhou Guiying 劉國光，周桂英 (主編). 1992. 中國改革全書：工業經濟卷 (An Encyclopedia of China's Reform: Volume on the Industrial Economy). 大連：大連出版社.

Liu Hongru and Wang Peizhen 劉鴻儒，王佩真 (主編). 1992. 中國改革全書：金融體制改革卷 (An Encyclopedia of China's Reform: Volume on Reforms of the Financial and Banking System). 大連：大連出版社.

Liu Kegu and Wang Zheng 劉克崮，王徵 (主編). 1995. 中國稅收制度 (China's Taxation System). 北京：中國財政經濟出版社.

Liu Qian 劉倩. 1998. "南街經濟分析" ("An Analysis of the Economy in Nanjie Village"). 鄭州：河南省社會科學院社會學研究所 (unpublished manuscript).

Liu Suinian 柳隨年. 1991. 物資工作與物資體制改革 (The Management and Reform of Capital Goods Allocation System). 北京：中國物資出版社.

Liu Suinian 柳隨年 (主編). 1993. 當代中國的物資流通 (Capital Goods Distribution in Contemporary China). 北京：當代中國出版社.

Liu Suinian and Cai Ninglin 柳隨年，蔡寧林 (主編). 1993. 中國物資系統概況 (An Overview of China's Capital Goods Allocation System). 北京：中國物資出版社.

Liu Suinian and Wu Qungan. 柳隨年，吳群敢. 1985. 中國社會主義經濟簡史：1949–83 (A Brief History of China's Socialist Economy: 1949–83). 哈爾濱：黑龍江人民出版社.

LNRB (Liaoning ribao) 遼寧日報 (*Liaoning Daily*).

Luan Tao and Li Zhengzhi 樂濤，李正志. 1993. 中國大中型企業的困境與出路 (China's Large and Medium Enterprises: Difficulties and Possible Solutions). 北京：中國財政出版社.

Ma Jiesan. 馬傑三 (主編). 1991. 當代中國的鄉鎮企業 (Township Enterprises in Contemporary China). 北京：當代中國出版社.

Ma Kai 馬凱. 1992. 從計劃價格到市場價格 (From Prices under the Plan to Market Prices). 北京：中國物價出版社.

Ma Rong, Huang Chaohan, Wang Hansheng, and Yang Mu. 馬戎，黃朝翰，

王漢生，楊沐（主編）. 1994. 九十年代中國鄉鎮企業調查 (Case Studies in Chinese Township Enterprises in the 1990s). 香港：牛津大學出版社.

Mao Hongjun 毛宏君. 1994. 中國金融體制改革新舉措 (New Measures in China's Financial and Banking Reform). 北京：北京大學出版社.

MP (Ming Pao) 明報 (Hong Kong) (daily).

MZYFZ (Minzhu yu fazhi) 民主與法制 (*Democracy and Law*) (monthly).

NFZM (Nanfang zhoumo) 南方週末 (*Southern Weekend News*).

Niu Renliang and Song Guangmao 牛仁亮，宋光茂 （主編）. 1992. 公務員制度：國家公職人員的重新安排 (The Civil Service System: A New Arrangement for State Functionaries). 北京：中國財政經濟出版社.

NJRB (Nanjing ribao) 南京日報 (*Nanjing Daily*).

Pan Shi 潘石 （主編）. 1991. 當代中國私營經濟研究 (A Study of Private Economic Activities in Contemporary China). 太原：山西經濟出版社.

Peng Guilan and Huang Shutian. 彭桂蘭，黃書田 （主編）. 1992. 中國改革全書：投資體制改革卷. (An Encyclopedia of China's Reforms: Volume on Reform of the Investment System). 大連：大連出版社.

Pu Xingzu, Ding Rongsheng, Sun Guanhong, and Hu Jinxing 蒲興祖，丁榮生，孫關宏，胡金星. 1995. 中華人民共和國政治制度 (Political System of the People's Republic of China). 香港：三聯書店.

QS (Qianshao) 前哨 (Hong Kong) (monthly).

QYJ (Qiye jia) 企業家 (*Entrepreneurs*) (monthly).

QYGL (Qiye guanli) 企業管理 (*Enterprise Management*) (monthly).

QYJB (Qiye jia bao) 企業家報 (*Entrepreneur News*).

RMLT (Renmin luntan) 人民論壇 (*People's Forum*).

RMRB (Renmin ribao) 人民日報 (*People's Daily*).

SCB (Shichang bao) 市場報 (*Market News*).

SDC (Shidai chao) 時代潮 (*Tides of the Time*).

Shang Jiguang 商季光 （主編）. 1993. 中國金融體制改革綜論 (On the Reform of China's Financial System). 北京：中國物價出版社.

Shang Ming 尚明 （主編）. 1989. 當代中國的金融事業 (The Financial Sector in Contemporary China). 北京：中國社會科學出版社.

Shao Zunting, Zhang Shengshu, and Xie Minggan 邵俊亭，張聲書，謝明幹 （主編）. 1992. 中國改革全書：物資流通體制改革卷 (An Encyclopedia of China's Reforms: Reform of the Industrial Material Distribution System). 大連：大連出版社.

Shen Jueren 沈覺人 （主編）. 1989. 當代中國的對外貿易 (Foreign Trade in Contemporary China). 北京：中國社會科學出版社.

Shi Lin 石林 （主編）. 1989. 當代中國的對外經濟合作 (International Economic Cooperation in Contemporary China). 北京：中國社會科學出版社.

Shi Xianmin 時憲民. 1993. 體制的突破：北京市西城區個體戶研究 (A Breakthrough in the System: A Study of Self-employed Individuals in the Western District of Beijing). 北京：中國社會科學出版社.

SJCYJS (Shuji chu yanjiu shi) 書記處研究室. 1982. 當前我國工人階級狀況調查資料匯編 (A Collection of Survey Findings on the Current Situation of Workers in Our Country). 北京：中共中央黨校出版社.

SJSFGS (Shenji shu fagui si) 審計署法規司. 1995. 三亂治理與收費管理法規匯編 (A Collection of Laws and Regulations on Fee Collection and Correction of "Three Types of Arbitrary Levies"). 北京：中國審計出版社.

Song Defu 宋德福 (主編). 1994. 當代中國的人事管理 (Personnel Management in Contemporary China). 北京：當代中國出版社.

Song Yi 宋毅 (主編). 1993. 中國傑出企業家列傳 (Biographies of Outstanding Entrepreneurs in China). 北京：海洋出版社.

Tong Wansheng and Zou Xiangqun 童宛生，鄒向群 (主編). 1992. 中國改革全書：價格體制改革卷 (An Encyclopedia of China's Reforms: Volume on Price Reform). 大連：大連出版社.

Wang Haibo 汪海波 (主編). 1994. 新中國工業經濟史 (A History of the Industrial Economy of New China). 北京：經濟出版社.

Wang Hansheng and Liu Shiding 王漢生，劉世定. 1995. 中國企業家：構成，特徵，態度與行為 (Chinese Entrepreneurs: Composition, Characteristics, Attitudes, and Behavior). 北京大學社會學系 (unpublished manuscript).

Wang Jingsong 王勁松. 1995. 中華人民和國政府與政治 (Politics and Government of the PRC). 北京：中共中央黨校出版社.

Wang Shaoguang and Hu Angang 王紹光，胡鞍鋼. 1994. 中國國家能力報告 (A Report on China's State Capacity). 香港：牛津大學出版社.

Wang Shiyuan 王仕元 (主編). 1993. 中國改革開放事典 (A Handbook of Important Events in China's Reform and Opening). 廣州：廣東人民出版社.

Wang Shiyuan, Li Xiuyi, and Yang Shiwen 王仕元，李修義，楊世文 (主編). 1992. 中國改革全書：農村改革卷 (An Encyclopedia of China's Reforms: Volume on Rural Reform). 大連：大連出版社.

Wang Sibin and Wang Hansheng 王思斌，王漢生 (主編). 1998. 街區政府，經濟與社會 (Government, Economy and Society in an Urban District). 北京大學社會學系 (unpublished manuscript).

Wu Jinglian 吳敬璉. 1993. 大中型企業改革：建立現代化企業制度 (Reforming Large and Medium Enterprises: Establishment of a Modern Enterprise System). 天津：天津人民出版社.

WWP (Wen Wei Po) 文匯報 (Hong Kong) (daily).

WZGL (Wuzi guanli) 物資管理 (*Capital Goods Management*) (monthly).

WZSQ (Wuzi shangqing) 物資商情 (*Market News on Industrial Materials*).

Xia Xingguo 夏興國. 1994. 地下經濟學概論 (An Analysis of Underground Economic Activities). 武漢：湖北人民出版社.

Xiang Huaicheng 項懷誠 (主編). 1994. 中國財政體制改革 (Reforming China's Fiscal System). 北京：中國財政經濟出版社.

Xiang Huaicheng and Jiang Weizhuang 項懷誠，姜維壯 (主編). 1992. 中國改革全書：財政體制改革卷 (An Encyclopedia of China's Reforms: Volume on Fiscal Reform). 大連：大連出版社.

Xing Bensi 邢賁思 (主編). 1992. 中國改革全書：鄧小平改革思想卷 (An Encyclopedia of China's Reforms: Volume on Deng Xiaoping's Views on Reform). 大連：大連出版社.

Xu Dixin 許滌新 (主編). 1988. 當代中國的人口 (Population in Contemporary China). 北京：中國社會科學出版社.

Xu Mu and Zhang Xiaohua 許牧，張曉華 (主編). 1995. 中國土地管理利用史 (A History of Land Use and Management in China). 北京：中國農業科技出版社.

Xu Weiguo 徐衛國. 1993. 我國第三次公司熱透視 (An In-depth Analysis of China's Third Wave of "Company Rush"). 經濟研究資料 8: 1–6.

YCWB (Yangcheng wanbao) 羊城晚報 (*Evening News of the Goat City*).

Yu Ying-shih 余英時. 1984. 史學與傳統 (Historical Research and the Chinese Tradition). 台北：聯經出版社.

1987. 中國近世宗教倫理與商人精神 (Premodern Chinese Religious Beliefs and Merchant Ethics). 台北：聯經出版社.

Yuan Shouqi 袁守啟. 1993. 中國與外國勞動工資社會保險制度比較 (A Comparative Study of Chinese and Foreign Systems of Wages and Social Security). 北京：中國廣播電視出版社.

ZGCJB (Zhongguo caijing bao) 中國財經報 (*China Financial and Economic News*).

ZGCSFZYJH (Zhongguo chengshi fazhan yanjiuhui) 中國城市發展研究會 (主編). 1998. 中國城市年鑒 (Yearbook of China's Cities). 北京：中國統計出版社.

ZGGLKXYCJS (Zhongguo guanli kexue yuan caijing suo) 中國管理科學研究院財經所 (主編). 1994. 社會主義市場經濟與會計制度改革 (Socialist Market Economy and Reform in the Accounting System). 北京：中國財經出版社.

ZGGSB (Zhongguo gongshang bao) 中國工商報 (*Industrial and Commercial News of China*).

ZGJJSB (Zhongguo jingji shibao) 中國經濟時報 (*China Economic Times*).

ZGJJTZGG (Zhongguo jingji tizhi gaige) 中國經濟體制改革 (*China's Economic System Reform*).

ZGJRXH (Zhongguo jinrong xuehui) 中國金融學會. Various years. 中國金融年鑒 (Almanac of China's Finance and Banking). 北京：中國金融年鑒編輯部.

ZGQN (Zhongguo qingnian) 中國青年 (*Chinese Youth*) (monthly).

ZGQNB (Zhongguo qingnian bao) 中國青年報 (*Chinese Youth Daily*).

ZGQYJB (Zhongguo qiye jia bao) 中國企業家報 (*Chinese Entrepreneur News*).

ZGRMYHJRTZGGS (Zhongguo renmin yinhang jinrong tizhi gaige si) 中國人民銀行金融體制改革司. 1991. 開拓奮進：中國金融體制改革 (Pressing Ahead: Reforms in China's Financial System). 北京：中國金融出版社.

ZGWZB (Zhongguo wuzi bao) 中國物資報 (*China Capital Goods News*).

ZGXZQYNJBJWYH (Zhongguo xiangzhen qiye nianjian bianji weiyuan hui). 中國鄉鎮企業年鑒編輯委員會. 1987–99. 中國鄉鎮企業年鑒 (Yearbook of China's Township Enterprises). 北京：中國農業出版社.

Zhang Delin 張德霖. 1993. 產權：國有企業改革與國有資產監督 (Property Rights: Reform of State-owned Enterprises and Monitoring of State-owned Assets). 北京：中國財政經濟出版社.

Zhang Lingyuan and Zhu Weiping 張玲元，朱薇平. 1988. 企業法講話 (A Study Guide to the *State-owned Enterprise Law*). 北京：清華大學出版社.

Zhang Shaojie 張少傑. 1986. 雙軌環境下的企業經濟行為 (Economic Behavior of Enterprises under the Dual-track Price System). 走向未來 1.

Zhang Xiaohua 張曉華. 1993. 土地行政法 (Land Administration Laws). 北京：中國人事出版社.

Zhang Xuwu, Li Ding, and Xie Minggan 張緒武，李定，謝明幹 (主編). 1994. 中國私營經濟年鑒 (Yearbook of China's Private Sector Economy). 香港：香港經濟導報出版社.

1996. 中國私營經濟年鑒 (Yearbook of China's Private Sector Economy). 北京：中華工商聯合出版社.

Zhang Yi 張毅. 1990. 中國鄉鎮企業：歷史的必然 (China's Township Enterprises: A Historical Inevitability). 北京：法律出版社.

Zhang Yichun 張亦春 (主編). 1994. 中國金融改革沉思錄 (Reflections on China's Financial and Banking Reform). 北京：中國社會科學出版社.

Zhang Zuoji 張左己 (主編). 1994. 中國勞動體制改革研究 (A Study of Reforms in the Labor Employment System of China). 北京：中國勞動出版社.

Zhao Haikuan 趙海寬. 1993. 中國金融業大變革 (Great Changes in China's Financial Sector). 鄭州：河南人民出版社.

Zheng Haihang 鄭海航. 1998. 中國國有企業虧損研究 (A Study of Losses Incurred by State-owned Enterprises). 北京：經濟管理出版社.

Zheng Yushuo and Xie Qingkui 鄭宇碩，謝慶奎 (主編). 1992. 當代中國政府 (Government in Contemporary China). 香港：天地圖書.

ZHGSB (Zhonghua gongshang bao) 中華工商報 (*Chinese Industrial and Commercial News*).

Zhou Taihe 周太和 (主編). 1984. 當代中國的經濟體制改革 (Economic System Reform in Contemporary China). 北京：中國社會科學出版社.

ZHQGZGG (Zhonghua quanguo zong gonghui) 中華全國總工會. 1987. 全國職工隊伍狀況調查 (A National Survey on Urban Employees). 北京：工人出版社.
    1993. 走向社會主義市場經濟的中國工人階級 (The Chinese Working Class on Way toward a Socialist Market Economy). 北京：工人出版社.

Zhu Rongji 朱鎔基 (主編). 1985. 當代中國的經濟管理 (Economic Management in Contemporary China). 北京：中國社會科學出版社.

Zou Yuchuan 鄒玉川 (主編). 1998. 當代中國的土地管理 (Land Administration in Contemporaty China). 北京：當代中國出版社.

Part II. English Materials (Cited by Last Name of Author or Full Title of Publication)

Adelman, Irma, and David Sunding. 1987. Economic Policy and Income Distribution in China. *Journal of Comparative Economics* 11: 444–61.

Akerlof, George A. 1984. *An Economic Theorist's Book of Tales: Essays that Entertain the Consequences of New Assumptions in Economic Theory.* Cambridge University Press.

Alt, James E., and Kenneth A. Shepsle, eds. 1990. *Perspectives on Positive Political Economy.* Cambridge University Press.

Andors, Stephen. 1977. *China's Industrial Revolution: Politics, Planning and Management.* New York: Pantheon Books.

Aoki, Masahiko, Bo Gustafsson, and Oliver E. Williamson, eds. 1990. *The Firm as a Nexus of Treaties.* London: Sage Publications Ltd.

Apter, David. 1972. *Choice and the Politics of Allocation.* New Haven: Yale University Press.
    1987. *Rethinking Development.* Beverly Hills, CA: Sage Publications, Inc.

Arrow, Kenneth J. 1974. *The Limits of Organization.* New York: W. W. Norton.

Axelrod, Robert. 1984. *The Evolution of Cooperation.* New York: Basic Books.

Babbie, Earl. 1992. *The Practice of Social Research.* Belmont, CA: Wadsworth Publishing Company.

Bardhan, Pranab K. 1997. Corruption and Development: A Review of Issues. *Journal of Economic Literature* 35: 1320–46.

Barnett, A. Doak, and Ralph N. Clough, eds. 1986. *Modernizing China: Post-Mao Reform and Development*. Boulder, CO: Westview Press.

Barnett, A. Doak, and Ezra Vogel. 1967. *Cadres, Bureaucracy, and Political Power in Communist China*. Columbia University Press.

Bartlett, Randall. 1989. *Economics and Power: An Inquiry into Human Relations and Markets*. Cambridge University Press.

Bates, Robert H. 1981. *Markets and States in Tropical Africa: The Political Basis for Agricultural Policies*. Berkeley: University of California Press.

Bates, Robert H., and Anne O. Krueger, eds. *Political and Economic Interactions in Economic Policy Reform: Evidence from Eight Countries*. Oxford: Blackwell.

Bell, Michael W., Hoe Ee Khor, and Kalpana Kochhar. 1993. *China at the Threshold of a Market Economy*. Washington DC: International Monetary Fund.

Bendix, Reinhard. 1974. *Work and Authority in Industry*. Berkeley: University of California Press.

Bernstein, Thomas P., and Xiaobo Lu. 2000. Taxation without Representation: Peasants, the Central and the Local States in Reform China. *The China Quarterly* 163: 742–63.

Bhagwati, Jagdish N. 1982. Directly Unproductive, Profit-seeking (DUP) Activities. *Journal of Political Economy* 90: 988–1002.

Bian, Yanjie. 1994. *Guanxi* and the Allocation of Urban Jobs in China. *The China Quarterly* 140: 971–99.

1997. Bringing Strong Ties Back In: Indirect Ties, Network Bridges, and Job Searches in China. *American Sociological Review* 61: 266–85.

Blecher, Marc, and Vivienne Shue. 1996. *Tethered Deer: Government and Economy in a Chinese County*. Stanford: Stanford University Press.

Blejer, Mario I., Guillermo A. Calvo, Fabrizio Coricelli, and Alan H. Gelb. 1993. Eastern Europe in Transition: From Recession to Growth? *World Bank Discussion Papers* 196. Washington, DC: The World Bank.

Boisot, Max, and John Child. 1996. From Fiefs to Clans and Network Capitalism: Explaining China's Emerging Economic Order. *Administrative Science Quarterly* 41: 600–28.

Bowles, Paul, and Gordon White. 1993. *The Political Economy of China's Financial Reforms: Finance in Late Development*. Boulder, CO: Westview Press.

Brus, Wlodzimierz, and Kazimierz Laski. 1989. *From Marx to the Market: Socialism in Search of an Economic System*. Oxford: Oxford University Press.

Bruun, Ole. 1993. *Business and Bureaucracy in a Chinese City: An Ethnography of Private Business Households in Contemporary China*. Berkeley: Institute of East Asian Studies, University of California.

Buchanan, James M. 1980. Profit Seeking and Rent Seeking. In *Toward a Theory of the Rent-Seeking Society*, eds. James M. Buchanan, Robert D. Tollison, and Gordon Tullock, 3–15. College Station: Texas A&M University Press.

1985. *Liberty, Market, and State.* New York: New York University Press.

Byrd, William. 1987. The Impact of Two-tier Plan/Market System in Chinese Industry. *Journal of Comparative Economics* 11: 295–308.

1989. Plan and Market in the Chinese Economy: A Simple General Equilibrium Model. *Journal of Comparative Economics* 13: 177–204.

1991. *The Market Mechanism and Economic Reforms in China.* Armonk, New York: M. E. Sharpe, Inc.

ed. 1992. *Chinese Industrial Firms under Reform.* New York: Oxford University Press.

Byrd, William A., and Lin Qingsong, eds. 1990. *China's Rural Industry: Structure, Development, and Reform.* New York: Oxford University Press.

Chamberlain, Heath B. 1987. Party-management Relations in Chinese Industries. *The China Quarterly* 112: 631–61.

Chang, Chun, and Yijiang Wang. 1994. The Nature of the Township-village Enterprise. *Journal of Comparative Economics* 19: 434–52.

Chen, Kuan, Gary Jefferson, Thomas Rawski, Wang Hongchang, and Zheng Yuxin. 1988a. New Estimates of Fixed Capital Stock for Chinese State Industry. *The China Quarterly* 114: 243–66.

1988b. Productivity Change in Chinese Industry: 1953–1985. *Journal of Comparative Economics* 12: 570–91.

Cheung, Steven N. S. 1995. A Simplistic General Equilibrium Theory of Corruption. *Contemporary Economic Policy* 16: 1–5.

Ch'i, Hsi-sheng. 1991. *Politics of Disillusionment: The Chinese Communist Party under Deng Xiaoping.* Armonk, NY: M. E. Sharpe, Inc.

China Daily (Beijing).

Chow, Gregory. 1985. *The Chinese Economy.* New York: Harper & Row.

1994. *Understanding China's Economy.* Singapore: World Scientific.

Christiansen, Flemming, and Zhang Junzuo. 1998. *Village Inc.: Chinese Rural Society in the 1990s.* Surrey: Curzon Press.

Chu, Godwin C., and Yanan Ju. 1993. *The Great Wall in Ruins: Communication and Cultural Change in China.* Albany: State University of New York Press.

CND-Global (China News Digest-Global) (Internet publication).

Coase, R. H. 1988. *The Firm, the Market, and the Law.* Chicago: The University of Chicago Press.

Comisso, Ellen, and Laura D'Andrea Tyson, eds. 1986. *Power, Purpose and Collective Choice: Economic Strategy in Socialist States.* Ithaca: Cornell University Press.

Cox, T. 1986. *Peasants, Cadres, and Capitalism.* New York: Oxford University Press.

Crook, Frederick. 1975. The Commune System in the People's Republic of China, 1963–74. In *China: A Reassessment of the Economy,* ed. Joint Economic Committee, US Congress, 366–410. Washington, DC: US Government Printing Office.

Cyert, Richard, and James March. 1966. *A Behavioral Theory of the Firm.* Englewood Cliffs, NJ: Prentice-Hall.

Dalton, George, ed. 1968. *Primitive, Archaic and Modern Economies: Essays of Karl Polanyi.* New York: Anchor Books.

Davis, Deborah, and Ezra Vogel, eds. 1990. *Chinese Society on the Eve of Tiananmen*. Cambridge, MA: Harvard University Press.

Dickson, Bruce J. 1990. Conflict and Non-compliance in Chinese Politics: Party Rectification 1983–7. *Pacific Affairs* 63: 170–90.

Ding. X. L. 2000. The Informal Asset Stripping in China's State Firms. *The China Journal* 43: 1–28.

Dittmer, Lowell. 1987. *China's Continuous Revolution*. Berkeley: University of California Press.

Duckett, Jane. 1998. *The Entrepreneurial State in China: Real Estate and Commerce Developments in Reform Era Tianjin*. London: Routledge.

Eckstein, Alexander. 1977. *China's Economic Revolution*. Cambridge University Press.

Eggertsson, Thrainn. 1990. *Economic Behavior and Institutions*. Cambridge University Press.

Elster, Jon. 1989. *Nuts and Bolts for the Social Sciences*. Cambridge University Press.

Eng, Irene, and Yi-min Lin. 1997. "Agent as Partner: Enterprise-led Institutional Change in a Chinese Prefecture." Working paper, Social Science Division, Hong Kong University of Science and Technology.

2000. "Religious Festivities, Communal Rivalry, and Restructuring of Authority Relations in Rural Chaozhou, Southeast China." Working paper, Social Science Division, Hong Kong University of Science and Technology.

Evans, Peter B. 1995. *Embedded Autonomy: States and Industrial Transformation*. Princeton: Princeton University Press.

Evans, Peter B., Dietrich Rueschemeyer, and Theda Skocpol, eds. 1985. *Bringing the State Back In*. Cambridge University Press.

Far Eastern Economic Review.

Field, Robert Michael. 1983. Slow Growth of Labor Productivity in Chinese Industry, 1952–1981. *The China Quarterly* 96: 641–64.

1986. The Performance of Industry during the Cultural Revolution: Second Thoughts. *The China Quarterly* 108: 625–42.

Francis, Corinna-Barbara. 1999. Unit Ownership in China's Market Transition: Spin-offs in the Computer and High Technology Sector. In *Property Rights and Economic Reform in China*, eds. Jean Oi and Andrew Walder, 226–47. Stanford: Stanford University Press.

Friedman, Milton. 1990. *Friedman in China*. Hong Kong: The Chinese University Press.

Galbraith, John K. 1967. *The New Industrial State*. London: Hamish Hamilton.

Gerschenkron, Alexander. 1962. *Economic Backwardness in Historical Perspective: A Book of Essays*. Cambridge, MA: Harvard University Press.

Gold, Thomas B. 1985. After Comradeship: Personal Relations in China since the Cultural Revolution. *The China Quarterly* 104: 657–75.

Goldstein, Avery. 1991. *From Bandwagon to Balance-of-Power Politics: Structural Constraints and Politics in China, 1949–1978*. Stanford: Stanford University Press.

Gong, Ting. 1994. *The Politics of Corruption in Contemporary China*. Westport, CT: Praeger.

Gore, Lance. 1998. *Market Communism: The Institutional Foundation of China's Post-Mao Hyper-Growth*. Hong Kong: Oxford University Press.

1999. The Communist Legacy in Post-Mao Economic Growth. *The China Journal* 41: 25–54.

Gouldner, Alvin. 1967. *Patterns of Industrial Bureaucracy*. New York: The Free Press.

Grampp, William D. 2000. What Did Smith Mean by the Invisible Hand? *Journal of Political Economy* 108: 441–65.

Granick, David. 1990. *Chinese State Enterprises: A Regional Property Rights Analysis*. Chicago and London: The University of Chicago Press.

Granovetter, Mark. 1985. Economic Action and Social Structure: The Problem of Embeddedness. *American Journal of Sociology* 91: 481–510.

Gregory, Paul, and Robert Stuart. 1985. *Comparative Economic Systems*. Boston: Houghton Mifflin Company.

Guthrie, Doug. 1997. Between Markets and Politics: Organizational Responses to Reform in China. *American Journal of Sociology* 102: 1258–1304.

1998. The Declining Significance of Guanxi in China's Economic Transition. *The China Quarterly* 154: 254–82.

1999. *Dragon in a Three-piece Suit: The Emergence of Capitalism in China*. Princeton: Princeton University Press.

Hardin, Russell. 1982. *Collective Action*. Baltimore: The Johns Hopkins University Press.

Harding, Harry. 1981. *Organizing China*. Stanford: Stanford University Press.

1987. *China's Second Revolution*. Washington, DC: The Brookings Institution.

Hirschman, Albert O. 1957. *Strategy of Economic Development*. New Haven: Yale University Press.

1970. *Exit, Voice, and Loyalty*. Cambridge, MA: Harvard University Press.

Ho, Samuel P. S. 1994. *Rural China in Transition: Non-agricultural Development in Rural Jiangsu, 1978–1990*. Oxford: Clarendon Press.

Holz, Carsten, and Yi-min Lin. 2000. "Pitfalls of Chinese Industrial Statistics: Inconsistencies and Specification Problems." Working paper, Social Science Division, Hong Kong University of Science and Technology.

Hsing, You-tien. 1998. *Making Capitalism in China: The Taiwan Connection*. New York: Oxford University Press.

Huang, Yasheng. 1990. Web of Interests and Patterns of Behavior in Chinese Local Economic Bureaucracies and Enterprises during Reforms. *The China Quarterly* 123: 431–58.

1995. Administrative Monitoring in China. *The China Quarterly* 143:828–43.

1996. *Inflation and Investment Controls in China: The Political Economy of Central-local Relations in the Reform Era*. Cambridge University Press.

Huntington, Samuel P. 1968. *Political Order in Changing Societies*. New Haven: Yale University Press.

Hwang, Kwang-kuo. 1987. Face and Favor: The Chinese Power Game. *American Journal of Sociology* 92: 944–74.

Jackson, Sukhan. 1986. Reform of State Enterprise Management in China. *The China Quarterly* 107: 405–32.

1992. *Chinese Enterprise Management: Reforms in Economic Perspective.* Berlin and New York: Walter de Gruyter.

Jefferson, Gary H., and Thomas G. Rawski. 1994a. Enterprise Reform in Chinese Industry. *Journal of Economic Perspectives* 8: 47–70.

1994b. How Industrial Reform Worked in China: The Role of Innovation, Competition, and Property Rights. *Proceedings of the World Bank Annual Conference on Development Economics*: 129–56.

Jefferson, Gary H., and Inderjit Singh, eds. 1999. *Enterprise Reform in China: Ownership, Transition, and Performance.* New York: Oxford University Press.

Jia, Hao, and Zhimin Lin, eds. 1994. *Changing Central-local Relations in China: Reform and State Capacity.* Boulder, CO: Westview Press.

Joint Economic Committee (US Congress), ed. 1982. *China under the Four Modernizations.* Washington, DC: US Government Printing Office.

Kamath, Shyam J. 1990. Foreign Direct Investment in a Centrally Planned Developing Economy: The Chinese Case. *Economic Development and Cultural Change* 39: 107–30.

Kelliher, Daniel. 1992. *Peasant Power in China: The Era of Rural Reform, 1979–1989.* New Haven: Yale University Press.

Khan, Z. S. 1991. Patterns of Direct Foreign Investment in China. *World Bank Discussion Papers* 130. Washington, DC: The World Bank.

King, Ambrose Y. C. 1991. Kuan-hsi and Network Building: A Sociological Interpretation. *Daedalus* 120: 63–84.

Kitching, G. 1982. *Development and Underdevelopment in Historical Perspective.* London and New York: Methuen.

Knight, Jack. 1992. *Institutions and Social Conflict.* Cambridge University Press.

Kohli, Atul. 1990. *Democracy and Discontent: India's Growing Crisis of Governability.* Cambridge University Press.

Kornai, Janos. 1980. *Economics of Shortage.* Amsterdam: North Holland Publishing Company.

1985. *Contradictions and Dilemmas: Studies on the Socialist Economy and Society.* Cambridge, MA: The MIT Press.

1990. *Vision and Reality, Market and State: Contradictions and Dilemmas Revisited.* London and New York: Harvester Wheatsheaf.

Korzec, Mickel, and Martin Whyte. 1981. Reading Note: The Chinese Wage System. *The China Quarterly* 86: 248–73.

Krueger, Anne. 1974. The Political Economy of the Rent-seeking Society. *American Economic Review* 64: 291–303.

Kueh, Y. Y. 1992. Foreign Investment and Economic Change in China. *The China Quarterly* 111: 638–90.

Kung, James, and Yi-min Lin. 1999. "The Evolving Ownership Structure of China's Transitional Economy: An Analysis of the Rural Nonfarm Sector." Working paper, Social Science Division, Hong Kong University of Science and Technology.

Kwong, Julia. 1997. *The Political Economy of Corruption in China.* Armonk, New York: M. E. Sharpe, Inc.

Laaksonen, Oiva. 1988. *Management in China during and after Mao.* Berlin and New York: Walter de Gruyter.

Lampton, David, ed. 1987. *Policy Implementation in Post-Mao China.* Berkeley: University of California Press.

Lane, David. 1976. *The Socialist Industrial State: Toward a Political Sociology of State Socialism.* London: Allen and Unwin.

Lardy, Nicholas. 1978. *Economic Growth and Distribution in China.* Cambridge University Press.

1995. The Role of Foreign Trade and Investment in China's Economic Transformation. *The China Quarterly* 144: 1065–82.

1998. *China's Unfinished Economic Revolution.* Washington, DC: Brookings Institution Press.

Latham, Richard J. 1985. The Implications of Rural Reforms for Grass-roots Cadres. In *The Political Economy of Reform in Post-Mao China*, eds. Elizabeth Perry and Christine Wong, 157–73. Cambridge, MA: Harvard University Press.

Lavoie, Don. 1985. *Rivalry and Central Planning: The Socialist Calculation Revisited.* Cambridge University Press.

Lazonick, William. 1991. *Business Organization and the Myth of the Market Economy.* Cambridge University Press.

Lee, Hung Yong. 1978. *The Politics of the Chinese Cultural Revolution.* Berkeley: University of California Press.

1990. *From Revolutionary Cadres to Party Technocrats in Socialist China.* Berkeley: University of California Press.

Lee, Keun. 1991. *Chinese Firms and the State in Transition: Property Rights and Agency Problems in the Reform Era.* Armonk, NY: M. E. Sharpe, Inc.

Lee, Peter N. S. 1987. *Industrial Management and Economic Reform in China, 1949–1984.* Hong Kong: Oxford University Press.

1990. Bureaucratic Corruption during the Deng Xiaoping Era. *Corruption and Reform* 5: 29–47.

Leff, Nathaniel. 1964. Economic Development through Bureaucratic Corruption. *American Behavoral Scientist* 8: 8–14.

Levi, Margaret. 1988. *Of Rule and Revenue.* Berkeley: University of California Press.

Li, Lianjiang, and Kevin J. O'Brien. 1996. Villagers and Popular Resistance in Contemporary China. *Modern China* 22 (1): 28–61.

1999. The Struggle over Village Elections. In *The Paradox of China's Post-Mao Reforms*, eds. Merle Goldman and Roderick MacFarquhar, 129–45. Cambridge, MA: Harvard University Press.

Li, Lin-nei, ed. 1993. *English-Chinese Dictionary of New Economic Terms Used in Contemporary China.* Hong Kong: Shangwu yinshu guan.

Lieberthal, Kenneth. 1995. *Governing China: From Revolution through Reform.* New York: W. W. Norton.

Lieberthal, Kenneth, and David Lampton, eds. 1992. *Bureaucracy, Politics, and Decision Making in Post-Mao China*. Berkeley: University of California Press.

Lieberthal, Kenneth, and Michel Oksenberg. 1988. *Policy Making in China: Leaders, Structures, and Processes*. Princeton: Princeton University Press.

Lin, Nan. 1995. Local Market Socialism: Local Corporatism in Action in Rural China. *Theory and Society* 24: 301–54.

Lin, Nan, and Chih-jou Jay Chen. 1999. Local Elites as Officials and Owners: Shareholding and Property Rights in Daqiuzhuang. In *Property Rights and Economic Reform in China*, eds. Jean Oi and Andrew Walder, 145–70. Stanford: Stanford University Press.

Lin, Yi-min. 2000. Rethinking China's Economic Transformation. *Contemporary Sociology* 29: 608–13.

Lin, Yi-min, and Zhanxin Zhang. 1999. The Private Assets of Public Servants: Profit-seeking Entities Sponsored by State Agencies. In *Property Rights and Economic Reform in China*, eds. Jean Oi and Andrew Walder, 203–25. Stanford: Stanford University Press.

Lin, Yi-min, and Tian Zhu. 2001. Ownership Restructuring in Chinese State Industry: An Analysis of Evidence on Initial Organizational Changes. *The China Quarterly* 166: 298–334.

Lindblom, Charles. 1959. The "Science" of Muddling Through. *Public Administration Review* 19: 79–88.

——— 1977. *Politics and Markets: The World's Political-economic Systems*. New York: Basic Books.

Link, Perry, Richard Madsen, and Paul G. Pickowicz, eds. 1989. *Unofficial China: Popular Culture and Thought in the People's Republic*. Boulder, CO: Westview Press.

Little, Daniel. *Understanding Peasant China: Case Studies in the Philosophy of Social Science*. New Haven: Yale University Press.

Liu, Binyan. 1983. *People or Monsters?* (ed. Perry Link). Bloomington: Indiana University Press.

Liu, Yia-ling. 1992. Reform from Below: The Private Economy and Local Politics in the Rural Industrialization of Wenzhou. *The China Quarterly* 130: 293–316.

Lo, Dic. 1997. *Market and Institutional Regulation in Chinese Industrialization, 1978–94*. London: Routledge.

Lu, Xiaobo. 2000. *Cadres and Corruption: The Organizational Involution of the Communist Party*. Stanford: Stanford University Press.

Lyons, Thomas P., and Victor Nee, eds. 1994. *The Economic Transformation of South China: Reform and Development in the Post-Mao Era*. Ithaca: Cornell East Asia Program.

Ma, Stephen K. 1989. Reform Corruption: A Discussion on China's Current Development. *Pacific Affairs* 62: 40–52.

——— 1999. Man of Efficiency and Man of Ethics: Can China's Administrative Reform Produce Both for Her Economic Development? *Policy Studies Review* 16: 133–46.

238   *Bibliography*

McMillan, John, and Barry Naughton. 1992. How to Reform a Planned Economy: Lessons from China. *Oxford Review of Economic Policy* 8: 130–43.

McMillan, John, John Whalley, and Lijing Zhu. 1989. The Impact of China's Economic Reforms on Agricultural Productivity Growth. *Journal of Political Economy* 97: 781–807.

MacMurray, T., and J. Woetzel. 1994. The Challenge Facing China's State-owned Enterprises. *The McKinsey Quarterly* 2: 61–74.

Madsen, Richard. 1984. *Morality and Power in a Chinese Village.* Berkeley: University of California Press.

1997. *China's Catholics: Tragedy and Hope in an Emerging Civil Society.* Berkeley: University of California Press.

Manion, Melanie. 1993. *Retirement of Revolutionaries in China: Public Policies, Social Norms, Private Interests.* Princeton: Princeton University Press.

1996a. The Electoral Connection in the Chinese Countryside. *American Political Science Review* 90: 736–48.

1996b. Corruption by Design: Bribery in Chinese Enterprise Licensing. *Journal of Law, Economics, and Organization* 12: 167–95.

1997. Corruption and Corruption Control: More of the Same in 1996. In *China Review 1997*, eds. Maurice Brosseau, Kuan Hsin-chi, and Y. Y. Kueh, 34–56. Hong Kong: Chinese University Press.

March, James. 1978. Bounded Rationality, Ambiguity and the Engineering of Choice. *Bell Journal of Economics* 9: 587–608.

March, James, and Johan Olsen. 1976. *Ambiguity and Choice in Organizations.* Bergen, Norway: Universitetsforlaget.

March, James, and Herbert Simon. 1958. *Organizations.* New York: John Wiley.

Mauro, Paolo. 1995. Corruption and Growth. *Quarterly Journal of Economics* 110: 681–712.

Meaney, Connie Squires. 1989. Market Reform in a Leninist System: Some Trends in the Distribution of Power, Status, and Money in Urban China. *Studies in Comparative Communism* 22: 203–20.

Meier, Gerald M. 1984. *Leading Issues in Economic Development.* New York: Oxford University Press.

Meisner, Maurice. 1982. *Marxism, Maoism, and Utopianism.* Madison: University of Wisconsin Press.

1984. *Mao's China and After.* New York: The Free Press.

Meyer, Marshall, and Lynn Zucker. 1989. *Permanently Failing Organizations.* Beverly Hills, CA: Sage Publications, Inc.

Milgrom, Paul, and John Roberts. 1992. *Economics, Organization and Management.* Englewood Cliffs, NJ: Prentice-Hall.

Mills, C. W. 1956. *The Power Elite.* New York: Simon and Schuster.

Montinola, Gabriella, Yingyi Qian, and Barry R. Weingast. 1995. Federalism, Chinese Style: The Political Basis for Economic Success in China. *World Politics* 48: 50–81.

Mueller, Dennis C. 1989. *Public Choice II: A Revised Edition of Public Choice.* Cambridge University Press.

Murphy, Kevin, Andrei Shleifer, and Robert W. Vishny. 1993. Why Is Rent-seeking So Costly to Growth? *American Economic Association Papers and Proceedings* 83: 409–14.

Myrdal, Gunnar. 1968. *Asian Drama: An Enquiry into the Poverty of Nations.* New York: Pantheon.

Nathan, Andrew. 1985. *Chinese Democracy.* New York: Knopf.

Naughton, Barry. 1988. The Third Front: Defense Industrialization in the Chinese Interior. *China Quarterly* 115: 351–86.

1992a. Implications of the State Monopoly over Industry and Its Relaxation. *Modern China* 18: 14–41.

1992b. Hierarchy and the Bargaining Economy: Government and Enterprise in the Reform Process. In *Bureaucracy, Politics, and Decision-making in Post-Mao China*, eds. Kenneth G. Lieberthal and David M. Lampton, 245–79. Berkeley and Los Angeles: University of California Press.

1994a. What Is Distinctive about China's Economic Transition? State Enterprise Reform and Overall System Transformation. *Journal of Comparative Economics* 18: 470–90.

1994b. China's Institutional Innovation and Privatization from Below. *AEA Papers and Proceedings* 84: 266–70.

1995a. *Growing Out of the Plan: Chinese Economic Reform, 1978–1993.* Cambridge University Press.

1995b. China's Macroeconomy in Transition. *The China Quarterly* 144: 1084–104.

Nee, Victor. 1989. A Theory of Market Transition: From Redistribution to Markets in State Socialism. *American Sociological Review* 54: 663–81.

1991. Social Inqualities in Reforming State Socialism: Redistribution and Markets in China. *American Sociological Review* 56: 267–82.

1992. Organizational Dynamics of Market Transition: Hybrid Forms, Property Rights, and Mixed Economy in China. *Administrative Science Quarterly* 37: 1–27.

1996. The Emergence of a Market Society: Changing Mechanisms of Stratification in China. *American Journal of Sociology* 101: 908–49.

Nee, Victor, and Peng Lian. 1994. Sleeping with the Enemy: A Dynamic Model of Declining Political Commitment in State Socialism. *Theory and Society* 23: 253–96.

Nee, Victor, and David Stark, eds. 1989. *Remaking the Economic Institutions of Socialism: China and Eastern Europe.* Stanford: Stanford University Press.

Nee, Victor, and Sijin Su. 1990. Institutional Change and Economic Growth in Rural China. *Journal of Asian Studies* 49: 3–25.

Nelson, Daniel N., ed. 1983. *Communism and the Politics of Inequalities.* New York: Lexington Books.

Nelson, Richard, and Sidney Winter. 1982. *An Evolutionary Theory of Economic Change.* Boston: Belknap Press.

Niou, Emerson M. S. 1998. "An Introduction to the Electoral Systems Used in Chinese Village Elections." Unpublished manuscript, Department of Political Science, Duke University.

Nolan, Peter, and Robert F. Ash. 1995. China's Economy on the Eve of Reform. *The China Quarterly* 144: 980–98.

Nolan, Peter, and Gordon White. 1984. Urban Bias, Rural Bias or State Bias? Urban-rural Relations in Post-revolutionary China. *Journal of Development Studies* 20: 52–81.

Noonan, John T., Jr. 1987. *Bribes*. Berkeley and Los Angeles: University of California Press.

North, Douglass C. 1977. Markets and Other Allocation Systems in History: The Challenge of Karl Polanyi. *European Economic History Review* 6: 703–16.

1981. *Structure and Change in Economic History*. New York: W. W. Norton.

1990. *Institutions, Institutional Change and Economic Performance*. Cambridge University Press.

Nove, Alec. 1983a. *The Soviet Economic System*. London: Allen and Unwin.

1983b. *The Economics of Feasible Socialism*. London: Allen and Unwin.

1990. "Market Socialism" and "Free Economy": A Discussion of Alternatives. *Dissent* 37: 443–6.

Nye, Joseph S. 1967. Corruption and Political Development: A Cost-benefit Analysis. *American Political Science Review* 61: 417–27.

O'Brien, Kevin J., and Lianjiang Li. 2000. Accommodating "Democracy" in a One-Party State: Introducing Village Elections in China. *The China Quarterly* 162: 467–89.

Odgaard, Ole. 1992. *Private Enterprises in Rural China: Impact on Agriculture and Social Stratification*. Aldershot: Avebury.

Oi, Jean. 1988. The Chinese Village, Inc. In *Chinese Economic Policy: Economic Reform at Midstream*, ed. Bruce Reynolds, 67–87. New York: Paragon House.

1989a. *State and Peasant in Contemporary China: The Political Economy of Village Government*. Berkeley: University of California Press.

1989b. Market Reform and Corruption in Rural China. *Studies of Comparative Communism* 22: 221–33.

1992. Fiscal Reform and the Economic Foundations of Local State Corporatism in China. *World Politics* 45: 99–126.

1995. The Role of the Local State in China's Transitional Economy. *The China Quarterly* 144: 1132–49.

1998. The Evolution of Local State Corporatism. In *Zouping in Transition: The Process of Reform in Rural North China*, ed. Andrew G. Walder, Chapter 2. Cambridge, MA: Harvard University Press.

1999. *Rural China Takes Off: Institutional Foundations of Economic Reform*. Berkeley: University of California Press.

Oksenberg, Michel, and James Tong. 1991. The Evolution of Central-Provincial Fiscal Relations in China, 1971–1984. *The China Quarterly* 125: 1–32.

Okun, Arthur. 1975. *Equality and Efficiency: The Big Trade-off*. Washington, DC: The Brookings Institution.

Olson, Mancur. 1965. *The Logic of Collective Action*. Cambridge, MA: Harvard University Press.

1982. *The Rise and Decline of Nations.* New Haven: Yale University Press.

2000. *Power and Prosperity: Outgrowing Communist and Capitalist Dictatorships.* New York: Basic Books.

Parish, William, and Ethan Michelson. 1996. Politics and Markets: Dual Transformations. *American Journal of Sociology* 101: 1042–59.

Parish, William, and Martin K. Whyte. 1978. *Village and Family in Contemporary China.* Chicago: University of Chicago Press.

Pearce, David W., ed. 1986. *The MIT Dictionary of Modern Economics.* Cambridge, MA: The MIT Press.

Pearson, Magaret M. 1991a. The Erosion of Controls over Foreign Capital in China, 1979–1988. *Modern China* 17: 122–50.

1991b. *Joint Ventures in the People's Republic of China.* Princeton: Princeton University Press.

1997. *China's New Business Elite: The Political Consequences of Economic Reform.* Berkeley: University of California Press.

Pelzman, Sam. 1990. How Efficient Is the Voting Market? *Journal of Law and Economics* 33: 27–63.

Perkins, Dwight Heald. 1988. Reforming China's Economic System. *Journal of Economic Literature* 26: 601–45.

1994. Completing China's Move to the Market. *Journal of Economic Perspectives* 8: 23–46.

Perrow, Charles. 1985. *Complex Organizations: A Critical Essay.* New York: Random House.

Perry, Elizabeth J. 1989. State and Society in Contemporary China. *World Politics* 41: 579–91.

1994. Trends in the Study of Chinese Politics: State-society Relations. *The China Quarterly* 139: 704–13.

Perry, Elizabeth, and Christine Wong, eds. 1985. *The Political Economy of Reform in Post-Mao China.* Cambridge, MA: Harvard University Press.

Pfeffer, Jeffrey. 1981. *Power in Organizations.* Boston: Pitman.

Polanyi, Karl. 1957 (1944). *The Great Transformation.* New York: The Free Press.

Pomfret, R. 1991. *Investing in China.* Ames: Iowa State University Press.

Portes, Alejandro, Manuel Castells, and Lauren A. Benton, eds. 1989. *The Informal Economy: Studies in Advanced and Less Developed Countries.* Baltimore: The Johns Hopkins University Press.

Powell, Walter W., and Paul J. DiMaggio, eds. 1991. *The New Institutionalism in Organizational Analysis.* Chicago: University of Chicago Press.

Prybyla, Jan S. 1987. *Market and Plan Under Socialism: The Bird in the Cage.* Stanford, CA: The Hoover Institution Press.

1989. China's Economic Experiment: Back from the Market? *Problems of Communism* 38: 1–18.

Pryor, Frederic. 1973. *Property and Industrial Organization in Communist and Capitalist Nations.* Bloomington: Indiana University Press.

Qian, Yingyi, and Chenggang Xu. 1993. Why China's Economic Reforms Differ: The M-form Hierarchy and Entry/Expansion of the Non-state Sector. *Economics of Transition* 2: 135–70.

Ramseyer, J. Mark, and Francis McCall Rosenbluth. 1993. *Japan's Political Marketplace.* Cambridge, MA: Harvard University Press.

Rawski, Thomas. 1975. China's Industrial System. In *China: A Reassessment of the Economy,* ed. Joint Economic Committee, US Congress, 175–98. Washington, DC: US Government Printing Office.

1994a. Chinese Industrial Reform: Accomplishments, Prospects, and Implications. *AEA Papers and Proceedings* 84: 271–5.

1994b. Progress without Privatization: The Reform of China's State Industries. In *Changing Political Economies: Privatization in Post-Communist and Reforming Communist States,* ed. Vedat Milor, 27–52. Boulder, CO: Lynne Rienner.

1994c. "China's Industrial Growth and Performance (1978–1992)." Unpublished manuscript.

1995. Implications of China's Reform Experience. *The China Quarterly* 144: 1150–73.

1999. Reforming China's Economy: What Have We Learned? *The China Journal* 41: 139–56.

2000. "China's GDP Statistics – A Caveat Lector?" Working paper, Department of Economics, University of Pittsburgh.

Redding, S. Gordon, 1990. *The Spirit of Chinese Capitalism.* Berlin and New York: Walter de Gruyter.

Reynolds, Bruce, ed. 1988. *Chinese Economic Reform: How Far, How Fast?* Boston: Academic Press.

Riskin, Carl. 1987. *China's Political Economy: The Quest for Development since 1949.* Oxford: Oxford University Press.

Rocca, Jean-Louis. 1992. Corruption and Its Shadow: An Anthropological View of Corruption in China. *The China Quarterly* 130: 402–16.

Rose-Ackerman, Susan. 1978. *Corruption: A Study in Political Economy.* New York: Academic Press.

1999. *Corruption and Government: Causes, Consequences, and Reform.* Cambridge University Press.

Rudolph, Lloyd I., and Susanne Hoeber Rudolph. 1987. *In Pursuit of Lakshmi: The Political Economy of the Indian State.* Chicago: University of Chicago Press.

Sachs, Jeffrey D., and Wing Thye Woo. 1994a. Structural Factors in the Economic Reforms of China, Eastern Europe, and the Former Soviet Union. *Economic Policy* 18: 102–31.

1994b. Experiences in the Transition to a Market Economy. *Journal of Comparative Economics* 18: 271–5.

Samuelson, Paul, and William Nordhaus. 1985. *Economics.* New York: McGraw-Hill.

Sandler, Todd. 1992. *Collective Action: Theory and Applications.* Ann Arbor: University of Michigan Press.

Sands, Barbara. 1989. Market-clearing by Corruption: The Political Economy of China's Recent Economic Reform. *Journal of Institutional and Theoretical Economics* 145: 116–26.

Schell, Orville. 1989. *Discos and Democracy: China in the Throes of Reform.* New York: Anchor Books.

Schelling, Thomas C. 1978. *Micromotives and Macrobehavior.* New York: W. W. Norton.

Schumpeter, Joseph A. 1975. *Capitalism, Socialism, and Democracy.* New York: Harper and Row.

Schurmann, Franz. 1968. *Ideology and Organization in Communist China.* Berkeley and Los Angeles: University of California Press.

Scott, W. Richard. 1992. *Organizations: Rational, Natural, and Open Systems.* Englewood Cliffs, NJ: Prentice-Hall.

Shambaugh, David, ed. 1998. *Is China Unstable?: Assessing the Factors.* Washington, DC: Sigur Center for Asian Studies.

Shan, Weijian. 1992. The Hybrid System and Continued Marketization of the Chinese Economy. *China Economic Review* 3: 57–74.

Shen, Xiaofang. 1990. A Decade of Direct Foreign Investment in China. *Problems of Communism* 39: 61–74.

Shi, Tianjian. 1997. *Political Participation in Beijing.* Cambridge, MA: Harvard University Press.

1999. Village Committee Elections in China: Institutionalist Tactics for Democracy. *World Politics* 51: 385–412.

Shim, Jae K., and Joel G. Siegel. 1995. *Dictionary of Economics.* New York: John Wiley.

Shirk, Susan. 1982. *Competitive Comrades: Career Incentives and Student Strategies in China.* Berkeley: University of California Press.

1993. *The Political Logic of Economic Reform in China.* Berkeley: University of California Press.

1994. *How China Opened Its Door: The Political Success of the PRC's Foreign Trade and Investment Reforms.* Washington, DC: The Brookings Institution.

Shleifer, Andrei, and Robert W. Vishny. 1993. Corruption. *Quarterly Journal of Economics* 83: 599–617.

Shue, Vivienne. 1988. *The Reach of the State: Sketches of the Chinese Body Politic.* Stanford: Stanford University Press.

Sicular, Terry. 1995. Redefining State, Plan and Market: China's Reforms in Agricultural Commerce. *The China Quarterly* 144: 1020–46.

Simon, Herbert. 1976. *Administrative Behavior.* New York: The Free Press.

Skocpol, Theda. 1979. *State and Social Revolutions.* Cambridge University Press.

Solinger, Dorothy J. 1991a. *From Lathes to Looms: China's Industrial Policy in Comparative Perspective, 1979–1982.* Stanford: Stanford University Press.

1991b. Urban Reform and Relational Contracting in Post-Mao China: An Interpretation of the Transition from Plan to Market. In *Reform and Reaction in Post-Mao China: The Road to Tiananmen,* ed. Richard Baum, 104–23. New York and London: Routledge.

1993. *China's Transition from Socialism: Statist Legacies and Market Reforms, 1980–1990.* Armonk, NY: M. E. Sharpe, Inc.

1999. *Contesting Citizenship in Urban China: Peasant Migrants, the State, and the Logic of the Market.* Berkeley: University of California Press.

South China Morning Post.

Steinfeld, Edward S. 1998. *Forging Reform in China: The Fate of State-owned Industry.* Cambridge University Press.

Stiglitz, Joseph E. 1993. *Economics.* New York and London: W. W. Norton.

Stinchcombe, Arthur. 1983. *Economic Sociology.* New York: Academic Press.

Sun, Yan. 1991. The Chinese Protests of 1989: The Issue of Corruption. *Asian Survey* 31: 762–82.

Szelenyi, Ivan. 1988. *Socialist Entrepreneurs: Embourgeoisement in Rural Hungary.* New York: Polity Press.

Tang, Jianzhong, and Laurence J. C. Ma. 1985. Evolution of Urban Collective Enterprises in China. *The China Quarterly* 104: 614–40.

Tang, Wen Fang. 1994. "Post-socialist Transition and Environmental Protection." Unpublished manuscript, Department of Political Science, University of Pittsburgh.

Tidrick, Gene, and Chen Jiyuan, eds. 1987. *China's Industrial Reform.* Oxford: Oxford University Press.

Tollison, Robert D. 1982. Rent Seeking: A Survey. *Kyklos* 35: 575–602.

Tollison, Robert D., and Roger D. Congleton, eds. 1995. *The Economic Analysis of Rent Seeking.* Aldershot, UK: Edward Elgar Publishing Limited.

Tsao, King K., and John Abbott Worthley. 1995. Chinese Public Administration: Change with Continuity during Political and Economic Development. *Public Administration Review* 55: 169–74.

Tsui, Anne S., and Larry J. L. Farh. 1997. Where Guanxi Matters: Relational Demography and Guanxi in the Chinese Context. *Work and Occupations* 24: 56–79.

Tullock, Gordon. 1967. The Welfare Costs of Tariffs, Monopolies, and Theft. *Western Economic Journal* 3: 224–32.

1990. The Costs of Special Privilege. In *Perspectives on Positive Political Economy*, eds. James E. Alt and Kenneth A. Shepsle, 195–211. Cambridge University Press.

Unger, Jonathan. 1996. "Bridges": Private Business, the Chinese Government and the Rise of New Associations. *The China Quarterly* 147: 795–819.

Useem, Michael. 1984. *The Inner Circle: Large Corporations and the Rise of Business Political Activity in the US and the UK.* New York: Oxford University Press.

Vogel, Ezra. 1965. From Friendship to Comradeship: The Change in Personal Relations in Communist China. *The China Quarterly* 21: 46–60.

1989. *One Step Ahead in China: Guangdong under Reform.* Cambridge, MA: Harvard University Press.

Wade, Robert. 1990. *Governing the Market: Economic Theory and the Role of Government in East Asian Industrialization.* Princeton: Princeton University Press.

Walder, Andrew. 1986. *Communist Neo-traditionalism: Work and Authority in Chinese Industry.* Berkeley: University of California Press.

1987. Wage Reform and the Web of Factory Interests. *The China Quarterly* 109: 22–41.

1989a. Factory and Manager in an Era of Reform. *The China Quarterly* 118: 242–64.

1989b. Post-revolution China. *Annual Review of Sociology 1989*. Palo Alto: Annual Reviews Inc.

1992a. Local Bargaining Relationships and Urban Industrial Finance. In *Bureaucracy, Politics, and Decision-making in Post-Mao China*, eds. Kenneth G. Lieberthal and David M. Lampton, 308–33. Berkeley and Los Angeles: University of California Press.

1992b. Property Rights and Stratification in Socialist Redistributive Economies. *American Sociological Review* 57: 524–39.

1994. Corporate Organization and Local Government Property Rights in China. In *Changing Political Economies: Privatization in Post-Communist and Reforming Communist States*, ed. Vedat Milor, 54–66. Boulder, CO: Lynne Rienner.

1995a. Local Governments as Industrial Firms: An Organizational Analysis of China's Transitional Economy. *American Journal of Sociology* 101: 263–301.

1995b. China's Transitional Economy: Interpreting Its Significance. *The China Quarterly* 144: 963–79.

1996. Markets and Inequality in Transitional Economies: Toward Testable Hypotheses. *American Journal of Sociology* 101: 1060–73.

1997. The State As an Ensemble of Economic Actors: Some Inferences from China's Trajectory of Change. In *Transforming Post-communist Political Economies*, eds. Joan M. Nelson, Charles Tilly, and Lee Walker, 432–52. Washington, DC: National Academy Press.

ed. 1998. *Zouping in Transition: The Process of Reform in Rural North China*. Cambridge, MA: Harvard University Press.

Wang, James C. F. 1995. *Contemporary Chinese Politics*. Englewood Cliffs, NJ: Prentice-Hall.

Wang, Shaoguang. 1995. The Decline of Central State Fiscal Capacity in China. In *The Waning of the Communist State: Economic Origins of Political Decline in China and Hungary*, ed. Andrew G. Walder, 87–113. Berkeley and Los Angeles: University of California Press.

1996. "The Institutional Foundation of China's Fiscal Reform." Paper presented at Social Science Division, Hong Kong University of Science and Technology (October).

1997. China's 1994 Fiscal Reform: An Initial Assessment. *Asian Survey* 37: 801–17.

Wank, David L. 1995. Bureaucratic Patronage and Private Business: Changing Networks of Power in Urban China. In *The Waning of the Communist State: The Economic Origins of Political Decline in China and Hungary*, ed. Andrew G. Walder, 153–83. Berkeley: University of California Press.

1996. The Institutional Process of Market Clientelism: *Guanxi* and Private Business in a South China City. *The China Quarterly* 144: 820–38.

1999. *Commodifying Communism: Business, Trust, and Politics in a Chinese City*. Cambridge University Press.

Ward, Peter M., ed. 1989. *Corruption, Development and Inequality: Soft Touch or Hard Graft?* London and New York: Routledge.

Wasserstrom, Jeffrey N., and Elizabeth J. Perry, eds. 1994. *Popular Protest and Political Culture in Modern China*. Boulder, CO: Westview Press.

Weber, Max. 1978. *Economy and Society: An Outline of Interpretive Sociology*. Berkeley: University of California Press.

Wedeman, Andrew. 1996. Corruption and Politics. In *China Review 1996*, eds. Maurice Brosseau, Suzanne Pepper, and Tsang Shu-ki, 62–94. Hong Kong: The Chinese University Press.

Weingast, Barry R. 1995. The Economic Role of Political Institutions: Market-Preserving Federalism and Economic Growth. *Journal of Law, Economics and Organization* 11: 1–31.

Weitzman, Martin, and Chenggang Xu. 1994. Chinese Township Village Enterprises as Vaguely Defined Cooperatives. *Journal of Comparative Economics* 18: 121–45.

White, Gordon, ed. 1988. *Developmental States in East Asia*. New York: St. Martin's Press.

Whiting, Susan H. 1995. "The Micro-Foundation of Industrial Change in Reform China: Property Rights and Revenue Extraction in the Rural Industrial Sector." Ph.D. dissertation, Department of Political Science, University of Michigan.

———. 1996. Contract Incentives and Market Discipline in China's Rural Industrial Sector. In *Reforming Asian Socialism: The Growth of Market Institutions*, eds. John McMillan and Barry Naughton, 53–110. Ann Arbor: University of Michigan Press.

———. 1999. The Regional Evolution of Ownership Forms: Shareholding Cooperatives and Rural Industry in Shanghai and Wenzhou. In *Property Rights and Economic Reform in China*, eds. Jean C. Oi and Andrew G. Walder, 171–202. Stanford: Stanford University Press.

Whyte, Martin K., and William Parish. 1984. *Urban Life in Contemporary China*. Chicago: University of Chicago Press.

Williamson, Oliver. 1985. *The Economic Institutions of Capitalism*. New York: The Free Press.

Wolf, Charles, Jr. 1993. *Markets or Governments: Choice between Imperfect Alternatives*. Cambridge, MA: The MIT Press.

Wong, Christine. 1987. Between Plan and Market: The Role of the Local Sector in Post-Mao China. *Journal of Comparative Economics* 11: 385–98.

———. 1991. Central-local Relations in an Era of Fiscal Decline: The Paradox of Fiscal Decentralization in Post-Mao China. *The China Quarterly* 128: 691–715.

———. ed. 1997. *Financing Local Government in the People's Republic of China*. Hong Kong: Oxford University Press.

Wong, Christine, Christopher Heady, and Wing T. Woo. 1995. *Fiscal Management and Economic Reform in the People's Republic of China*. Hong Kong: Oxford University Press.

Woo, Wing Thye. 1994. The Art of Reforming Centrally Planned Economies: Comparing China, Poland, and Russia. *Journal of Comparative Economics* 18: 276–308.

———. 1999. The Real Reasons for China's Growth. *The China Journal* 41: 115–37.

Woo, Wing Thye, Wen Hai, Jin Yibiao, and Fan Gang. 1994. How Successful Has Chinese Enterprise Reform Been? Pitfalls in Opposite Biases and Focus. *Journal of Comparative Economics* 18: 410–37.

Woo-Cumings, Meredith, ed. 1999. *The Developmental State.* Ithaca, NY: Cornell University Press.

World Bank. 1990. *China: Macroeconomic Stability and Industrial Growth under Decentralized Socialism.* Washington, DC.

1992. *China: Reform and the Role of the Plan in the 1990s.* Washington, DC.

1994. *China: Internal Market Development and Regulation.* Washington, DC.

1996. *World Development Report 1996: From Plan to Market.* New York: Oxford University Press.

1997. *Clear Water, Blue Skies: China's Environment in the New Century.* Washington, DC.

1998. *World Development Report 1998: Knowledge for Development.* New York: Oxford University Press.

Wu, Jinglian. 1995. "China's Economic Reform: Retrospect and Prospect." Paper presented at the Chinese Economic Reform Workshop, Social Science Division, Hong Kong University of Science and Technology.

Wu, Jinglian, and Zhao Renwei. 1987. On the Dual Price System in China's Industry. *Journal of Comparative Economics* 11: 309–18.

Xiao, Geng. 1991. Managerial Autonomy, Fringe Benefits, and Ownership Structure: A Comparative Study of Chinese State and Collective Enterprises. *China Economic Review* 2: 47–73.

Xin, Kathrine R., and Jone L. Pearce. 1996. Guanxi: Connections as Substitutes for Formal Institutional Support. *Academy of Management Journal* 39: 1641–58.

Xu, Wenyi, Gary Jefferson, and Dhilip Rathja. 1993. "China Data Documentation." Unpublished manuscript. Transition and Macro-Adjustment Division, World Bank.

Yan, Yun-xiang. 1996. *The Flow of Gifts: Reciprocity and Social Networks in a Chinese Village.* Stanford: Stanford University Press.

Yang, Mayfair Mei-hui. 1994. *Gifts, Favors, and Banquets: The Art of Social Relationships in China.* Ithaca and London: Cornell University Press.

Young, Susan. 1995. *Private Business and Economic Reform in China.* Armonk, NY: M. E. Sharpe, Inc.

Zhang, Weiying, and Gang Yi. 1997. China's Gradual Reform: A Historical Perspective. In *China's Economic Growth and Transition: Macroeconomic, Environmental and Social/Regional Dimensions,* eds. Clement A. Tisdell and Joseph C.H. Chai, 19–53. Commack, NY: Nova Science Publishing, Inc.

Zheng, Shiping. 1997. *Party vs. State in Post-1949 China: The Institutional Dilemma.* Cambridge University Press.

Zweig, David. 1989. *Agrarian Radicalism in China, 1968–1981.* Cambridge, MA: Harvard University Press.

Index

administrative units (*jiguan danwei*), 99n2, 215
advertisement, 4
Africa, 181
Agricultural Bank, 139
Anti-Corruption Bureau, 2, 211
arbitrage, 93, 102–6, 200
asset stripping, 118–20, 168, 170, 187–91, 204
authority relations, 5–7, 12, 56, 123–5, 131–2, 144–5, 164, 197–9
autonomy: in enterprise decision making, 33–5, 70, 115–16, 204

backyard profit centers, 98–102, 130, 140–1, 147, 156–7, 201, 203, 207
bank loans, 68–9, 83–5, 175, 189
Bardhan, Pranab K., 19, 180
bargaining, 11n18, 198; in the reform, 102, 104–5, 155n6, 176–8; under central planning, 7, 54–6, 126
Bates, Robert, 169, 181
bending the rules (to get through) (*biantong*), 138
Bernstein, Thomas, 192, 193n51
Bhagwati, Jagdish, 204n2
Bian, Yanjie, 155, 161
Blecher, Marc, 145
Bolshevik Revolution, 159
bonus, 37n35, 125, 133

borrowing contract: regulation on, 69n5
bribes, 2, 11, 155n6
brokerage: of state agents, 110–12, 120, 178, 197
Buchanan, James, 19n31
Byrd, William, 7, 28, 160, 174, 186

capacity: overbuilding and underutilization of, 183–7
capital goods (*wuzi*), 72–3, 86–7, 103–5
CESS (China's Entrepreneurs Survey System), 35–6, 67, 109
Central Discipline Inspection Commission: of the CCP, 2n3, 210
central planning, 1, 4, 6–8, 24, 32, 47, 53–6, 66, 68, 70, 72–3, 99, 120, 171–2, 181, 197, 204–5
Chen, Chih-jou Jay, 163, 182n21
Chen Xitong (Mayor of Beijing), 2, 78
Cheng Kejie, 2
China Strategic Holdings (*Zhongce*), 119
Chow, Gregory, 73
chronic shortage, 172
Chu, Godwin C., 154, 161
civil service, 210
cleanup campaigns: against profit seeking by officials, 101
coercion: in transaction, 112–15